WESTERN CANADA
TRAVEL ✦ SMART™

Lyn Hancock

D0071436

John Muir Publications
Santa Fe, New Mexico

Dedication
To Frank Hedingham with love

Acknowledgments
The author wishes to thank Chris Maartens of Virtual Research, for getting the ball rolling, and Frank Hedingham, my long-suffering assistant, for keeping it in the air despite the year-long hurricane that raged around us as this book was researched and written. No matter what he volunteered to do—phoning, driving, writing, filming, searching for computer gremlins that wiped out whole chapters, even fighting a rogue black bear that was killing tourists in the western wilderness—Frank supported this enterprise with rare dedication. Thanks, Frank.

John Muir Publications, P.O. Box 613, Santa Fe, New Mexico 87504

Printed in the United States of America.
First edition. First printing March 1998.

ISSN: 1096-4061
ISBN: 1-56261-320-0

Editors: Dianna Delling, Sarah Baldwin, Nancy Gillan
Graphics Editor: Tom Gaukel
Production: Mladen Baudrand
Design: Janine Lehmann and Linda Braun
Cover design: Janine Lehmann
Typesetting: Fabian Cooperman West
Map style development: American Custom Maps—Albuquerque, N.M., U.S.A.
Map illustration: Kathy Sparkes, White Hart Designs—Albuquerque, N.M., U.S.A.
Printing: Publishers Press
Front cover photo: *small*—© Jean Higgins/Unicorn Stock Photos
          large—Leo deWys, Inc./Steve Vidler
Back cover photo: Calgary CVB/Calgary Stampede

Distributed to the book trade by
Publishers Group West
Emeryville, California

WESTERN CANADA
TRAVEL ✦ SMART™

Stone Mountain Provincial Park

HOW TO USE THIS BOOK

The *Western Canada Travel•Smart* guidebook is organized in 17 destination chapters, each covering the best sights and activities, restaurants, and lodging available in that specific destination. Thanks to thorough research and experience, the author is able to bring you only the best options, saving you time and money in your travels. The chapters are presented in geographic sequence so you can follow an easy route from one to the next. If you were to visit each destination in chapter order, you'd enjoy a complete tour of the best of Western Canada.

Each chapter contains:

• User-friendly maps of the area, showing all recommended sights, restaurants, and accommodations.
• "A Perfect Day" description—how the author would spend her time if she had just one day in that destination.
• Sightseeing highlights, each rated by degree of importance:
  ★★★ Don't miss; ★★ Try hard to see; ★ See if you have time; and No stars—Worth knowing about.
• Selected restaurant, lodging, and camping recommendations to suit a variety of budgets.
• Helpful hints, fitness and recreation ideas, insights, and random tidbits of information to enhance your trip.

The Importance of Planning. Developing an itinerary is the best way to get the most satisfaction from your travels, and this guidebook makes it easy. First, read through the book and choose the places you'd most like to visit. Then, study the color map on the inside cover flap and the mileage chart (page 12) to determine which you can realistically see in the time you have available and at the travel pace you prefer. Using the Planning Map (pages 10–11), map out your route. Finally, use the lodging recommendations to determine your accommodations.

Some Suggested Itineraries. To get you started, six itineraries of varying lengths and based on specific interests follow. Mix and match according to your interests and time constraints, or follow a given itinerary from start to finish. The possibilities are endless. *Happy travels!*

SUGGESTED ITINERARIES

With the *Western Canada Travel•Smart* guidebook, you can plan a trip of any length—a one-day excursion, a getaway weekend, or a three-week vacation—around any special interest. To get you started, the following pages contain six suggested itineraries geared toward a variety of interests. For more information, refer to the chapters listed—chapter names are bolded, and chapter numbers appear inside black bullets. You can follow a suggested itinerary in its entirety, or shorten, lengthen, or combine parts of each, depending on your starting and ending points.

Discuss alternative routes and schedules with your travel companions—it's a great way to have fun, even before you leave home. And remember: don't hesitate to change your itinerary once you're on the road. Careful study and planning ahead of time will help you make informed decisions as you go, but spontaneity is the extra ingredient that will make your trip memorable.

Mountain goat kid

Lyn Hancock

The Best of Western Canada Tour

① Vancouver
② Whistler and the Sea to Sky Highway
③ Victoria
④ Highway Loops and Islands
⑤ West Coast of Vancouver Island
⑥ Port Hardy to the Cariboo
⑦ Queen Charlotte Islands
⑧ Northern British Columbia

⑨ Jasper National Park
⑩ Edmonton
⑪ Northern Alberta
⑫ Calgary
⑬ Drumheller Valley
⑭ Kananaskis Country
⑮ Banff/Lake Louise
⑯ Kootenay Country
⑰ The Okanagan Similkameen

Time needed: 3 to 4 weeks

Nature Lover's Tour

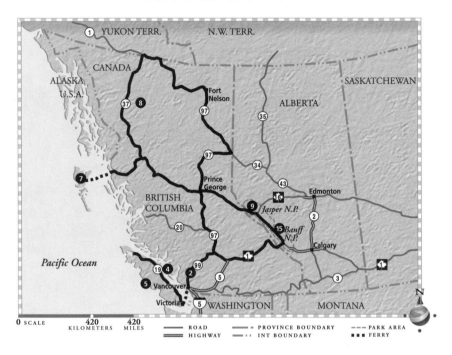

The whole of Western Canada is a nature lover's tour, from the rich marine life, rugged fjords, and forests of the West Coast to the lakes and rivers of the semi-desert interior, from the glaciers and ice sheets of the Rocky Mountains to the rolling prairie beyond.

❷ Whistler and the Sea to Sky Highway (parks, wintering eagles)
❹ Highway Loops and Islands (whales, wintering sea birds, spawning salmon, marmots, Nanaimo Sea Lion Festival)
❺ West Coast of Vancouver Island (Cathedral Grove, Pacific Rim National Park Reserve, Pacific Rim Whale Festival)
❼ Queen Charlotte Islands (Gwaii Haanas National Park Reserve, Naikoon Provincial Park, Delkatla Wildlife Sanctuary)
❽ Northern British Columbia (Photo Safari Tour, provincial parks)
❾ Jasper National Park (Icefields Parkway, Columbia Icefield, Mount Edith Cavell, Maligne Lake)
⓯ Banff/Lake Louise (Bow Valley Parkway, lakes, hot springs)

Time needed: 3 weeks

Aboriginal Culture Tour

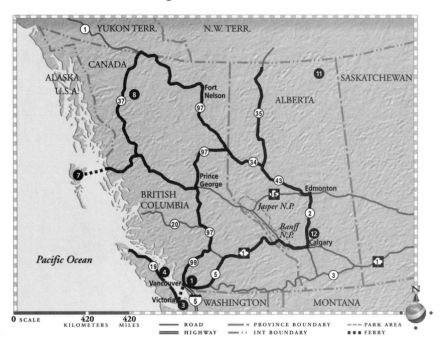

With land claims negotiations as a background, there has been a recent resurgence of interest and pride in First Nations (formerly called Indian) culture. Visit the following museums, cultural centres, and villages to learn more about Western Canada's aboriginal people.

- ❶ **Vancouver** (UBC Museum of Anthropology)
- ❸ **Victoria** (Royal British Columbia Museum, Thunderbird Park)
- ❹ **Highway Loops and Islands** (Native Heritage Centre, U'mista CulturalCentre, Duncan City of Totems)
- ❼ **Queen Charlotte Islands** (Gwaii Haanas National Park Reserve, Haida Gwaii Museum, Ninstints, Old Masset)
- ❽ **Northern British Columbia** (Hands of History tour through Gitskan Wet-Suweten villages)
- ⓫ **Northern Alberta** (Fort Chipewyan)
- ⓬ **Calgary** (Head-Smashed-In Buffalo Jump near Fort McLeod)

Time needed: 10 days

Wine Lover's Tour

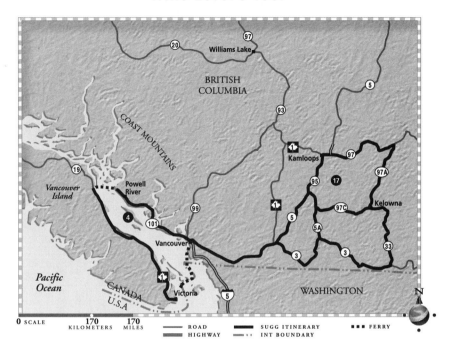

Take this tour in October, when the Okanagan Similkameen has its annual wine festival. Drive Highway 3 through the Similkameen to the Okanagan Valley; follow the highway signs to the wineries of your choice (there are over 25), pick up local guides at various information centres along the way, and stop often to participate in wine tastings, special dinners, vineyard picnics, and horse-drawn orchard tours.

❹ **Highway Loops and Islands** (Mill Bay, Cobble Hill, Cowichan Valley, Duncan)
⓱ **The Okanagan Similkameen** (Keremeos, Osoyoos, Okanagan Falls, Naramata, Summerland, Peachland, Westbank, Kelowna, Vernon)

Time needed: 1 to 2 weeks

Family Fun Tour

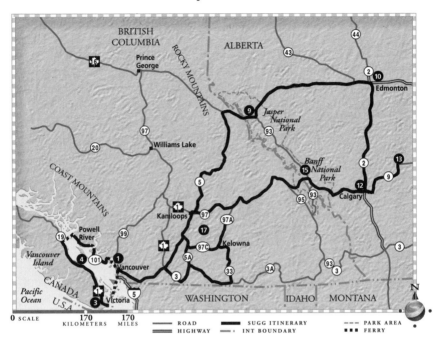

● **Vancouver** (Public Aquarium, Stanley Park, Science World, Kids Festival)
● **Victoria** (Old Town, Royal B.C. Museum, Craigdarroch Castle)
● **Highway Loops and Islands** (Newcastle Island Provincial Marine
  Park, Coombs Emporium, Cyber City Adventures)
● **Jasper National Park** (camping, canoeing, white-water rafting)
● **Edmonton** (Space and Science Center, West Edmonton Mall, Valley
  Zoo, Alberta Aviation Museum, Klondike Days in July)
● **Calgary** (Calgary Science Centre, Stampede, Calgary Zoo, Heritage
  Park Historical Village, Aerospace Museum, Calaway Park)
● **Drumheller Valley** (Rosebud Theatre, Royal Tyrrell Museum, Dinosaur
  Museum, Reptile World, Badlands Go-Kart Park, Funland Amusements,
  Drumheller Aquaplex, Dinosaur Provincial Park)
● **Banff/Lake Louise** (hiking, fishing, wildlife watching, gondola riding)
● **The Okanagan Similkameen** (swimming, boating, water sliding,
  ballooning, Kettle Valley Steam Railway)

Time needed: 2 to 3 weeks

Skier's Tour

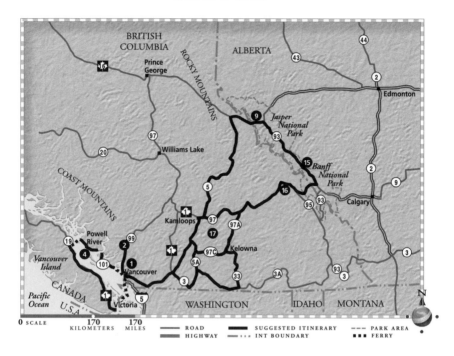

With its many mountains, high plateaus, mild climate, and staggering scenery, Western Canada is a skier's paradise.

- **❶ Vancouver** (Grouse Mountain)
- **❷ Whistler and the Sea to Sky Highway** (Whistler Resort)
- **❹ Highway Loops and Islands** (Mount Washington Ski Resort)
- **❾ Jasper National Park** (Marmot Basin)
- **⑮ Banff/Lake Louise** (Mount Norquay, Sunshine Village)
- **⑯ Kootenay Country** (Red Mountain)
- **⑰ The Okanagan Similkameen** (Silver Star Mountain Resort, Big White Ski Resort, Apex Resort)

Time needed: 2 weeks

USING THE PLANNING MAP

A major aspect of itinerary planning is determining your mode of transportation and the route you will follow as you travel from destination to destination. The Planning Map on the following pages will allow you to do just that.

First read through the destination chapters carefully and note the sights that intrigue you. Then photocopy the Planning Map so you can try out several different routes that will take you to these destinations. (The mileage chart that follows will help you to calculate your travel distances.) Decide where you will be starting your tour of Western Canada. Will you fly into Vancouver, Calgary, or Edmonton, or will you start from somewhere in between? Will you be driving from place to place or flying into major transportation hubs and renting a car for day trips? The answers to these questions will form the basis for your travel route design.

Once you have a firm idea of where your travels will take you, copy your route onto one of the additional Planning Maps in the Appendix. You won't have to worry about where your map is, and the information you need on each destination will always be close at hand.

Lyn Hancock

Alaska Highway, mile 401

Planning Map: Western Canada

Tatshenshini-Alsek
Wilderness Park

Yukon Territory

1

Atlin
Provincial
Park

37

97

Juneau

Muncho Lake
Provincial Park

Telegraph
Creek

8

Alaska

Mount Edziza
Provincial Park

Spatsizi Plateau
Wilderness Provincial
Park

37

Tatlatui
Provincial Park

Ketchikan

Stewart

Hazelton

Naikoon
Provincial
Park

Prince
Rupert

British
Columbia

16

Queen
Charlotte
Islands

7

Hecate Strait

Kitimat Ranges

16

Tweedsmuir
Provincial
Park

Pacific Ocean

South Moresby
National Park
Reserve

6

Bella
Coola

20

Cape Scott
Provincial
Park

Port Hardy

Ts'ylpos
Provincial
Park

Campbell
River

Vancouver
Island

Strathcona
Provincial
Park

19

4

4

5

Pacific Rim National Park

Nanaimo

0 SCALE   250   250
            KILOMETERS   MILES

— ROAD
══ DIVIDED HIGHWAY

········ FERRY
----- AREA OR PARK BOUNDARY

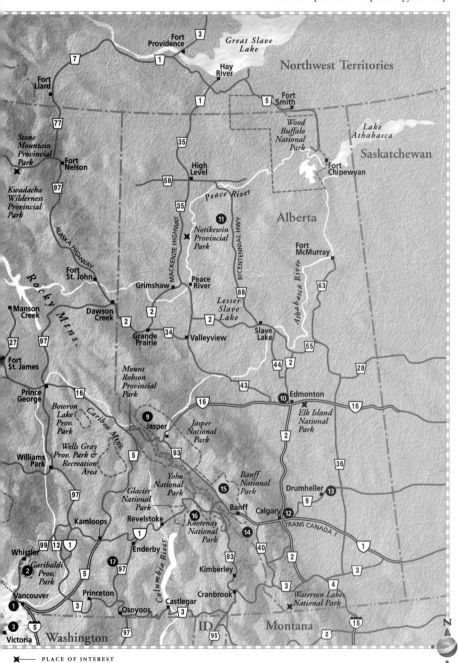

Fort Providence `3`
Great Slave Lake
`7` `1`
Hay River
Fort Liard
Northwest Territories
`1` `5` Fort Smith
`77`
Wood Buffalo National Park
Lake Athabasca
Stone Mountain Provincial Park
`35`
Fort Nelson
High Level
Saskatchewan
Fort Chipewyan
Kwadacha Wilderness Provincial Park `97`
`58`
Peace River
`35`
ALASKA HIGHWAY
Notikewin Provincial Park `11`
Alberta
Rocky Mtns.
Fort St. John
MACKENZIE HIGHWAY
Grimshaw
Peace River
BICENTENNIAL HWY
Fort McMurray
Athabasca River
Manson Creek
Dawson Creek
`2`
Lesser Slave Lake
`88`
`63`
`27` `97`
`2`
Grande Prairie `34`
Valleyview
`2`
Slave Lake
`55`
Fort St. James
`44` `2`
`28`
Prince George
`16`
Mount Robson Provincial Park
`43`
`16`
Edmonton `10`
`16`
Bowron Lake Prov. Park
Cariboo Mtns.
`9` Jasper
Jasper National Park
Elk Island National Park
Wells Gray Prov. Park & Recreation Area
`5`
`93`
`2`
Williams Park
`97`
Yoho National Park
Banff National Park
`36`
Glacier National Park
`15`
Drumheller `13`
Kamloops
Revelstoke
`1`
Banff
Calgary `12`
`9`
`16`
Kootenay National Park
`14`
TRANS CANADA 1
`99` `12` `1`
Enderby
Columbia River
`40`
`1`
Whistler
`17` `97`
`93`
`2`
Garibaldi Prov. Park
`2`
`5`
Kimberley
`3`
Vancouver
Princeton
`3`
Castlegar
Cranbrook
`3`
`4`
Waterton Lakes National Park
`1`
Osoyoos
`3`
`3` `5`
`97`
ID
Montana
`15`
Victoria
Washington
`95`
`2`

N

✶━━ PLACE OF INTEREST

	Banff	Calgary	Drumheller	Edmonton	Ft. McMurray	Jasper	Kananaskis Village	Kelowna	Nelson	Prince George	Prince Rupert	Terrace	Vancouver	Watson Lake	Whistler
Calgary	128/80														
Drumheller	263/164	138/86													
Edmonton	401/249	295/183	279/174												
Fort Mcmurray	840/522	733/456	703/475	439/273											
Jasper	287/179	413/257	547/340	361/225	796/495										
Kanaskis Village	257/160	129/80	249/155	339/211	778/484	372/231									
Kelowna	474/295	602/374	740/460	897/558	1314/817	602/374	559/348								
Nelson	496/309	624/388	762/474	919/572	1336/831	701/436	581/361	338/210							
Prince George	661/411	789/491	927/577	737/458	1206/750	376/234	746/464	685/426	979/609						
Prince Rupert	1385/861	1513/941	1651/1027	1461/909	1930/1201	1100/684	1470/914	1409/876	1703/1059	724/450					
Terrace	1238/770	1366/850	1504/935	1314/817	1783/1109	953/593	1323/823	1262/785	1556/968	577/359	147/91				
Vancouver	847/527	975/606	1113/692	1155/718	1687/1049	794/494	932/580	395/246	657/409	778/484	1502/934	227/141			
Watson Lake	1889/1175	1870/1163	2008/1249	1575/980	2104/1309	1604/998	1974/1228	1913/1190	2207/1373	1228/764	988/615	1500/933	1492/928		
Whistler	967/601	1095/681	1233/764	1275/793	1807/1124	914/569	1052/654	515/320	777/483	898/559	1622/1009	308/192	192/119	2126/1322	
Williams Lake	779/485	907/564	1045/650	904/562	1444/898	543/338	864/537	447/278	741/461	238/148	962/598	757/471	583/363	1466/912	660/411

WHY VISIT WESTERN CANADA?

Several decades ago I left my home in Australia and set off to see the world, traveling through Asia, Africa, and Europe before ending up in Canada. I lived in Eastern Canada for a year, but it wasn't until I went to Western Canada that I was lured to stay. I call it God's Country; others call it Lotus Land or Shangri-la.

What's so alluring about Western Canada? What does it have that attracts immigrants and tourists alike and makes it the fastest-growing region in the country? Diversity—of climate, landscapes, wildlife; of people, cities, cultures. Immensity—of mountains, forests, prairies; of sky and light that lift your spirits and trigger your dreams. Beautiful British Columbia. Wild Rose Country Alberta.

It takes less than an hour to jet across Western Canada—from the reef-ridden beaches and rainforest jungles of the Pacific Coast and the island-studded fjords of the Inland Passage; over the ice-capped mountains of the Coast Range, the sagebrush hills and rolling grasslands, the lakes and rivers of the Interior Plateau; over more ice-capped mountains—this time the world-famous Canadian Rockies; and then to flat, patterned prairie. West of the Rockies is the magnificent chaos of British Columbia; east of the Rocky Mountains is the contrasting orderliness of Alberta.

Yet it takes more than one lifetime to see it all. Despite Western Canada's vast network of roads and ferries, it is still largely unexplored. You will have to make choices.

Take a boat trip through the Gulf Islands or the Inland Passage. Hike and camp in a Rocky Mountain national park. Ride a horse or raft a river in the Cariboo-Chilcotin or the Red Deer Valley. Ski at Whistler, Kelowna, or Jasper. Visit a vineyard along Okanagan Lake. Drive the Alaska Highway or the Icefields Parkway. Fish for salmon on the Queen Charlotte Islands or for trout in one of myriad northern lakes. Connect with human history by viewing totem poles in Ninstints or a buffalo jump at Head-Smashed-In, hiking the Chilkoot Gold Rush Trail, or visiting a fur-trading post or heritage park.

The main reason for visiting Western Canada is the great outdoors, but even its cities are attractive. See cosmopolitan Vancouver, dynamic Calgary, mega-malled Edmonton, or fabled Victoria, and seek out other towns such as charming Kimberley, spectacular Atlin, or picturesque Telegraph Cove.

"Go West" is advice as good today as it was yesterday.

HISTORY AND CULTURES

In earlier times the two provinces of Western Canada—British Columbia and Alberta—were kept largely separate by the two north-south series of mountain ranges: the Coast Range and Rockies. Aboriginals, now called First Nations people, occupied the lands on either side of these barriers for at least 10,000 years. To the west lived the Coast Salish, Nootka, Kwakiutl, Bella Coola, Haida, Tsimshian, and Tlingit; to the east, the Interior Salish, Beaver, Chipewyan, Blackfoot, Blood, Cree, Peigan, and Sarcee.

Coastal tribes fished for salmon, hunted whales, gathered berries, and harvested furs and cedar trees for clothing and canoes. Easy living produced a rich culture. Inland tribes, living in a harsher climate, had to work harder. They moved around a lot more and traded such things as obsidian, buffalo skins, and mountain-goat wool for the much-valued eulachon oil of their coastal cousins.

Europeans looking for the Northwest Passage and rich trade items of their own began exploring Western Canada in the late 1700s. From the west by sea came Russians, Spaniards, Americans, and British, who established a fiercely competitive trade with China in the sea-otter furs that they obtained from natives along the Pacific Coast.

From the east by land came British and Americans who set up fur-trading posts for the Northwest Company and Hudson's Bay Company. The Northwest Company's Alexander Mackenzie used native trading routes to find his way across Western Canada to the Pacific Ocean. In 1793 he became the first person to cross the continent. As the sea otter and beaver were vital trade items in what was to become British Columbia, so was the buffalo (or plains bison) in what was to become Alberta.

Few visitors settled in Western Canada until the Gold Rush, which began in 1858, first in the Fraser River, then the Cariboo, and by 1898, the Yukon. In 1866 the two colonies of Vancouver Island and mainland British Columbia became one colony, and in 1871 British Columbia joined other provinces to became partners in the Dominion of Canada—after very nearly joining the United States!

The next great influx of settlers came to Western Canada after 1886, when the Canadian Pacific Railway reached the Pacific Coast. A year later the logging settlements in Burrard Inlet became part of the new port city of Vancouver, which quickly outstripped Victoria as the capital of British Columbia. Other railway lines followed, and lumbering became the province's most important industry.

Meanwhile, in Alberta, the Northwest Mounted Police, who came west to maintain law and order, built Fort Macleod and Fort Calgary; the once-vast throngs of plains bison were decimated through overhunting; treaties were signed with the native peoples; and in the 1880s, surveyors marked the prairie into 160-acre (65-hectare) squares. The foothills and short-grass prairie, combined with the railway and warm chinook winds from the west, were found to be ideal for agriculture and ranching.

In the early years of the twentieth century, settlers from such places as the Ukraine, Great Britain, Germany, Scandinavia, and the United States streamed into Western Canada in response to the Canadian government's offer of free land. In 1905 Alberta became a province and, with Saskatchewan, joined the Confederation. As a result of its strategic location for people heading north to the Klondike gold-diggings and, later, the Alaska Highway and Canol pipeline construction, Edmonton flourished and became the provincial capital.

It was the discovery of oil at Turner Valley in 1914 and, more importantly, at Leduc in 1947 that really put Alberta on the map. Alberta's economy shifted from agriculture to oil and gas. Western Canada's natural resources—fish, lumber, grain, oil, gas, and coal—combined with an abundance of energetic immigrants have brought it wealth.

Today tourism is being encouraged to lessen the impact of what has been a boom-and-bust economy. Tourists flock to Western Canada in response to its geography: to climb mountains, camp in parks, raft rivers, watch whales, or catch fish. Adventure travel and ecotourism are the fastest-growing segments of the industry.

Tourists also come to sample Western Canada's many different cultures, after a recent increase in interest and pride in aboriginal cultures. On the Queen Charlotte Islands, they watch Haida artists at work; at the Gitxsan villages of the Skeena River ('Ksan), they view longhouses and watch masked dancers; at Writing-on-Stone Provincial Park on the Milk River, they see North America's largest concentration of pictographs and petroglyphs; and at Head-Smashed-In Buffalo, they learn how Plains Indians killed and used bison.

The arts and cultures brought to Western Canada by various immigrant groups make it a fascinating place to live and visit. See Victoria for things British, Calgary and the Calgary Stampede to experience American West culture, Cardston to learn about the Mormon way of life, Edmonton to savor the Ukrainian lifestyle, or Castlegar for Doukhobor culture.

The newest wave of immigrants comes from Asia. British Columbia, a Pacific Rim province, and the port city of Vancouver are benefiting most from Asian influence. Asia buys 40 percent of British Columbia's exports, and Hong Kong Chinese in particular have bought land and invested in business in Greater Vancouver. Vancouver's Chinatown is the second largest on North America's West Coast. To celebrate Chinese New Year, the Chinese community in Vancouver puts on a colorful parade and Lion Dance that winds through downtown streets.

CUISINE

The diversity of Western Canada's ethnic character naturally leads to an equally diverse cuisine. British Columbia salmon and seafood dominate West Coast restaurants. Alberta steaks big as dinner plates are touted on the prairie.

An increasing number of restaurants in Greater Vancouver serves Northwest Coast First Nations cuisine such as bannock bread, alder-grilled salmon, and soapberry ice cream. Fresh lamb is a specialty of Saltspring Island. Fresh Okanagan fruit is bought in boxes from roadside stands, and Okanagan grapes are the basis for a thriving wine industry. Armstrong cheeses are highly regarded. Lake trout and buffalo are served commonly in the north.

The effects of immigration on cuisine are seen everywhere. The British custom of afternoon tea is a popular ritual at the Empress Hotel and dozens of other restaurants in Ye Olde Victoria. Ukrainian perogies and cabbage rolls are easy to find in Edmonton, Russian borscht in Grand Forks. Thai food is the most recent flavor of the month.

ARTS

The arts are alive and very well in Western Canada. Along with a recent resurgence in and greater appreciation of indigenous art such as Haida carving, there has been a tremendous growth in all arts. There is likely no community on either side of the Rockies, however small, without its own art, music, theater, or dance group. Ballroom dancing is making a big comeback in British Columbia, and of course, square dancing has always been big in Alberta.

The arts flourish particularly on the West Coast and even more particularly on the Gulf Islands. Attracted by the diverse scenery, more and more Hollywood films are being produced in Western Canada,

especially in Vancouver, Victoria, and Nelson. Each town's daily newspapers and weekly tabloids list current arts and entertainment events. In addition, Vancouver has an Arts Hotline at (604) 684-ARTS.

It's worth taking in a show or symphony at Vancouver's refurbished Orpheum Theatre just to see this concert hall's original splendor. Visit the Vancouver Art Gallery and Victoria's Emily Carr Gallery to view the works of Emily Carr, an eccentric painter who captured the essence of the wild West Coast. Shows of international significance take place at Vancouver's Queen Elizabeth Theatre, Victoria's MacPherson Playhouse, Calgary's Centre for the Performing Arts, the Calgary Jubilee Auditorium, and the Edmonton Jubilee Auditorium. Sometimes the showcase is as intriguing as the event, as in the Vancouver Symphony's annual performance on the top of Whistler Mountain, and Victoria Symphony's performance on a barge in Victoria's Inner Harbor.

Festivals of all kinds are held everywhere, especially in summer. Check out the Edmonton Folk Music Festival, the Edmonton Jazz City International Festival, the Edmonton Street Performers Festival, and Edmonton Dreamspeakers. Try the Whistler Country and Blues Festival, Whistler's Showcase of Street Entertainment Festival, the Victorian International Festival, Banff Festival of the Arts, Harrison Hotsprings Festival of the Arts, and Chemainus Festival of Murals. Don't miss the Fringe Festival of streetside theatrical events held in Victoria, Vancouver, and often other Western Canadian towns. A new festival is Victoria's First People's Festival in early August. There are also zillions of arts and crafts fairs and venues where you can see local artists in action.

Museums you shouldn't miss are Victoria's Royal British Columbia Museum, Calgary's Glenbow Museum, B.C. Forest Museum in Duncan, Head-Smashed-in Buffalo Jump Interpretive Centre near Fort Macleod, Vancouver's Museum of Anthropology, the Royal Tyrrell Museum in Drumheller, and Passing of the Legends Museum in Kananaskis Country.

FLORA

Timber covers almost two-thirds of British Columbia. Huge trees, some 300 feet tall and over 1,000 years old—Douglas fir, western red cedar, western hemlock, Sitka spruce—dominate Western Canada's wild and wet west coast. Take a walk through Cathedral Grove or follow a trail in Clayuquot Sound to appreciate the best of these world-famous rainforests. Gnarled Garry oak and smooth shiny arbutus grow

in pockets of rocky outcroppings on Vancouver and the Gulf Islands. On the rain-shadow side of the mountains, at higher elevations or more northerly latitudes, the coast and boreal forests give way to parklands or grasslands dotted with groves of alder, birch, and aspen. Most of the southern prairie, however, has no trees at all.

There is a greater variety of flowering plants in British Columbia than anywhere else in Canada. Southwestern British Columbia's mild climate brings flowers out earlier than in other parts of Western Canada; Victorians like to boast of roses blooming at Christmas and the highest flower count in the country each February. Spectacular displays of wildflowers appear in spring on high alpine meadows such as Manning Park or Mount Revelstoke. The provincial flower of British Columbia is the Pacific dogwood; Alberta's is the wild rose.

FAUNA

No place in Canada is home to as many wild animal species as British Columbia: including fish, there are 1,083 different species. Off the west coast, many tour operators will take you to see seals, sea lions, orcas, grey whales, and even sea otters (now making a comeback after virtual extermination). The forests in both British Columbia and Alberta are home to cougars, deer, elk, moose, wolves, and black bear; the mountains shelter mountain sheep and goats. Many of these can be seen from over 60 Wildlife Viewing Areas being set up throughout British Columbia by the government. Contact the Wildlife Branch, B.C. Environment, 780 Blanshard Street, Victoria, British Columbia V8V 1X5, (250) 387-9767. Tour operators take visitors to see the rare white kermode bear on Princess Royal Island and the endangered grizzlies of the Khutzeymateen Valley. But you don't necessarily have to trek to the wilderness to see Western Canada's famous wildlife—cougars have been spotted on several occasions on the grounds of the Empress Hotel in downtown Victoria!

Birders flock to see Western Canada's birds. More than a million birds migrate along the Pacific Flyway, and hundreds of thousands stop to nest. Victoria and Vancouver are favorite wintering areas for ducks, geese, and eagles, and Victoria's Christmas bird count is often the highest in Canada.

Popular viewing areas are the Reifel Refuge at the mouth of the Fraser River, Brackendale near Vancouver, and Witty's Lagoon near Victoria. Visitors are often amazed to see colorful tropic-like birds such

as tufted puffins and rhinoceros auklets swimming close to shore or nesting in offshore seabird colonies along the west coast. The many sloughs and potholes in British Columbia's Cariboo region and on the Alberta prairie provide nesting grounds for many species of ducks, geese, swans, and white pelicans. Some towns celebrate the annual return of their wildlife, such as Parksville's Brant Festival, Nanaimo's Sea Lion Festival, and Ucluelet's and Tofino's Whale Festivals.

Alberta is well known for its bird-conservation efforts, especially regarding birds of prey. Several centers encourage visitors to have a close-up look at the raptors in their care. Try Alberta Birds of Prey Centre near Lethbridge (800-661-1222) and the Canadian Wildlife Service Peregrine Falcon Hatchery near Wainwright (403-842-5513). McLennan, north of Edmonton, calls itself the Bird Capital of Canada: it's at the center of three major flyways and hosts some 17,000 shorebirds and 250,000 landbirds yearly. For guided tours, check out Kimiwan Birdwalk (403-324-3065). In the far north, Wood Buffalo National Park is the last natural nesting grounds of the rare whooping crane.

THE LAY OF THE LAND

British Columbia, the westernmost province of Western Canada, is known around the world for beautiful landscapes. The words on B.C. license plates are true: Beautiful British Columbia. Visitors who are inhibited by high snowcapped mountains may prefer Alberta, which shares the Rocky Mountains on its southwestern edge but stretches east to the Great Plains and north to the rocky Canadian Shield. Whichever route you take, you will be awestruck by the variety of landscapes in Western Canada.

In the far west, the land rises from the Pacific Ocean in a necklace of islands, the largest of which are the Queen Charlotte Islands, Vancouver Island, and the Gulf Islands. These islands help to protect British Columbia's deeply fjord-indented coastline and are part of the Inland Passage to Alaska. Towering over the islands are the Coast Mountains, the highest in North America (Mount Waddington is 13,175 feet/4,016 meters).

The only flat parts of British Columbia are the rich Fraser River delta and areas of the Peace River Lowland in northeast British Columbia, which merge with the Peace River Lowland in northwestern Alberta.

British Columbia's drier interior, between the coast and the Rocky Mountains, is a region of high plateaus (the Cariboo-Chilcotin), deep lakes and valleys (the Okanagan), and even more mountain ranges (Cassiar, Omineca, Monashee, Selkirk, and Purcell).

Between the interior plateau and the next wall of mountains (the Rockies) lies the Rocky Mountain Trench, a huge gash in the landscape through which major rivers such as the Columbia flow. The Rockies mark the Continental Divide, a height from which some rivers flow west to the Pacific Ocean, others flow north to the Arctic Ocean, and still others flow east across Canada to empty eventually into the Atlantic Ocean. Mount Robson, at 13,048 feet (3,977 meters), is the Rockies' highest point. Remnants of the last Ice Age can be seen in the popular Columbia Ice Fields and the Athabasca Glacier.

Sloping eastward from the Rockies are the forested foothills of Alberta. About three-quarters of Alberta is flat prairie grasslands, now tamed into neat farmlands. The plain is gashed by deep valleys, such as the North and South Saskatchewan Rivers, and by dry gulches, such as the Badlands near Drumheller. In the north the prairie gives way to boreal forest and the ancient rocks and lakes of the Canadian Shield.

OUTDOOR ACTIVITIES

You name it, you can do it—depending on the season—and stores offer guidebooks galore to tell you where and how to do it: walking, hiking, mountaineering, climbing, cycling, swimming, canoeing, kayaking, white-water rafting, Sea-Dooing (marine motorbiking), powerboating, sailboating, houseboating, scuba diving, windsurfing, gliding, parachuting, parasailing, hot-air ballooning, horseback-riding, hunting, fishing, bird-watching, wildlife-watching, whale-watching, golfing, caving, gold-panning, snowmobiling, snowshoeing, skiing— or just suntanning and hot-springs soaking.

And what spectacular settings for outdoor activities! British Columbia has five national parks, over 450 provincial parks and provincial and recreation areas, 131 ecological reserves, an increasing number of specially protected areas, additional Forest Service recreation areas, and municipal recreation areas. Alberta has four national parks, 143 provincial parks, 159 Forest Service recreation areas, and additional municipal recreation areas. Note: Be sure to plan early— some of the more popular national parks trails restrict numbers.

PRACTICAL TIPS

HOW MUCH WILL IT COST?

Traveling in Western Canada is less expensive than in Europe but more expensive than in the United States. Goods and services are generally dearer anywhere in Canada and, except in the Yukon, Northwest Territories, Nunavut, and Alberta, additional taxes must be paid: the Provincial Sales Tax (PST), which is 7 percent in British Columbia; the much-hated Goods and Services Tax (GST), also 7 percent on most goods and services; and an additional nonrefundable tax on hotel and motel accommodations: 8 percent in British Columbia and 5 percent in Alberta.

Still, nonresidents can have the GST refunded on some accommodations and nonconsumable products if the goods are bought for use outside Canada and taken out of the country within 60 days of purchase, and if the rebate is claimed within a year of purchase. You must buy a minimum of $100 worth of goods (i.e., have paid at least $7 GST) and must submit original receipts. Rebate application forms are available from most Canadian duty-free shops, tourist information centers, and Canadian embassies and consulates; or you can mail your application to Revenue Canada, Customs and Excise, Visitor Rebate Programme, Ottawa, Ontario K1A 1J5. For further information, call (800) 66-VISIT in Canada or (613) 991-3346 outside Canada.

American visitors have the advantage of a U.S. dollar that is usually worth one-third more than the Canadian dollar. At the time of this writing, American visitors received approximately $1.38 Canadian for every U.S. dollar; shop around for the best exchange rates. All prices quoted in this book are given in Canadian dollars. (To convert to approximate U.S. dollars, divide by 1.4.) Besides the usual $5, $10, $20, $50, $100, and larger bills, Canada uses a couple of intriguing coins: the "loonie," worth $1 and engraved with a loon, and the "toonie," worth $2 and engraved at the center with a "gold" polar bear. They're so striking you may want to keep one or two as souvenirs.

Prices for hotel and motel accommodations vary hugely according to where and when you go—from less than $30 a night in the off-season in the backwoods or on the edge of town, to more than $2,000 a night in high season for a suite in a top-flight Banff resort. The average price for a motel or hotel room is $80–$125, but competition for the tourist dollar permits a variety of specials based on location and time of year and week, and such add-ons as free breakfasts and dinners. You can get good rooms for $30–$50. Bed and breakfast accommodations usually cost less. Camping costs range $10–$20 per party, one vehicle per site, and these prices include the GST. Hostel prices are similar to those at campsites. Prices quoted are based on summer 1997 research; invariably, there will be some increases, so be sure to call for current rates.

Meals vary greatly in price as well. You can get a filling breakfast for as little as $2.99 at a neighborhood cafe and a gourmet dinner for about $40 or more at a ritzy hotel, but an average dinner at a good restaurant costs about $20 (excluding drinks, appetizers, and desserts). Buffets and chain restaurants are economical. Often, the higher the price for a meal, the less food on your plate. Perhaps that's why I prefer buffets—you see what you get beforehand. I particularly like trendy Mongolian stir-fry places where you pick your meat, vegetables, and sauces; watch them being cooked; and pay by weight.

Elderhostel Canada is an excellent way to enjoy a rewarding holiday. For as little as $400 a week all-inclusive, you live on college campuses or in conference centers, marine biology field stations, or environmental study centers, and enjoy all the accompanying cultural and recreational resources. Elderhostel is a blend of education and travel for participants who are usually in their mid-fifties and beyond. You listen to lectures for about 90 minutes a day, but you have no homework or exams and enjoy many extracurricular activities suited to the elderhostel's location.

There are programs to suit every interest in Western Canada. You might study Pacific Coast marine life from the Bamfield Marine Station or aboard a 65-foot motor vessel; explore Vancouver gardens from a college campus; capture the Kootenays with a camera or paintbrush from a platformed, double-walled tipi; learn about the Ukrainian culture from a hotel in Smoky Lake; or explore Calgary by bicycle. For information, contact Diane Osberg, Box 31, RR1 Site 7, Priddis, Alberta T0L 1W0, (403) 949-2165; or Loretta Krauter, Okanagan University College, Box 68, 13211 Henry Street, Summerland, British Columbia V0H 1Z0, (250) 494-4469.

To save money traveling in Western Canada, take buses and trains, choose housekeeping facilities at motels, use campgrounds in provincial and national parks, watch for specials on transportation, and travel midweek to get free rides on government ferries if you're a British Columbia senior over 65.

GETTING THERE

The major airports of Vancouver, Calgary, and Edmonton are served by just about every major airline, notably Air Canada and Canadian Airlines International. Cut costs by using advance purchase bookings, by being alert to special deals, and by flying with no-frills discount charter airlines such as Greyhound Air and Canada 3000. If you leave from Vancouver's International Airport, you have to pay a controversial Airport Improvement Tax of $10 (provincial) and $15 (international). This tax has made so much money for Vancouver, that Edmonton now has one and Calgary plans one, too.

Once in Western Canada, the best way to travel is either by car or in some kind of recreational vehicle (RV). The scenery is ever-changing, there's much to see and do in concentrated areas, and the highways are constantly being improved. In British Columbia, myriad logging roads provide after-hours and weekend access to a variety of outback countryside and free camping areas. Maps are freely available from the B.C. Forest Service, Recreation Section, 4595 Canada Way, Burnaby, British Columbia V5G 4L9, (604) 660-7500. A four-wheel-drive vehicle is usually necessary only in the more remote and mountainous off-road areas or in accessing snow activity areas in season.

Ferries are an integral part of the highway system; B.C. Ferries runs many routes that interconnect and provide a delightful way of hopping between the islands and the mainland. The Inside Passage Ferry between Port Hardy and Prince Rupert and the new Discovery Coast Ferry between Port Hardy and Bella Coola are really minitours. Between June and September, artists are often on board to entertain or to display and sell their work. Inland ferries are free for all, and on other ferries, seniors with B.C. Pharmacare cards can travel free Monday through Thursday (excluding holidays). Count on lines in summer on the more popular routes. It is possible to reserve space under certain conditions. For more information, contact B.C. Ferries, 1112 Fort Street, Victoria, British Columbia V8V 4V2; phone Vancouver (604) 669-1211, Victoria (250) 386-3431, or from anywhere in British Columbia (800) 663-7600. Other ferries ply the waters between Victoria, Seattle, and Port Angeles; and between Sidney and Anacortes.

U.S. drivers must carry proof of financial responsibility. The Yellow Card is accepted as a nonresident interprovincial motor-vehicle liability insurance, obtainable from your own insurance company. Radar detection of speeders is controversial, but it's widely used in British Columbia.

Seat belts and child restraints for children under 6 are mandatory in Western Canada, as are helmets for cyclists and motorcyclists. The Alaska Highway and Mackenzie Highway are paved (or as good as paved), but watch your windshields and avoid logging trucks on the Liard Highway, which is still gravelled.

Gas is cheaper in the U.S. than Canada, so if you're close to the U.S. border, fill up on the American side. Gas is also cheaper east of the Rockies. Officially, Canada is metric, but there has been some resistance to changing from Imperial measurement, and recently Canadians have begun using both, especially in grocery stores.

All major cities are linked by Greyhound Bus, and smaller bus companies provide economical connections between many other communities. Train travel is more costly and limited in scope, but it's more relaxing and often follows more scenic routes. The Rocky Mountain Railtour between Vancouver and Jasper, Banff, and Calgary is highly regarded as the most spectacular train trip in the world. For further information, contact VIA Rail at (800) 561-8630 in Canada, B.C. Rail at (604) 631-3500, and Rocky Mountaineer Railtours at (800) 665-7245 (Canada and the U.S.).

WHEN TO GO

Western Canada's weather is as varied as its geography, but generally it rains a lot more on the west side of the mountains, is drier in the central interior and the prairie, and is cooler the farther north or the higher you go. British Columbia is the rainiest (and the balmiest) province, and Alberta is the sunniest.

June to August are the most popular months to travel in Western Canada. It's vacation time, when the weather is warmest, a lot warmer than southern visitors expect in a country world-renowned for its cold. In fact, in July the prairie sizzles, and in the Osoyoos desert you can fry an egg on the pavement. But summer months can be crowded, so consider the advantages of shoulder seasons. Spring and fall are beautiful in the Okanagan Similkameen and are also wine-tasting time. Spring, when the flowers burst into blossom, is probably the best time of year in Victoria and Vancouver. If you visit the northern half of Western Canada in fall, when the leaves turn gold and orange, you avoid mosquitoes and can catch more fish. Winter in the Rockies and the Okanagan is ideal for skiing.

Remember to dress in layers and be ready for everything—a light, hooded jacket and windbreaker for the unpredictable mountains, especially at night; gumboots and umbrellas for rain on the west coast at any time of year; and bathing suits and shorts for the dry, lake-splashed interior in summer.

WHERE TO STAY AND EAT

This book includes a wide variety of food and lodging places, and many more are listed in the resources provided free by government travel departments and private businesses. But places get bought and sold and people change their jobs so quickly that it's always wise to ask local residents for suggestions about lodgings and restaurants.

Try one of each region's conversation pieces. Have a drink and watch the world go by from a streetside table in the village of Whistler; take in tea and crumpets at Victoria's Empress Hotel; at least walk through the lobby and grounds of famous hotels such as Chateau Lake

WESTERN CANADA CLIMATE

Average daily high and low temperatures in degrees Celsius, plus monthly precipitation in millimeters (inches in parentheses). To convert degrees Celsius to degrees Fahrenheit, multiply by 1.8 and add 32.

	Victoria	Vancouver	Banff	Calgary
Jan.	6.5/0.3	6.3/0.2	-5.3/-14.9	-3.6/15.4
	141 (5.6)	149.8 (6.0)	31 (1.2)	12.2 (0.5)
Mar.	10.2/1.9	10.1/1.8	3.8/-7.9	3.3/-8.4
	72 (2.9)	108.8 (4.4)	21.5 (0.9)	14.7 (0.6)
May	16.3/6.5	16.8/6.4	14.2/1.5	16.4/3.0
	33.5 (1.3)	61.7 (2.5)	57.5 (2.3)	52.9 (2.1)
July	21.8/10.4	22.0/11.1	22.1/7.4	23.2/9.5
	17.6 (0.7)	36.1 (1.4)	51.2 (2.1)	69.9 (2.8)
Sept.	19.1/8.4	19.0/8.3	16.1/2.4	17.4/3.8
	36.6 (1.5)	64.4 (2.6)	43.8 (1.8)	48.1 (1.9)
Nov.	9.4/2.5	9.2/2.3	0.5/-8.2	2.9/-9.0
	139.2 (5.6)	169.9 (6.8)	30.4 (1.2)	11.6 (0.5)

Louise, Banff Springs, or Jasper Park Lodge in the Rockies; splurge on a fishing resort off one of the West Coast islands; watch the sun set from a sandy beach on the Pacific Ocean; dine in a revolving "view" restaurant, such as the top of the Calgary Tower or Vancouver's Cloud Nine; or do something—anything—at the Edmonton Mall. The budget traveler may have to choose a campsite, but in Western Canada this may be the most rewarding place of all.

Help for the handicapped is fairly widespread in Western Canada. Several British Columbia parks are set up for people in wheelchairs. The Access Canada logo on a property means that seniors and people with disabilities are assured of special facilities and service.

Note that British Columbia has new area codes for its phone lines: the code in Vancouver, east to Hope, north to D'Arcy, as well as all of the Sunshine Coast, remains 604, but the area code for the rest of the province is now 250.

RECOMMENDED READING

A plethora of books on Western Canada is available from an abundance of bookstores and publishers. People who live in, or even visit, this area are smitten with a love of the landscapes and their inhabitants, and feel compelled to write about them. In this space I can mention only a smattering, and new titles keep replacing the old in a bewildering array. My list concentrates mainly on the newest releases.

Kim Goldberg's recent *Where to See Wildlife on Vancouver Island* (Harbour Publishing, 1997) is a welcome addition to the British Columbia government's own guide to the province's wildlife viewing areas.

Wild Mammals of Western Canada, by Arthur and Candace Savage (Western Producer Prairie Books, 1981), gives a scientific but popular overview of western wildlife.

There are oodles of books available for different ages on specific Western Canadian animals. *There's a Seal in My Sleeping Bag*, by Lyn Hancock (HarperCollins, 1972) is a Canadian classic, if I do say so myself . . . ! It describes the author's life flying, boating, and meeting Western Canada's people and wildlife. My other books, *There's a Raccoon in My Parka*, *Love Affair with a Cougar*, and *An Ape Came out of My Hatbox*, are out of print but available in libraries. See also *Tell Me, Grandmother*, *The True Story of Jane and Sam Livingston*, about the first settlers in what was to become Calgary.

The Fraser River, by Alan Haig-Brown (Harbour Publishing,

1996), is the most recent book about a river that flows through much of British Columbia's landscape. In its historical, geographical, cultural, and economical importance, the Fraser *is* British Columbia.

For a racy raconteur's rendition of life on the West Coast, read the Raincoast Chronicles (there are more than 17), by Howard White of Harbour Publishing. You'll find a similar look inland in *Down the Road: Journeys through Small-Town British Columbia* and *Backroading Vancouver Island*, both by Rosemary Neering (Whitecap Books, 1991).

A Traveller's Guide to Aboriginal B.C., by Cheryl Coull (Whitecap Books, 1995), is the latest of many books featuring Western Canada's original inhabitants. Any books by author and illustrator Hilary Stewart on Western Canada's First Nations people and their culture are well worth reading. Try *Cedar* and *Looking at Totem Poles* (Douglas and McIntyre, 1993).

Kids will enjoy *Fun BC Facts for Kids*, by Mark Zuelke (Whitecap Books, 1995), and the novel *Buffalo Sunrise*, by Diane Swanson (Whitecap Books, 1995). Zuelke also wrote *The BC Fact Book*, *Everything You Ever Wanted to Know*, and *The Alberta Fact Book* (Whitecap Books, 1995).

For history, a classic is *British Columbia, A History of the Province*, by well-respected George Woodcock (Whitecap Books, 1993). For a lighter look, try *Bowering's BC, A Swashbuckling History*, by poet George Bowering; and *British Columbia, An Illustrated History*, by Geoffrey Molyneux. Heather Harbord concentrates on *Nootka Sound* (Heritage House,1996), where the non-native discovery of British Columbia began. This book is both a history and a paddling guide for kayakers.

For an airborne look at a grandiose province, you can't do better than *Over Beautiful British Columbia* and its accompanying video, recently released by *Beautiful British Columbia* magazine (Pacific Publishers, 1996). It's heavy on photographs and too light on text but great stuff for the coffee-table.

The Rocky Mountains inspire a flood of pictorials and guides. Try Bruce Obee's *The Canadian Rockies* (Whitecap Books). Altitude Press publishes most of the Rockies books, such as *Classic Hikes in the Canadian Rockies*, by Paul Graeme.

RESOURCES

There's a multitude of resources for people planning a trip to Western Canada; this book will help you make some sense out of

the chaos. British Columbia is divided into nine official tourism regions, each led by a local tourism association. Alberta has six tourism
regions, with similar agencies. In addition, many communities throughout the region run summer travel infocenters. So first, gather the free
maps and literature provided by Tourism British Columbia and Travel
Alberta, and, if you're a member, get a copy of the free handbook,
maps, "trip-tiks," and other material provided by the British Columbia
and Alberta Automobile Associations. Then use this book to make
choices. Here are some important resources:

Alberta Economic Development and Tourism, 10155 102nd Street,
Edmonton, Alberta T5J 4L6; (403) 427-4321 or (800) 661-8888.

Alberta Environmental Protection Fish and Wildlife Services, 9920 108th
Street, Edmonton, Alberta T5K 2M4; (403) 944-0313.

Alberta Environmental Protection Parks Service, Standard Life Centre,
10405 Jasper Avenue, Edmonton, Alberta T5J 3N4; (403) 427-6781.

British Columbia Ferries, 1112 Fort Street, Victoria, British Columbia V8V
4V2. For recorded schedule information, phone: Nanaimo
(250) 753-6626, Vancouver (604) 685-1021, and Victoria
(250) 656-0757.

British Columbia Forest Service, Recreation Section, 4595 Canada Way,
Burnaby, British Columbia V5G 4L9; (604) 660-7500.

British Columbia Provincial Parks, 800 Johnson Street, Victoria, British
Columbia V8V 1X4; (250) 387-5002.

Calgary Convention and Visitors Bureau, Main Floor, Calgary Tower, Tower
Centre, 9th Avenue and Centre Street, South Calgary, Alberta T2G
0K8; (403) 263-8510 or (800) 661-1678 (North America).

The Canadian Paraplegic Association, 780 South West Marine Drive,
Vancouver, British Columbia V6P 5Y7; (604) 324-3611; for
wheelchair-accessibility information.

Canadian Parks Service, Information Services, Western Regional Office,
Room 520, 220 4th Avenue SE, Box 2989, Station M, Calgary,
Alberta T2P 3H8; (403) 292-4401.

Cariboo Tourism Association, 190 Yorston Street, Box 4900, Williams
Lake, British Columbia V2G 2V8, (250) 392-2226 or
(800) 663-5885.

Department of Fisheries and Oceans, 555 West Hastings Street, Vancouver,
British Columbia V6B 5G3; (604) 666-3545.

Discover Camping British Columbia, (800) 689-9025. Quick call for
booking campsites between March 15 and October 15.

Edmonton Tourism, 104-9797 Jasper Avenue, Edmonton, Alberta T5J 1N9; (403) 496-8400 or (800) 463-4667.

Guides and Outfitters Association of B.C., Box 94675, Richmond, British Columbia V6Y 4A4; (604) 278-2688, fax (604) 278-3440, e-mail GOABC@dowco.com.

Heritage Canada, (800) 651-7959. Quick call for National Park information.

Kelowna Visitor's and Convention Bureau, (800) 663-4345; Penticton Information Centre, (800) 663-5052; Vernon Tourism, (250) 542-1415; Vernon Reservations, (800) 665-0795.

Ministry of the Environment, 780 Blanshard Street, Victoria, British Columbia V8V 1X4; (250) 387-9717.

Northern Alberta, (800) 661-8888 or (800) 756-4351 for information on this vast region.

SPARC, 106-2182 West 12th Avenue, Vancouver, British Columbia V6K 2N4; (604) 736-4367; for parking permits for people with physical disabilities.

Tourism British Columbia, Parliament Buildings, Victoria, British Columbia V8V 1X4; (800) 663-6000, international and local callers, (604) 663-6000. In the United States, write Box C-34971, Seattle, Washington 98124-1971. In England, write 1 Regent Street, London, England SW1Y 4NS. Advance reservations for accommodations, advice on British Columbia travel, events, points of interest, publications.

Tourism Rockies, Box 10, Kimberley, British Columbia V1A 2Y5; (250) 427-4838 or (250) 427-3344.

Travel Alberta, Box 2500, Edmonton, Alberta T5J 2Z4; (800) 661-8888 (North America), (403) 427-4321, via the Internet: www.discoveralberta.com/ATP.

Vancouver Infocentre, Plaza Level, Waterfront Centre, 200 Burrard Street, Vancouver, British Columbia V6C 3L6; (604) 683-2000, from the United States (800) 888-8835.

Victoria Infocentre, 812 Wharf Street, Victoria, British Columbia V8W 1T3; (250) 382-2127.

1
VANCOUVER

Ahh, Vancouver. Lotus Land! Shangri-la! City of Dreams! Clichés? Yes, but for this gateway to Western Canada, the superlatives are really true. Consider the statistics: Vancouver is British Columbia's largest city, Canada's third-largest city, and the fastest-growing city in North America, with a 1.8 million population and a 3 percent annual growth rate. According to the Corporate Resources Group of Geneva, it's the world's second-best city in which to live: a healthy, clean environment where you can sail or golf in the morning, ski in the afternoon, and still pick roses in winter. For tour buses, it's the number-one destination in North America. A favorable dollar exchange gives Americans every third day of their stay for free. Can 7 million visitors a year be wrong?

Vancouver sprawls across islands and peninsulas separated by rivers, inlets, fjords, and bays, between a dramatic backdrop of rugged mountains and a lush apron of fertile farmland. It's one of the top ten —some say the top three—most beautiful cities in the world. And the variety of its terrain makes it third only to Los Angeles and New York as a North American film and TV production center. Vancouver caters not only to lovers of sports and the outdoors, but also to connoisseurs of good books, coffee, wine, restaurants, and the arts. Boasting the highest ratio of foreign-born residents of any city in the world, its mix of many cultures only adds to its appeal. ∎

VANCOUVER

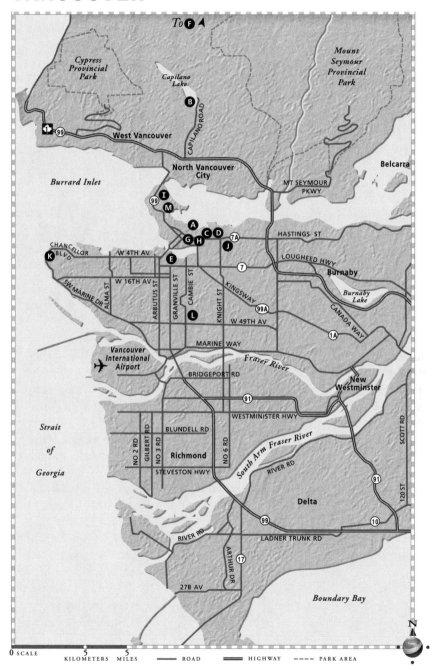

To **F** ▲

Cypress Provincial Park

Capilano Lake

B

Mount Seymour Provincial Park

1 99

West Vancouver

CAPILANO ROAD

North Vancouver City

Belcarra

Burrard Inlet

MT SEYMOUR PKWY

I 99
M

A
G **C** **D**
H **J** 7A

HASTINGS ST

CHANCELLOR BLVD
K

W 4TH AV

E

LOUGHEED HWY

7

Burnaby

SW MARINE DR

ALMA ST

W 16TH AV

ARBUTUS ST

GRANVILLE ST

CAMBIE ST

KNIGHT ST

KINGSWAY

Burnaby Lake

CANADA WAY

99A

L

W 49TH AV

1A

MARINE WAY

Vancouver International Airport

Fraser River

BRIDGEPORT RD

New Westminster

91

WESTMINSTER HWY

SCOTT RD

Strait

of

Georgia

NO 2 RD

GILBERT RD

NO 3 RD

BLUNDELL RD

Richmond

NO 6 RD

South Arm Fraser River

STEVESTON HWY

RIVER RD

Delta

91

120 ST

99

10

RIVER RD

LADNER TRUNK RD

ARTHUR DR

17

27B AV

Boundary Bay

N

0 SCALE 5 5
KILOMETERS MILES   ━━━ ROAD   ▬▬▬ HIGHWAY   ---- PARK AREA

Sights

Ⓐ Canada Place

Ⓑ Capilano Canyon and Lynn Canyon

Ⓒ Chinatown

Ⓓ Gastown

Ⓔ Granville Island

Ⓕ Grouse Mountain

Ⓖ Library Square

Ⓗ Science World

Ⓘ Stanley Park

Ⓙ Sun Yat-Sen Classical Chinese Garden

Ⓚ University of British Columbia Museum of Anthropology

Ⓛ Van Dusen Botanical Gardens

Ⓜ Vancouver Public Aquarium

A PERFECT DAY IN VANCOUVER

Start the day at either the Georgia Street, Alberni, or the Beach Avenue entrance and walk the Seawall around Stanley Park (a Vancouver tradition). Avoid traffic jams and parking problems by walking (or biking). Stroll the beaches of English Bay to the Aquatic Centre, then take a False Creek ferry to Granville Island for lunch—either a stand-up snack at the Public Market or a sit-down meal at a dockside restaurant. False Creek, once a derelict industrial area, now hosts trendy cafes, condos, pubs, and marinas. It's not a creek but an inlet that can be circumnavigated by foot or ferry. If it rains, pop into the Maritime Museum, Science World, or a pub at Stamps Landing. Take the SkyTrain through downtown, from Main Street station to Waterfront Station at Canada Place, then the SeaBus ferry to the North Shore of Burrard Inlet. Finish your day with a Skyride up Grouse Mountain for dinner and dancing.

SIGHTSEEING HIGHLIGHTS

★★★ **Canada Place**—Georgia and Granville Streets used to mark the social center of downtown Vancouver. Now crowds stroll around stunningly beautiful Canada Place, a pier which juts into Burrard Inlet from the feet of Burrard, Hornby, Howe, and Granville Streets. A

series of illustrated plaques marks a Historic Walk along the promenades. The white, Teflon-coated sails that form the roof of the Vancouver Trade and Convention Centre and its ship-like shape are an
irresistible subject for camera-toting tourists and residents alike. The
largest cruise ships in the world tie up on either side of the convention
center, and the cruise-ship terminal is underneath. Saturday is the time
to watch the ships arrive and depart. The offices of the World Trade
Centre are beneath the Pan Pacific Hotel, which soars beside the sails.

Inside the convention center is the CN IMAX Theatre, with its
five-story screen and sensational films that pull you in with wraparound sound. Details: (604) 682-4629 for further information, (604)
280-4444 for tickets. Hourly features May through September noon to
6 p.m. and double features at 7 and 9 p.m.; rest of year, noon to 3 p.m.
and doubles at 7 and 9 p.m. Admission is adults $6.25 to $10.25, seniors
and students 13–17 $5.50 to $9.25, ages 3–12 $4.50 to $8.25. (2 hours)

★★★ **Granville Island**—A center for sawmills and other industries in
the 1920s and '30s, this mudflat island in False Creek was largely
deserted after World War II. In 1973 it received a cosmetic facelift and
became a popular people place—a houseboat community, a waterpark,
tennis courts, three theaters, a brewery, a Kids Only market, and an
unbeatable Public Market where you can watch artisans make pottery,
tapestries, silk paintings, and other arts and crafts. Details: (604) 666-
6655; open 9 a.m. to 6 p.m. year-round (except Monday in winter).

Getting to Granville Island is often an adventure. Moorage is free
for two hours if you arrive in your own boat, and AquaBus ferries leave
from the foot of Hornby Street every few minutes. Buses #50 and #51
are a better bet than using your own car, which is guaranteed to try
both your own patience and that of your passengers. (3 hours)

★★★ **Grouse Mountain**—From the city, 'tis Christmas every night—
ski runs in winter, hikes the rest of the year, a fun family outing or an
escape to paradise, and views, views, views: across the Lower Mainland,
over to Vancouver Island, and down to the United States. Of course,
such a "foreverland" can be seen only on a clear day.

A 100-passenger car glides smoothly up the mountainside to some
1,100 meters (3,600 ft) above sea level in just eight minutes at a cost of
$15, discounted for seniors, children, and families. Expensive? No—
not when it includes the Peak Chair lift, a multimedia presentation on
Haida folklore, the history of the toy city of Vancouver laid out below,

and a logger sports show. In winter, this price includes a horse-drawn sleigh ride. In summer, use the picnic spots or take the one-hour trail around Blue Grouse Lake. There's also an adventure playground for kids, a beer garden alongside the Peak Chair lift, and the Grouse Nest restaurant with its expectedly spectacular views (advance dinner reservations include the Skyride). (604) 984-0661.

Helicopter tours, (604) 270-1484, of the surrounding mountains range from $40 to $70 per person, depending on tour length. For skiers, there are two aerial trams, four double chairs, one T-bar, and two rope tows, on a total 13 runs of up to 2.4 km (1.5 mi). Other features include rentals, instruction, cafeteria, and night runs till 11 p.m. Details: 20 minutes by car over the Lions Gate Bridge, or take the #246 bus and transfer to #232 Grouse. (3 hours)

★★★ **Stanley Park**—The pride and centerpiece of Vancouver, Stanley is one of the finest and largest (405 hectares/1,000 acres) natural city parks in North America, a mecca for residents and visitors alike. Bordered on three sides by water, it guards the entrance to Vancouver's spectacular natural harbor and sets the scene for the rest of the city's attractions. The park is ringed by a paved road and a 10.5-km (6.5-mi) seawall walk/cycleway. Vehicle traffic runs one way, counterclockwise.

You can golf, bowl, or play tennis; watch cricket, rugby, or soccer; swim in a saltwater pool; or just relax on manicured lawns and smell the roses. You can identify birds in Beaver Lake and Lost Lagoon, photograph totem poles, ogle the boats at the Royal Vancouver Yacht Club, watch cruise ships sail under Lions Gate Bridge from Prospect Point, ride a miniature steam railway, take a horse-and-carriage tour, pet farmyard animals, see Theatre Under the Stars at the Malkin Bowl, watch the sun set from the Teahouse Restaurant at Ferguson Point, and listen to the firing of the Nine O'Clock Gun, a nightly tradition. But you can also escape into the park's heavily forested interior by a crisscross of trails and forget that a frenetic downtown is only minutes away. Be as social or as solitary as you like. Stanley Park appeals to people of all ages and interests, in all seasons. Details: At the foot of Georgia Street, Stanley Park is a peninsula in the Vancouver Harbour. Open daily, 24 hours. Admission is free, but there's a small parking fee. (minimum 4 hours)

★★★ **UBC Museum of Anthropology**—Drive the beaches to this award-winning building on the campus of the University of British

Columbia, brilliantly designed by famous Vancouver architect Arthur Erickson. Situated on the Point Grey Bluffs overlooking English Bay, the museum focuses on the art of the Northwest Coast First Nations. You will be awed by the carved front doors, monumental totem poles, and massive sculptures of the Great Hall. Details: 6393 N.W. Marine; (604) 822-3825; open Tuesday 11 a.m. to 9 p.m., Wednesday through Monday 11 a.m. to 5 p.m.; closed Monday in winter. Admission is $6 for adults, with discounts for children, seniors, and families. Free on Tuesday. (2 hours)

★★★ **Vancouver Public Aquarium**—This major must-see attraction in Stanley Park features orcas (killer whales), beluga whales (with a new baby beluga), seals, sea lions, and sea otters. Daily showings emphasize education, not exhibitionism. Details: Mailing address: Box 3232, Vancouver, British Columbia V6B 3X8; (604) 268-9900; open daily July 1 through Labor Day 9 a.m. to 8 p.m., the rest of the year 10 a.m. to 5:30 p.m. Admission: Adults $11, senior citizens and ages 13–18 $9.50; ages 4–12 $7.50, family rate (two adults and three children) $33. (2 hours)

★★ **Capilano Canyon and Lynn Canyon**—Capilano Canyon carves its tempestuous way through Capilano River Regional Park within minutes of downtown. Plunging cliffs, white-water rapids, and towering timbers and totem poles in a misty rainforest make it an awesome setting. Add a salmon hatchery with fish ladders and other outdoor displays, a 61-meter (200-ft) Giant Fir, and the famous Suspension Bridge. Details: Access is by car off Capilano Road, or by SeaBus to Lonsdale Quay, then bus #246 and #232 (in summer, #236 goes right by the park); (604) 985-7474; open daily mid-June through Labor Day 8 a.m. to 9 p.m.; day after Labor Day through September 30 8 a.m. to 8 p.m.; October 1–28 8.30 a.m. to 6.30 p.m.; October 29 through March 31 9 a.m. to 5 p.m. Admission: Adults $8.25, discounted for seniors and students.

If you want a similar experience for free, cross the 73-meter (240-ft) suspension bridge in Lynn Canyon Park. Walk the trails and visit the ecology center. Access is by car or by SeaBus and Phibbs Exchange/Westlynn bus #229. (1½ hours)

★★ **Chinatown and Sun Yat-Sen Classical Chinese Garden**— Step through time and space into this bustling "other world" centered

on East Pender Street between Carrall Street and Gore Street, where shops spilling out onto the sidewalks boast cheaper prices (but higher quality) than elsewhere. Vancouver's Chinatown is second only to San Francisco's in size, and some of its architecture (recessed balconies, ornamental rooflines, and curved roof tiles) is unique to this city. The Chinese began arriving in B.C. in 1858 with gold fever, became cheap labor for the construction of the Canadian Pacific Railway, and stayed on to cling to their culture as strongly as they did to their new homeland. Be sure to join local Chinese at restaurants such as the Floata, the Flamingo, or the New Diamond for a weekend dim-sum lunch or brunch. It's like taking an inexpensive trip to China without actually going there.

Nearby, beside a free public park, is the Sun Yat-Sen Classical Chinese Garden, the only such garden outside China. This beautiful walled sanctuary was designed and built by the People's Republic of China using only traditional methods and materials (no nails or screws). Details: 578 Carrall Street; (604) 662-3207; open 10 a.m. to late afternoon depending on the season; guided tours from 10:30 a.m. to 4 p.m. in summer and 10:30 a.m. to 2:30 p.m. in winter. Admission: Adults $4.50, discounted for children, seniors, and families. (1 hour)

✮✮ **Gastown**—"Gassy Jack" Deighton, a saloon owner and, in 1867, the first non-native inhabitant of the area, is Gastown's raison d'être. After a huge fire destroyed Vancouver in 1886, the area was rebuilt largely with hotels and warehouses that became an early Skid Row from the Great Depression through the early 1960s. A masterly plan turned this shopping area into a historic site, cobblestone streets and gas lamps lent authenticity, and trees added to the beauty when overhead wires were buried. Crowds gather to see the world's first steam clock, still operating, listen to its quarter-hour whistle, and see its on-the-hour spumes of steam, all within earshot of Gassy Jack's statue. Details: At the intersection of Water and Cambie Streets; free 90-minute tours led by costumed historians depart daily at 2 p.m. in summer. (2 hours)

✮✮ **Library Square**—A strangely modern nine-story Colosseum-type structure nestling beside a 22-story office tower and filling a complete city block, Vancouver's Public Library is either a building of grace and beauty or a hideously pretentious and controversial eyesore, depending on your point of view. The library has a six-story light-filled atrium, a vertical and horizontal electronic conveyor system to move books and

other materials, automated checkouts, a language library allowing self-tutoring in 90 languages, and a computerized lab, and is surrounded by promenades, shops, restaurants, espresso bars, and a bookstore. Details: Library Square is bounded by West Georgia, Hamilton, Robson, and Homer Streets; (604) 331-4045 for a tour of the library's interior; open May through September Monday through Wednesday 10 a.m. to 9 p.m., Thursday through Saturday 10 a.m. to 6 p.m., plus September through April Sunday 1 p.m. to 5 p.m. (1 hour)

★★ **Science World**—A sparkling geodesic dome houses hands-on exhibits that guarantee a blend of entertainment and education for all ages as well as diverse and intriguing daily demonstrations. The Omnimax Theatre features fascinating science and nature films on its domed screen, the largest screen in the world. Details: 1455 Quebec Street, near Terminal and Main Streets; (604) 268-6363; open daily in summer and every weekend year-round 10 a.m. to 6 p.m., winter weekdays 10 a.m. to 5 p.m. Museum admission is adults $9, discounted for seniors and children. Combined with Omnimax, adults $12 with similar discounts. (3 hours)

★★ **Van Dusen Botanical Gardens**—Once a golf course, this tranquil retreat is now ranked as one of the world's top ten botanical gardens. No matter the time of year, the garden blooms with fragrant beauty. Weather permitting, guided tours are offered afternoons from Easter to Thanksgiving, or pick up a self-guided tour sheet as you enter. Details: 5251 Oak Street at 37th Avenue; (604) 878-9274; open daily June through Labor Day 10 a.m. to 9 p.m., the rest of September 10 a.m. to 6 p.m.; the rest of the year 10 a.m. to 4 p.m.; during December Festival of Lights 5 p.m. to 9.30 p.m; closed December 25. Admission: Adults $5, discounted for seniors, children, and families. (2 hours)

FITNESS AND RECREATION

Vancouverites spend more money on sports equipment than any other Canadians. The possibilities are endless and easily accessible. You can walk and cycle the waterfront along Burrard Inlet, False Creek, and the Fraser River or through an impressive network of city parks; hike, ski, and climb in the North Shore mountains (Grouse Mountain, Cypress Bowl, and Mount Seymour, or the 41.5-km (26-mi) Baden-Powell Trail across the city's backdrop); sail, powerboat, paraglide, kayak, windsurf,

fish, dive, and swim in the city's many waterways; ride horses in Southlands, Vancouver's rural equestrian neighborhood; play tennis on dozens of free city park courts; and golf on a variety of scenic courses along Howe Sound and the Fraser River. Birders come from around the world to view more than 250 species of birds in peak season (April to October) at the George C. Reifel Bird Sanctuary on Westham Island. In-line skating is the current passion along the Vancouver waterfront.

FOOD

Vancouver is a culinary paradise, with an overwhelming choice of restaurants. Consult the weekly Vancouver newspaper, *Georgia Strait,* for updated listings at the time of your visit.

Popular for the dramatically presented but home-cooked quality of its West Coast menu, **Bishop's** is located at 2183 W. 4th Avenue, near Yew Street, (604) 738-2025. Specials are worth ordering, and desserts are special enough to be presented by a "dessert technician."

A summertime lunch or Sunday brunch favorite is **Bridge's**, 1696 Duranleau, Granville Island, (604) 687-4400, a dining room, bistro, and pub with a large patio overlooking the boats and ferries of False Creek.

You get a more industrial view of the Burrard Inlet waterfront at the refitted **Cannery,** 2205 Commissioner, near the north end of Victoria, (604) 254-9606. With a rustic decor in the style of the West Coast fishing industry, it's one of the city's oldest and most dependable seafood restaurants.

Perhaps the most panoramic view of downtown Vancouver and the North Shore mountains is **Seasons in the Park,** in Queen Elizabeth Park, W. 33rd Avenue and Cambie Street, (604) 874-8008. You can choose a seat in the dining room under a broad-leafed fig tree. The food is as good as the ambiance, especially the seafood. My favorites on the menu are B.C. grilled salmon and seared prawns and scallops.

Looking south, the view is tremendous at the long-established **Salmon House,** on the Hill at 2229 Folkestone Way, West Vancouver, (604) 926-3212. West Coast aboriginal artifacts adorn the walls, and the chef is known for such creations as alder-grilled salmon marinated in single-malt Scotch whiskey, lemon grass, and golden sugar with lemon and ginger butter. A newer, trendier place with the West Coast theme is the **Raintree Restaurant and Bar,** at the Landing on 375 Water Street near Cordova Street, (604) 688-5570.

VANCOUVER

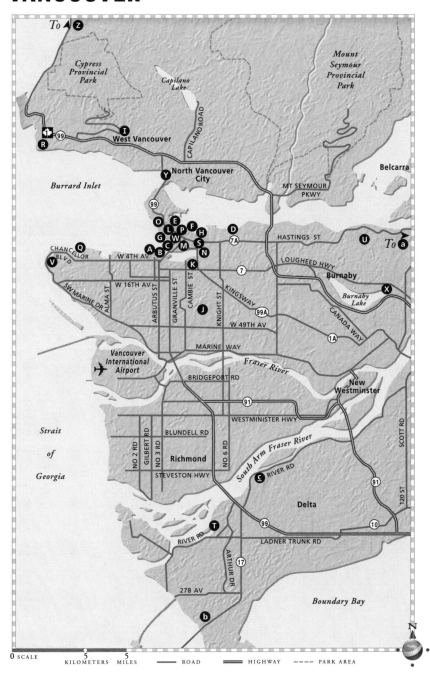

To **Z**

Cypress Provincial Park

Capilano Lake

Mount Seymour Provincial Park

CAPILANO ROAD

I
West Vancouver

99

R

North Vancouver City **Y**

Burrard Inlet

Belcarra

99

MT SEYMOUR PKWY

O **E** **F** **D**
L **P** **H**
G **W** **S** **7A**
A **B** **C** **M** **N**

HASTINGS ST

U

To **a**

CHANCELLOR BLVD
Q
V

W 4TH AV

K

LOUGHEED HWY

Burnaby

7

SW MARINE DR
ALMA ST
W 16TH AV

ARBUTUS ST
GRANVILLE ST
CAMBIE ST
KNIGHT ST

KINGSWAY

99A

Burnaby Lake

X

CANADA WAY

1A

J

W 49TH AV

MARINE WAY

Fraser River

Vancouver International Airport

BRIDGEPORT RD

New Westminster

91

WESTMINISTER HWY

Strait

of

Georgia

NO 2 RD
GILBERT RD
NO 3 RD

BLUNDELL RD

Richmond

NO 6 RD

South Arm Fraser River

SCOTT RD

STEVESTON HWY

C RIVER RD

91

Delta

120 ST

T

99

RIVER RD

LADNER TRUNK RD

10

ARTHUR DR
17

27B AV

Boundary Bay

b

N

0 SCALE   5   5
KILOMETERS MILES   —— ROAD   ═══ HIGHWAY   ---- PARK AREA

Food

A Bishop's

B Bread Garden

C Bridges

D Cannery

E Chartwell

F Five Sails Restaurant

G Il Giardino di Umberto

H Old Spaghetti Factory

H Raintree Restaurant and Bar

G Romano's Macaroni Grill

I Salmon House on the Hill

J Seasons in the Park

K Tojo's

L Tsunami Sushi

M William Tell

Lodging

N Backpackers Youth Hostel

O English Bay Inn

P Four Seasons Hotel

Q Hostelling International Vancouver

Lodging *(continued)*

P Hotel Vancouver

R Lighthouse Retreat Bed and Breakfast

S New Backpackers Hostel

F Pan Pacific Hotel Vancouver

T River Run Cottages Bed and Breakfast

U Simon Fraser University

O Sylvia Hotel

V Walter Gage Residence at UBC

W Wedgewood Hotel

W YMCA/YWCA

Camping

X Burnaby Cariboo RV Park

Y Capilano RV Park

Z Garibaldi Provincial Park

a Golden Ears Provincial Park

b Park Canada Recreational Vehicle Inn

c Richmond RV Park

Note: Items with the same letter are located in the same area.

Famous chef Umberto Menghi owns several popular restaurants that reflect his passion for traditional Italian food. **Il Giardino di Umberto,** 1382 Hornby Street at Pacific Avenue, (604) 669-2422, is known for its hearty pastas and game dishes. If you want family fare, go instead to the **Old Spaghetti Factory** in Gastown, 53 Water Street, near Abbott Street, (604) 684-1288, where you can sit in an old streetcar while you eat, and where you know that you won't have to wash the dishes.

Three elegant but expensive downtown dining rooms are the **Five Sails Restaurant,** in the Pan Pacific Hotel, 300-999 Canada Place, (604) 662-8111; **Chartwell,** in the Four Seasons Hotel, 791 W. Georgia Street, (604) 689-9333; and **William Tell,** in the Georgian Court Hotel, 765 Beatty Street, (604) 688-3504. Expect to pay around $30 for an entree and salad, but service is exceptional.

Tojo's, 777 W. Broadway Avenue, at Willow Street, (604) 872-8050, is regarded as the best of Vancouver's Japanese restaurants, but I like the floating sushi bar at **Tsunami Sushi,** 238-1025 Robson Street, (604) 687-8744. You sit on stools and select your dishes of sushi as they float along a river of flowing water set in the counter in front of you. Prices are reasonable—sushi a la carte averages $2.70 for two pieces.

The **Bread Garden** is a chain of budget eat-in or take-out restaurants for those who want healthy soups, sandwiches, and salads at any hour of the day or night. The waitfolk are friendly and energetic and love their job. I like their smoked salmon raviolini, carrot and basil soup, Mediterranean frittata, and the cheese-filled tortellini with pesto salad. The chocolate mousse cheesecake is legendary. Complete meals run $7–$8. There are four in Vancouver; try the one at 1880 W. 1st at Cypress, (604) 738-6684.

Romano's Macaroni Grill at the Mansion, 1523 Davie Street, (604) 689-4334, an affordable but distinctive restaurant, is in a wonderfully restored heritage house said to be haunted—a great place to eat on Halloween. Dishes and decor are based on Philip Romano's memories of his Mama Rosa's home in Italy, featuring an open kitchen, white gladiolas, and paper-covered tables. Weekend brunch is a good deal: all the Italian you can eat for $9.95, with Caesar salad and focaccia included.

LODGING

Out of Vancouver's more than 16,000 rooms, you can find one from as little as $15 to as much as $1,000 a night. The best deals are offered in the city's off-season, October 17 through May 31. During that time Alberta, Washington, and California residents can take advantage of "Discover the Spectacular" program rates of as much as 50 percent off, offered through Tourism Vancouver hotel partners.

One of the most spectacular of the newer hotels is the **Pan Pacific Hotel Vancouver** (Canada Place pier and convention center), 999 Canada Place at the foot of Howe Street; (800) 663-1515 in

Canada, (800) 937-1515 in the U.S., fax (604) 685-8690. Rooms range $195–$450 a night, but you get an outstanding downtown location, an eight-story atrium lobby lined with totem poles, a lounge and cafe with 40-foot glass walls, a panoramic view of Vancouver Harbor, and probably the best hotel health club in Canada. Even if you don't stay there, do visit.

Those who want nostalgia and tradition in the grand style will be more attracted to the newly renovated **Hotel Vancouver,** 900 W. Georgia Street, (604) 684-3131 or (800) 441-1414. On the Entree Gold floor, perks include secretarial services and computer hookups as well as crystal and chandeliers. Prices range $240–$495 a night for a room or suite.

The **Four Seasons Hotel,** 791 W. Georgia Street, (604) 689-9333, (800) 268-6282 in Canada, (800) 332-3442 in the U.S., $149–$495 a night, pampers children and pets as well as adults. Kids get complimentary milk and cookies on arrival, movie videos and toys; pets get bottled water and sterling silver dinner bowls.

Eleni Skalbania's intimate little **Wedgewood Hotel,** 845 Hornby Street, (604) 689-7777, highly recommended, $129–$520 a night, is noted for its elegant antique furniture and its Bacchus Ristorante and Lounge, which resembles an authentic Tuscan inn.

Another Vancouver landmark is the **Sylvia Hotel,** 1154 Gilford Street, (604) 681-9321. With views of English Bay beaches and sunsets, and rates of $65–$130, this ivy-cloaked stone, heritage hotel is understandably popular; reserve early.

The **English Bay Inn** is a quiet spot at 1968 Comox Street, a block from the beach and Stanley Park, (604) 683-8002. This 1930s house is renovated in British private-club style, with sherry and port offered in the parlor each afternoon. All but one of its five rooms have sleigh or eighteenth-century four-poster beds. Prices range $130–$250.

B&Bs are multiplying rapidly in Vancouver. For something different, try the **Lighthouse Retreat Bed and Breakfast,** 4875 Water Lane, (604) 926-5959, in a house designed by famed architect Arthur Erickson. True to its West Coast style, it's perched on a cliff above Lighthouse Park, with views of Bowen Island, Horseshoe Bay, and Vancouver Island, and is only 30 minutes from downtown. The huge double rooms cost $115 and $125. Children are not welcome. If you like sleeping on water and waking up with nature by your window, try a floating B&B called **Waterlily,** one of three River Run Cottages at 4551 River Road, West Ladner, (604) 946-7778. It has a queen-size loft bed, a claw-foot tub, potbellied stove, private deck, and a kayak, rowboat, and bicycle for exploring the surrounding farmland and fishing village. It's 30 minutes to downtown by freeway; doubles cost $125 a night.

University residences, YMCA/YWCAs, and youth hostels are abundant in this two-university city and provide good budget accommodations. In summer months the **Walter Gage Residence**, 5961 Student Union Boulevard, University of British Columbia, (604) 822-1010, rents a variety of rooms for $20–$72. At the other end of the city—on top of Burnaby Mountain—**Simon Fraser University**, Room 212, McTaggart-Cowan Hall, Burnaby, (604) 291-4201, rents accommodations for as little as $19 per night if you bring your own sleeping bag, and only $89 per night for four-bedroom townhouses.

The **YMCA** at 955 Burrard Street, (604) 681-0221, enjoys a central location, offering cheap, clean, dorm-style rooms to all. The new **YWCA**, 733 Beatty Street, (604) 895-5830, charges $44 for a single room and $64 for family rooms.

There are three hostel-type hotels in Vancouver. **Hostelling International Vancouver**, 1515 Discovery Street, (604) 224-3208, Canada's largest hostel and North America's second largest, is on Jericho Beach off Point Grey Road and adjacent to tennis courts, but it's a 30-minute bus ride to downtown. Members stay for $15 a day, nonmembers for $18.50. **Backpackers Youth Hostel**, 927 Main Street, near Chinatown, (604) 682-2441, has private rooms as well as dorm rooms. The **New Backpackers Hostel**, 347 W. Pender Street, near Gastown, (604) 688-0112, is more upscale with larger rooms.

CAMPING

You can pitch your tent or park your RV just minutes from downtown Vancouver. **Capilano RV Park** has an incredibly choice location by the Capilano River, under the Lions Gate Bridge, opposite Stanley Park, and beside a beach and the popular Park Royal shopping center. It's at 295 Tomahawk Avenue, West Vancouver, (604) 987-4722; high-season rates are $30 for a trailer and two people, and include full hookups. Another choice site at the southern end of the city is **Park Canada Recreational Vehicle Inn**, 4799 Hwy. 17 (exit north on 52nd Street) in Delta, (604) 943-5811. It's handy to the Tswassen ferry terminal for Victoria and Nanaimo, and costs $22. Also close to Vancouver are **Burnaby Cariboo RV Park**, 8765 Cariboo Place, Burnaby, (604) 420-

1722, and the **Richmond RV Park**, 6200 River Road, Richmond, (604) 270-7878. Vancouver's wraparound wilderness, of course, offers natural camping sites in such nearby provincial parks as **Garibaldi Provincial Park** and **Golden Ears Provincial Park**. Reservations can be made through Discover Camping at (604) 689-9025.

NIGHTLIFE

All the big-name artists come to Vancouver. It's more than probable that they want an excuse to see the city—and be paid for it—as much as they enjoy Vancouverites' enthusiastic reception.

You can watch a glorious display at the annual **Symphony of Fire International Fireworks** over the English Bay in the West End, (604-738-4304); or see a show at the **Queen Elizabeth Theatre and Playhouse**, corner of Hamilton and Georgia, (604) 665-3050; the **Ford Centre for the Performing Arts**, (604) 280-2222; **Vancouver East Cultural Centre**, 1895 Venabels, (604) 254-9578; or the **Theatre Under the Stars**, Malkin Bowl, Stanley Park, (604) 687-0174. Wine and dine as you revolve through the view in the **Cloud 9 Lounge**, Landmark Hotel, 1400 Robson Street, (604) 687-4322; or at **The Lookout**, Harbour Centre Tower, 555 W. Hastings Street, (604) 689-0421. The 1950s atmosphere of the **Waldorf Hotel**, 1489 E. Hastings Street, (604) 253-7141, is presently in vogue, as are the singing and dancing at the **Blarney Stone**, 216 Carrall Street, Gastown, (604) 687-4322. Vancouver has nightclubs to suit every taste. Sample some of the "in" spots with **Star Limousine Service**, (604) 983-5577.

The hottest nightspot in town is the **Purple Onion**, 15 Water Street, right in the heart of Gastown, (604) 602-9442. It has two rooms: the jazz cabaret is small, intimate, and furnished in 1950s style for the older clientele (though it often has a good mix of ages); and down the hall is a large nightclub for those who want to dance the night away. Cabaret acts change frequently—to the delight of the obviously "steady" patrons of this establishment. I don't care much for the Purple Onion's retro-ambiance, but the shows are first-class, and the food does set this spot apart.

Scenic Route: The Georgia Strait

From Horseshoe Bay in West Vancouver, take Highway 101 up the Sunshine Coast to Powell River via the Langdale and Saltery Bay ferries, cross Georgia Strait to Comox and Courtenay, and drive down the east side of Vancouver Island to Crofton. Then take the Saltspring Island ferry to Vesuvius Bay, meander through Saltspring Island to the charming village of Ganges, and take another ferry from Fulford Harbour across the strait to Tsawassen and Vancouver. Ask B.C. Ferries for schedules and special CirclePac rates.

This enchanting coastal run of about 300 km (180 mi) through cottage country appeals to artists and boaters. Take your time and spend several days poking into its many nooks and crannies. Explore the detours. It's worth the water-taxi ride from Lund to cruise to the distinctive white sandy beaches of tropical-looking Savary Island. Don't miss the marine parks in Desolation Sound and Princess Louisa Inlet, either in your boat or on a trip with Bluewater Adventures, (604) 980-3800. Gibson's Landing, on the Sechelt Peninsula between Langdale and Earls Cove is world-famous as the location for the internationally popular CBC Television series *The Beachcombers.* Reminisce with the locals over a cup of coffee at Molly's Reach Cafe, the same watering hole featured in the show. ◼

THE GEORGIA STRAIT

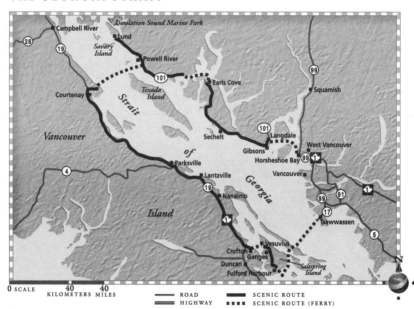

2

WHISTLER AND THE SEA TO SKY HIGHWAY

The Squamish Highway or, as it is more romantically called, the Sea to Sky Highway, climbs out of the picturesque seaside village and ferry terminal of Horseshoe Bay in West Vancouver, sidles along Howe Sound under a rim of overhanging mountains to Squamish, and slices up through forests to reach Whistler at 604 meters (2,100 ft).

Whichever season you choose, try to spend a few days at Whistler Resort. Named after the whistling marmots of Whistler Mountain, this is a world-class, European-style, four-season resort. Two top magazines have rated it the number-one ski resort in North America, not only for the greatest vertical drop in the continent (1,609 meters/5,280 ft), the largest ski area (more than 2,800 hectares/6,919 acres), and the most extensive high-speed lift system in the world (28 lifts serving 200-plus marked runs and 12 alpine bowls, including three glaciers), but also for its scenery, dining, value, service, and après-ski activities. Since Whistler Village opened in 1980 at the base of Whistler and Blackcomb Mountains, it has become a permanent, self-contained community with a year-round population of more than 6,800 (a number that jumps to almost 30,000 during peak winter periods). ∎

WHISTLER AND
THE SEA TO SKY HIGHWAY

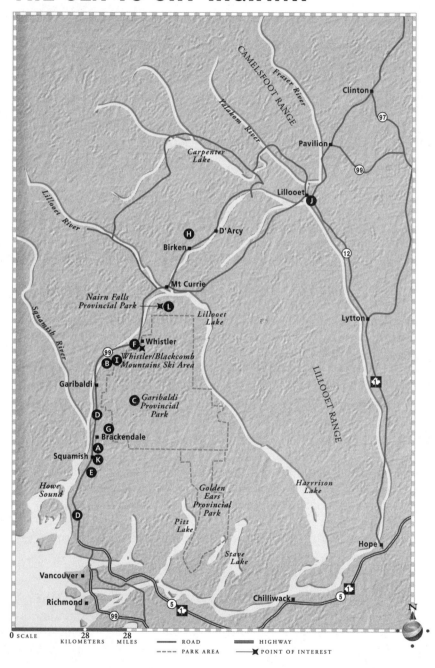

CAMELSFOOT RANGE

Fraser River

Yalakom River

Clinton

97

Pavilion

99

Carpenter
Lake

Lillooet

J

Lillooet River

H D'Arcy

Birken

Mt Currie

12

Nairn Falls
Provincial Park L

Lillooet
Lake

Lytton

Squamish River

F Whistler

99 I Whistler/Blackcomb
B Mountains Ski Area

Garibaldi

C Garibaldi
Provincial
Park

LILLOOET RANGE

D

G

Brackendale

A
K
Squamish

E

Howe
Sound

Golden
Ears
Provincial
Park

Harrrison
Lake

D

Pitt
Lake

Hope

Stave
Lake

1

Vancouver

N

Richmond

99

Chilliwack

5

5

1

0 SCALE   28   28
      KILOMETERS MILES   ROAD   HIGHWAY
                          ---- PARK AREA   POINT OF INTEREST

Sights

- **A** Brackendale and Squamish
- **B** Brandywine Falls Provincial Park
- **C** Garibaldi Provincial Park
- **D** Sea to Sky Highway
- **E** Stawamus Chief Provincial Park
- **F** Whistler Resort

Food

- **F** Bear Foot Bistro, Listel Hotel
- **F** Christine's
- **F** The Crab Shack
- **F** Il Caminetto di Umberto
- **F** Old Spaghetti Factory
- **F** Pika's Restaurant
- **F** Rendezvous
- **F** Thai One On
- **F** Trattoria di Umberto
- **F** Val D'Isere
- **F** Zeuski's Taverna

Lodging

- **F** Blackcomb Lodge
- **F** Canadian Pacific Chateau Whistler Resort
- **F** Chalet Luise B&B
- **F** Edelweiss Pension
- **F** Hostelling International-Whistler
- **F** Marriott Residence Inn
- **F** Shoestring Lodge
- **F** UBC Lodge

Camping

- **G** Alice Lake Provincial Park
- **H** Birkenhead Lake Provincial Park
- **B** Brandywine Provincial Park
- **I** Cal-Cheak Forest Service site
- **J** Cayoosh Creek Campground
- **C** Garibaldi Provincial Park
- **K** Klahanie Campground and RV Park
- **L** Nairn Falls Provincial Park

Note: Items with the same letter are located in the same town or area.

A PERFECT DAY IN WHISTLER

In summer, I would wake up from my slopeside suite as far up Blackcomb Mountain as possible, take a gondola or open-air chairlift ride to the top of either Whistler or Blackcomb Mountain, and then hike one of the alpine trails, which vary in length from 30 minutes to three hours or more. If weather permitted and the pocketbook allowed, I would join a helicopter tour to get even higher into the mountains for heli-hiking or a picnic lunch on one of the glaciers (Whistler Heli-copters, 604-932-3512). Then I'd descend the mountain (no mountain bikes for me!) and stroll through Whistler Village to browse the shops and art galleries, sip a drink at a cafe, listen to some streetside enter-tainment, then go to my hotel (or a village restaurant) for dinner.

HIGHWAY SAFETY

The Sea to Sky Highway is a spectacular mountain drive, but between Vancouver and Squamish it is squeezed between the sea and the moun-tains in a high rainfall area subject to mudslides. It is narrow, winding, and can be dangerous. For up-to-date road reports, phone Talking Yellow Pages, (604) 299-9000; listen to Mountain FM Radio West Vancouver-Squamish at 107.1; or watch hourly reports between November and April on the Weather Network Channel. For road safety assistance, phone the B.C. Automobile Association, (800) 663-2222.

SIGHTSEEING HIGHLIGHTS

★★★ **Brackendale**—This residential community is noteworthy for its Brackendale Art Gallery, which sponsors the annual January eagle count. Brackendale is home to the largest gathering of bald eagles in North America, though the number varies year to year. In 1994 a world record of more than 3,700 bald eagles was established in one day. Details: 10 km (6 mi) beyond Squamish. Gallery: (604) 898-3333; open afternoons and weekends. (4 hours)

★★★ **Garibaldi Provincial Park**—You can ski or walk from Whistler Mountain to neighboring Garibaldi Provincial Park via Singing Pass and Russet Lake, but it isn't easy. Better to access this stunningly beautiful park, with its striking volcanic peaks, lush alpine meadows, and remote lakes, via various signposted trails that take off from the Sea to Sky Highway. Or you can take the train to Garibaldi Station and hike from there.

I'd rather access the park on top by helicopter instead of trekking uphill through the trees, but my favorite Garibaldi hike is into Gari-baldi Lake from the Rubble Lake parking lot 39 km (23 mi) north of Squamish. I camp overnight in alpine meadows, then climb Black Tusk 2,315 meters (7,595 ft)—or as much of its rocky peak as I dare. Cheakamus Lake and Diamond Head are the park's other two main natural attractions. Late July through early September is the most popular visiting time; snow may linger on the ground until well into July. Details: District Manager, Alice Lake Provincial Park, Box 220, Brackendale, British Columbia V0N 1H0; (604) 898-3678. (1 day)

★★★ **Whistler Resort**—Whistler has rapidly become world-famous as a year-round playground for local families, not just celebrities or wealthy globetrotting skiers. It's also a convenient base for side trips to the rest of Sea and Sky country. Backdropped by two beautiful side-by-side mountains—Blackcomb and Whistler—Whistler Resort comprises several villages and residential neighborhoods, and more are being built all the time. There's no sign of a recession at this popular destination—and rightly so, considering Whistler's dramatic natural setting, pedestrian-only cobblestone plazas, and wide variety of easily accessible activities. Whistler Resort is third only to Vancouver and Victoria in terms of money generated from tourism; it attracts nearly 1.5 million visitors annually, the highest number of skier visits of any North America resort.

Whistler's abundant snowfall (an average of 11.5 m/35 ft) allows exceptional downhill, cross-country, and heli-skiing; snowboarding; snowshoeing; snowmobiling; ice skating; ice hockey; and sleigh-riding. Its mile-high vertical runs mean you can easily mountain-ski until late May and glacier-ski and snowboard mid-June to mid-August. By helicoptering to the glaciers, you can ski almost year-round. Buy dual mountain lift tickets so you can ski both mountains economically. A dual day pass costs $54 plus the usual 7 percent tax.

For 80 years before Whistler became a ski resort, the area was a local summer resort. It now boasts some of the world's best golf courses and mountain-bike trails. Whistler's mild coastal climate means golfing can begin in May. Chairlifts and gondolas to the top of the mountains make it easy to go alpine hiking, horseback-riding, and paragliding. July through October is the best time for hiking in alpine areas. If you prefer to stay at the base of the mountains, Whistler has many miles of marked hiking trails that wander along its lakes and valleys.

Until early August you can take a guided bus tour on Blackcomb Mountain through a forest at the edge of the alpine from the top of the Solar Coaster Express lift to the 7th Heaven Express lift. From there you're whisked up to the Horstman Glacier. Alternatively, you can take an ATV (all-terrain vehicle) tour. Daring mountain bikers switchback down the mountain under the chairlifts by a thrilling trail known simply as The Descent. Lift tickets cost $18 for adults, youths 13–18 and seniors 65-plus $15, and children under 12 free. Remember to use them for both mountains.

Five nearby lakes and numerous local streams encourage swimming, sunbathing, boardsailing, canoeing, kayaking, sailing, rafting, jet-boating, and fishing. Climbing is popular, whether it's on a granite rock face high in the mountains, a sport climb in such hinterlands as Nordic Bluffs and Cheakamus Canyon, or the Climbing Wall in Whistler Village itself. In-line skating is currently very trendy, and Whistler offers a paved 20-km (12-mi) Valley Trail shared by cyclists and walkers, as well as a 20,000-square-foot in-line skate park at the base of Wizard Chair on Blackcomb Mountain.

Anything is possible at Whistler Resort. Practically every month has its own festival or special event. From June through October, the streets come alive with constant entertainment. In August, the Vancouver Symphony Orchestra performs on a mountaintop. Children, especially, have lots to keep them occupied—from ski camps, day camps, and language camps, to climbing walls, windsurfing, and even a trapeze. An abundance of tours and tour guides are available if you want to leave the organization to others. Some tours, such as guided nature walks on the top of Blackcomb Mountain, are free.

Details: 120 km (75 mi) north of downtown Vancouver on Highway 99. To book tours and buy lift tickets, contact the Whistler Activity and Information Centre at the front doors of the Whistler Conference Centre in the main village, (604) 932-2394. For direct contact, call Whistler Mountain at (604) 932-3434 and Blackcomb Mountain at (604) 932-3141. Customized packages including lift tickets, lodging, and ground transportation to and from Vancouver International Airport are available from Whistler Resort, (800) 944-7853 or (604) 664-5625. Package prices vary depending on the season (e.g., a regular seven-night/six-day holiday is $899 in high season; $654 in low season). (1 day)

★★ **Brandywine Falls Provincial Park**—This park is worth visiting to walk the short trail to a viewpoint over 60-meter-high (195-ft) Brandywine Falls. Details: 37 km (23 mi) beyond Squamish on the Sea to Sky Highway; (604) 898-3678. (30 minutes)

★★ **Stawamus Chief Provincial Park**—Just south of Squamish is Stawamus Chief, which annually attracts more than 160,000 hikers and rock climbers. Its main feature is the 652-meter (2,139-ft) Stawamus Chief, one of the world's largest freestanding monoliths and a rock sacred to the Squamish First Nation. Details: 1km (.6mi) south of Squamish off the east side of the highway. (20 minutes)

FITNESS AND RECREATION

Unless you just sit in your car and look at the scenery or sit in a cafe and partake of the goodies Whistler has to offer, you can't help being fit in this area. In addition to all its outdoor activities, Whistler has several indoor fitness centers: **Delta Whistler Resort**, (604) 932-7336; **Meadow Park Sports Centre**, (604) 938-PARK; and the **Pumphouse Fitness Centre**, (604) 932-1984. Activities include indoor ice-skating, pool and spa facilities, squash courts, and fitness equipment.

FOOD

Many of the more cosmopolitan restaurants in Whistler Resort are expensive—as much as $100 for a full-course meal for two. I've chosen some of the most reasonable, where you get can the best value.

Val D'Isere, next to Whistler Village Centre, (604) 932-4666, serves expensive, classic French cuisine, but the food and ambiance are worth the price. Chef Umberto Menghi has two popular Italian restaurants at Whistler with moderate to high prices: **Trattoria di Umberto**, in Whistler Village, (604) 932-5858, and **Il Caminetto di Umberto**, at the Mountainside Lodge, (604) 932-4442. The **Bear Foot Bistro**, adjoining the Listel Hotel in Whistler Village, (604) 932-1133 or (604) 932-3433, serves incredible steaks ($2.25–$3 per ounce). Main dishes run about $18–$22 and desserts, $6.50. The Bistro has a separate room for drinking fine Scotch whiskey and smoking cigars, and artists-in-residence often create while you dine.

Thai One On, in the Upper Village at the base of Blackcomb Mountain, (604) 932-4822, serves trendy Thai food at reasonable prices; **Zeuski's Taverna** in Whistler's new Towne Plaza, (604) 932-6009, serves reasonably priced Greek food. The **Crab Shack**, formerly known as Jimmy D's Sports Bar, is across from the Whistler Fairways Hotel in Whistler Village, (604) 932-4451. It's a favorite for steak and seafood and has a separate pub side with an oyster bar and pool table. Families like the ever-popular **Old Spaghetti Factory** in the Crystal Lodge, (604) 932-1081.

You can eat your way up the mountains, from cafeteria-style fare at **Rendezvous,** at the top of the Solar Coaster lift on Blackcomb Mountain, (604) 932-3141; to **Pika's Restaurant** (604) 932-3434, at the top of the lift on Whistler Mountain, to the linen-and-silverware luncheon service at **Christine's,** in the Rendezvous Lodge on Blackcomb Mountain, (604) 932-3141. Try Sunday's all-you-can-eat brunch at Pika's (June 16 through October 13, 10:30 a.m. to 1:30 p.m.).

LODGING

With more than 70 lodgings available, Whistler offers something for everyone, from high-priced luxury hotels to friendly B&B inns and budget hostels. Off-season rates usually apply in November, December (excluding Christmas season), January, and in some places, April. Some hotels offer family packages. The quickest way to book accommodations is to call **Whistler Central Reservations,** (800) WHISTLER (944-7853).

Hotels such as **Canadian Pacific Chateau Whistler Resort,** 4599 Chateau Boulevard, (800) 268-9411 or (604) 938-8000, are worth visiting just to look at the architecture or furnishings, or to browse the shops. Prices range $299–$375 a night. The **Marriott Residence Inn,** a new ski-in/ski-out resort on the slopes of Blackcomb Mountain, 4899 Painted Cliff Road, (604) 905-3400 or (800) 331-3131, offers studios and one- and two-bedroom suites that look out onto the chairlift. The Marriott offers a complimentary serve-yourself breakfast and a shuttle to the town center. During my visit the hotel also provided generous servings of happy hour complimentary food. Prices range $199–$529 a night. **Blackcomb Lodge,** 4220 Gateway Drive in the town center, (604) 932-4155 or (800) 667-2855, is a good choice for its central location, good prices, and kitchens.

The closest pension-type B&B within walking distance of Whistler Village is **Chalet Luise,** 7461 Ambassador Crescent, (604) 932-4187. Its charm lies in its alpine-style architecture and Swiss hospitality. Rates range $75–$119 a person. The **Edelweiss Pension,** 7162 Nancy Green Drive, (604) 932-3641 or (800) 665-1892, is just as pretty and includes a full breakfast and a fondue dinner on request. Rates range $95–$220.

Whistler's lowest-priced accommodation is the **Shoestring Lodge,** about 2 km (1.3 mi) north of Whistler Village, (604) 932-3338. A bed in a shared quad is about $25 a night. Shoestring also offers rooms with two twin beds, one queen, or two sets of bunks at $95. **Hostelling International-Whistler**, 5678 Alta Lake Road, (604) 932-5492; and **UBC Lodge**, (604) 932-6604 or (604) 822-5851, offer good dormitory-style accommodations. Companies such as **Powder Resort Properties** rent out private condos; this one offers moderate to luxury studios and one- to three-bedroom suites, mainly in the Upper Village on Blackcomb Mountain. Contact Box 1044, Whistler, British Columbia V0N 1B0; (604) 932-2882 or (800) 777-0185.

CAMPING

Several provincial parks along the Sea to Sky Highway offer picnicking or overnight camping: **Porteau Cove, Shannon Falls, Alice Lake, Garibaldi, Brandywine Falls, Nairn Falls**, and **Birkenhead Lake**. All can be reached at (604) 898-3678. Prices range $9.50–$15.50 for four persons. **Klahanie Campground and RV Park**, (604) 892-3435, in Squamish, charges $15–$18 for two people. **Cayoosh Creek Campground**, (250) 256-4180, in Lillooet, costs $12 for two people.

You can set your tent against some wonderfully photogenic backdrops in **Garibaldi Provincial Park**, (604) 898-3678, and the haul to the top is well worth the struggle. Camping is restricted at Diamond Head to cleared tent spaces and a day shelter at Red Heather Campground, and to an overnight shelter with 34 bunks at Elfin Lakes Campground. At Garibaldi Lake and Black Tusk, camping is allowed only at Taylor Meadows and the west end of Garibaldi Lake, where there are cleared tent spaces and day shelters. Otherwise, camping is restricted to the west end of Cheakamus Lake and the northwest end of Wedgemount and Russet Lakes.

Close to Whistler Resort are several immaculate places for day picnicking and water sports: **Lost Lake, Alpha Lake**, and the largest, **Alta Lake**, which features **Rainbow Park, Lakeside Park**, and **Wayside Park**. (My personal favorite is Rainbow Park.) Often overlooked are the B.C. Forest Service's free campsites. Use them for their wilderness advantages or if alternative sites are unavailable. The **Cal-Cheak Forest Service** site is about 15 km (9.4 mi) south of Whistler, and it can be hard to find. (Past Brandywine Provincial Park on the way north, the highway become four lanes for about 2 km /1.3 mi. After it narrows back to two lanes, watch the right side for a dirt road and small sign. Cross the railroad tracks and follow the road to the campsites.)

NIGHTLIFE

Snow Country magazine ranks the big **Longhorn Saloon and Grill**, in the Carleton Lodge at the base of Whistler Mountain, (604) 932-5999, as the best après-ski bar in Canada. It has a ski-in location, substantial portions of food at fair prices, ice-cold draught beer, plus DJs spinning classic and modern rock during the week and live music on weekends. It offers 29 different burgers and perhaps the "best damn nachos in town." Its Live at the Longhorn Concert Series attracts world-class performers. Older people prefer **Buffalo Bill's Bar and Grill**, next to the Conference Centre in the heart of Whistler Village, (604) 932-6613, with lots of space for dancing, playing pool, eating lunch or dinner, watching sports events on a big-screen TV, trying out the ski simulator, or listening to the occasional live entertainment.

Another popular gathering place favored by locals is the **Cinnamon Bear Bar** in the Delta Whistler Resort, (604) 932-1982, open from 11 a.m. to 1 a.m. daily. The **Savage Beagle** in Whistler Village, (604) 932-3337, offers a variety of music, from hip-hop to jazz. **Garfinkel's**, (604) 932-2323, is a small Whistler Village club in which you can dance until 2 a.m.

3
VICTORIA

I n contrast to Vancouver, its boisterous big sister on the Lower
Mainland, Victoria on Vancouver Island is a sleepy English seaside
village—although that image is changing. It borrows its grandeur from
the Olympic Mountains in Washington, across the Strait of Juan de
Fuca. Victoria's hills are gentle, smooth, rocky outcrops softened by
glaciers and clothed with meadows of shiny arbutus, twisted oaks, and
glorious wildflowers. Victoria, like the Queen after whom the city is
named, is, well, genteel. Twenty percent of Victoria's residents are over
65, and in the past it's been said that the city rolls up its sidewalks at
night, but that image is changing, too.

Canadians fleeing eastern winters have discovered this mild-
tempered city of sea and gardens, and Victoria's population (330,000)
has more than doubled since the early 1960s. During the summer, the
city sees more than 4 million tourists. The site of a former Hudson's
Bay Company trading post (1843), Victoria is the oldest city in Western Canada and the capital of British Columbia. It's known worldwide for friendliness (the friendliest city in North America, according
to *Condé Nast Traveler* magazine), meticulously groomed year-round
gardens and hanging baskets, Victorian-era architecture, and the best
weather in Canada. The city attracts artists, naturalists, and retirees.
Travel writers call it the Garden of Eden. ∎

VICTORIA

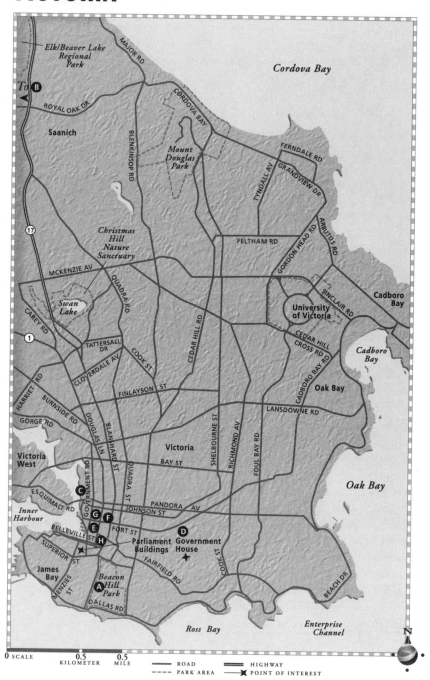

Elk/Beaver Lake Regional Park

Cordova Bay

To **B**

ROYAL OAK DR

MAJOR RD

CORDOVA BAY

Saanich

BLENKINSOP RD

Mount Douglas Park

FERNDALE RD

TYNDALL AV

GRANDVIEW DR

Christmas Hill Nature Sanctuary

FELTHAM RD

GORDON HEAD RD

ARBUTUS RD

17

MCKENZIE AV

QUADRA RD

SINCLAIR RD

Cadboro Bay

Swan Lake

CAREY RD

University of Victoria

CEDAR HILL RD

CEDAR HILL CROSS RD

Cadboro Bay

1

TATTERSALL DR

COOK ST

CADBORO BAY RD

Oak Bay

HARRIET RD

CLOVERDALE AV

FINLAYSON ST

BURNSIDE RD

LANSDOWNE RD

GORGE RD

DOUGLAS LN

BLANHARD ST

SHELBOURNE ST

RICHMOND AV

FOUL BAY RD

Victoria

Victoria West

BAY ST

Oak Bay

GOVERNMENT BD

QUADRA ST

ESQUIMALT RD

C

PANDORA AV

JOHNSON ST

Inner Harbour

G **F**

FORT ST

E

BELLEVILLE ST

H

D Government House

SUPERIOR ST

Parliament Buildings

COOK ST

James Bay

MENZIES ST

FAIRFIELD RD

BEACH DR

Beacon Hill Park

A

DALLAS RD

Ross Bay

Enterprise Channel

N

0 SCALE   0.5 KILOMETER   0.5 MILE   ROAD   HIGHWAY
--- PARK AREA   ✕ POINT OF INTEREST

Sights

Ⓐ Beacon Hill Park

Ⓑ Butchart Gardens

Ⓒ Chinatown

Ⓓ Craigdarroch Castle

Ⓔ Inner Harbor (Empress Hotel, Parliament Buildings)

Ⓕ Munro's Bookstore

Ⓖ Old Town

Ⓗ Royal British Columbia Museum

Ⓗ Thunderbird Park

Note: Items with the same letter are located in the same place.

A PERFECT DAY IN VICTORIA

Hit all the high spots in a London-style double-decker bus, horse-drawn carriage, or kabuki (pedicab), or walk and drive. A New York editor told me once that my love affair with Victoria reminded him of a kid with a candy cane. On that perfect day, we strolled the Inner Harbor to look at yachts and mingle with the crowds in the city's central core; eavesdropped on a wedding in Beacon Hill Park; followed the yellow footprints that mark the scenic Marine Drive and ducked golf balls across the golf course on the way to Oak Bay (the village behind Victoria's so-called Tweed Curtain); had a drink at the Snug in the Oak Bay Beach Hotel; dashed back for afternoon tea at the Empress Hotel; and meandered along every road to the water on the Saanich Peninsula. We capped the day with dinner and fireworks at Butchart Gardens. So much for traditional Victoria, but if you want a walk on the wild side . . . book an ecotour with the Royal British Columbia Museum (or any of the adventure travel operators) and spend a day offshore.

SIGHTSEEING HIGHLIGHTS

★★★ **Butchart Gardens**—Jenny Butchart started it in 1904 with a yen to beautify an old quarry. Now this 20-hectare (50-acre) showplace

near Brentwood Bay, 21 km (13 mi) north of Victoria, is a world-
famous destination featuring distinctive formal gardens, outdoor
musical and theatrical performances, the Ross Fountain, restaurants,
nightly illuminations June 15 through September 30, and a very
popular music-and-thrills fireworks display every Saturday night in July
and August. Your best bet is to spend Saturday at the gardens. Have a
picnic lunch or perhaps splurge on dinner, watch the fireworks, and
stroll the gardens in the moonlight. Details: Box 4010, Victoria, British
Columbia V8X 3X4; (604) 652-5256, 652-4422, or 652-8222; gate
opens every day at 9 a.m. (including holidays), and closing hour
depends on season. Admission: Adults $14.95, ages 13–17 $6.50, ages
5–12 $1.50; prices reduced November through March. (3 hours)

★★★ **Empress Hotel**—Built in 1908 by the Canadian Pacific
Railroad (CPR) in elegant château-style, the newly renovated Empress
is justly famous for the magnificence of its traditional decor, as in the
Palm Court and Crystal Ballroom. New traditions are seen in Tony
Hunt's Kwakiutl totem pole in the conference-center lobby beside the
rebuilt Conservatory. Afternoon tea in the Tea Lobby is expensive ($27
at last look), but it's a Victorian ritual that you shouldn't miss. (I once
had tea and crumpets with a cougar and one of the remaining dowagers
who had permanent rooms in the hotel. The cougar had milk.) Today
the Empress serves silver trays of cucumber, watercress, and egg salad
sandwiches; salmon and cream cheese pinwheels; scones with Devon-
shire cream; seasonal berries with crème Chantilly; and a tea blend
unique to the hotel. A string quartet provides soothing background
music. The Empress' afternoon tea is popular, so book three days in
advance, (250) 389-2727. You can get a cheaper version downstairs in
the Garden Cafe or at other locations in Victoria—but don't. Splurge,
and leave your jeans at home. Details: 721 Government Street; (250)
384-8111, reservations (800) 441-1414. (2 hours)

★★★ **The Inner Harbor**—It's worth being touristy in Victoria, so
make the stone-walled Inner Harbor your first stop. You may not want
to tour the Royal London Wax Museum, Miniature World, Crystal
Gardens, or Undersea Gardens—although your kids will—but do
wander the wheelchair-accessible waterfront, all of it. Pick up
brochures and free coupons at the Victoria Travel InfoCentre, 812
Wharf Street, (250) 953-2033, then read them on a bench overlooking
the harbor while listening to street-busker music or the museum's

carillon. Don't forget to take your own photo of Victoria's favorite postcard—the "Welcome to Victoria" sign on the lawn in front of the Parliament Buildings. Gaze up at the bronze statue of Captain Vancouver looking down from the roof of the legislature and holding the flag that he used in 1792 to claim this northwest corner of the continent in the name of the British Crown. Come back at night to snap the legislature outlined in lights. Details: The Inner Harbor is edged by Johnson, Wharf, Government, and Belleville Streets, in the heart of Victoria's downtown area. (minimum 2 hours)

★★★ **Old Town**—A flourishing seaport at the turn of the century, Victoria has preserved and remodeled more than 200 old warehouses, factories, offices, stores, and seedy hotels to produce a vibrant strolling area of colorful courtyards and alleyways that cater to historians, architects, artists, shoppers, and browsers. Bastion Square, where Sir James Douglas established Fort Victoria in 1843, houses the Maritime Museum, its vast collection of model ships, and the tiny but real vessels *Tilikum* and *Trekka* whose stories raise eyebrows—and hair! Multilevel Market Square has intriguing shops, bars, and restaurants surrounding a courtyard that often hosts free musical and other special events. Details: In the downtown area between Wharf and Government Streets; (250) 385-4222; open daily 9:30 a.m. to 4:30 a.m.; closed January 1 and December 25. Admission: Adults $5, seniors $4, ages 12–17 $3, ages 6–11 $2; discounts available. (2 hours)

★★★ **Royal British Columbia Museum**—One of the world's best museums, it's active enough to intrigue the whole family. The life-size hand-carved Haida canoe, with its naked Haida whalers, and the stunning rain-forest curtain that used to dominate the lobby have been relegated to storage; some say to avoid offending prudish sensibilities, others say to save space. However, the museum has plenty of other wonderfully realistic dioramas and three-dimensional sensory displays of the province's tidal marshes, seabird colonies, old-growth forests, aboriginal longhouses, sawmills, gold-diggings, and frontier towns. Real-life totem poles stand tall on either side of the escalator.

For an even more realistic adventure, take one of the museum's ecotours in the company of a qualified professional. Excursions include snorkeling with salmon, rafting wild rivers, sailing with whales, bird-watching, and viewing totem poles. Special kids' programs explore such topics as bugs and tidal pools. Details: 675 Belleville Street;

(250) 387-3701; open daily July through September 9:30 a.m. to 7:p.m., the rest of the year 10 a.m. to 5.30 p.m. Admission includes GST: Adults $5.35, seniors $3.21, youths $2.14, families $10.70. Free on Monday October through April. Audio tours in several languages available for a small fee. (2 hours)

★★ **Beacon Hill Park**—Once a swampy forest, this 74-hectare/183-acre inner-city park is now a mostly manicured retreat, walking destination, and birding spot for residents and tourists alike. It has formal flower beds, bird-filled ponds, graceful trees, stone-walled bridges, picnic sites, playing areas, and a children's farm. No food concessions, but there are free musical concerts in summer. Joggers, walkers, and dogs stretch their legs daily along the scenic Dallas Road waterfront, a very Victorian tradition. Details: The park entrance is at the foot of Douglas Street. (minimum 1 hour)

★★ **Chinatown**—It covers little more than Fisgard Street but is packed with shops and restaurants. Fan Tan Alley, Canada's narrowest thoroughfare, barely permits two people to stand side by side. The Gate of Harmonious Interest is an impressive entranceway to Chinatown. Details: The Gate of Harmonious Interest is at the intersection of Government and Fisgard Streets. (1 hour)

★★ **Craigdarroch Castle**—This sandstone extravagance, which looks as if it came from Disneyland, was built by coal baron Robert Dunsmuir for his wife in the late 1880s. He promised her a castle if she would go with him to Vancouver Island, but Dunsmuir died before he could live in it. The castle, overlooking the city, features turrets, leaded-glass windows, tiled floors, and intricately carved woodwork. It also houses Victorian furnishings and changing exhibits of the period. Details: 1050 Joan Crescent; (250) 592-5323; open daily June 15 through Labor Day 9 a.m. to 7 p.m., the rest of the year 10 a.m. to 4.30 p.m. Admission: Adults $6, students with ID $5, ages 6–12 $2. (1 hour)

★★ **Munro's Bookstore**—Probably the best-stocked bookstore in Victoria, it's also worth visiting for the elegance of its Neoclassical architecture. This restored 1909 heritage building once housed a bank. It has been touted as "the most magnificent bookstore in Canada, possibly North America." Details: 1108 Government Street; (250) 382-2464. (15 minutes plus browsing time)

⭐⭐ **Thunderbird Park**—Outside in Thunderbird Park are full-size totem poles, a half-size Kwakiutl ceremonial house, and a carvers' workshop. Listen to the Netherlands' Centennial Carillon, the gift of Dutch residents of British Columbia to commemorate Canada's centennial in 1967. It's the largest carillon in Canada. Details: On Belleville Street, outside the Royal British Columbia Museum. (½ hour)

FITNESS AND RECREATION

There's lots to do year-round in balmy, coastal Victoria. Walking or jogging the Dallas Road waterfront in all weather is a popular pastime. Golfers can't beat the scenery at **Victoria Golf Club**, situated on a peninsula jutting into the Juan de Fuca Strait, but to play at this exclusive course you'll need an introduction from another golf club. Birders head for **Clover Point, Whiffin Spit, Witty's Lagoon**, and the boardwalk of the **Swan Lake-Christmas Hill Nature Sanctuary**. The 42-km (26-mi) recently developed **Galloping Goose Trail** takes cyclists, hikers, and horseback-riders through the west coast communities. Swimmers use the magnificent new indoor **Saanich Commonwealth Place** aquatic center, built for the 1994 Commonwealth Games; nearby lakes such as **Thetis, Elk**, and **Beaver** (warmish); or such rare sandy beaches as **Willows** and **Island View** (a tad chilly). The new **Park Gowlland Tod Provincial** is a scenic hiking trail and day-use area on the edge of Finlayson Arm and Tod Inlet. Offshore offers many opportunities for boating, fishing, and the new passion for whale- and wildlife-watching—and, of course, in a city that caters to all ages, there are lawn bowling and croquet.

FOOD

When you're wondering where to go for a meal or nightclub in Victoria, pick up a copy of the weekly *Monday Magazine* (it comes out on Wednesday). Here are some of my favorite spots.

Barb's Fish and Ships (yes, really!) is a floating fish-and-chips shop in the middle of the fishing fleet on Fisherman's Wharf at 310 St. Lawrence Street, (250) 384-6515. It serves delicately battered halibut and homemade fries with the skins left on, all served traditionally—just as they should be—wrapped in traditional newspaper.

Whenever sweet-toothed guests come to town, I rush them to the **Dutch Bakery and Coffee Shop**, 718 Fort Street, (250) 385-1012, to

VICTORIA

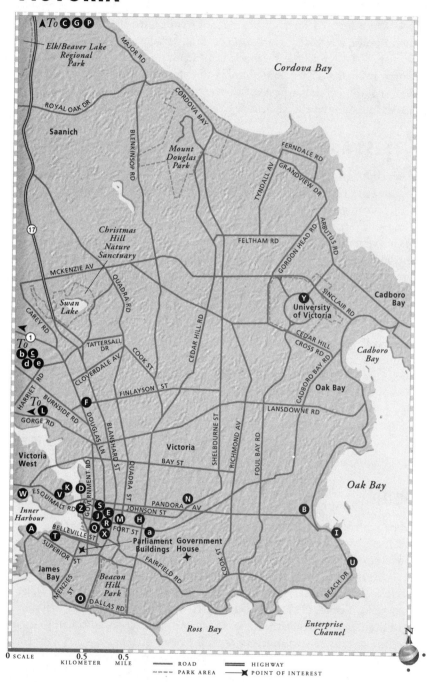

Elk/Beaver Lake Regional Park

Cordova Bay

MAJOR RD

ROYAL OAK DR

Saanich

BLENKINSOP RD

CORDOVA BAY

Mount Douglas Park

FERNDALE RD

TYNDALL AV

GRANDVIEW DR

ARBUTUS RD

17

Christmas Hill Nature Sanctuary

MCKENZIE AV

QUADRA RD

FELTHAM RD

GORDON HEAD RD

SINCLAIR RD

Cadboro Bay

Swan Lake

University of Victoria

CEDAR HILL CROSS RD

Cadboro Bay

CAREY RD

To 1

TATTERSALL DR

COOK ST

CEDAR HILL RD

CADBORO BAY RD

Oak Bay

CLOVERDALE AV

FINLAYSON ST

LANSDOWNE RD

HARRIET RD

BURNSIDE RD

To

GORGE RD

DOUGLAS LN

BLANSHARD ST

SHELBOURNE ST

RICHMOND AV

FOUL BAY RD

Victoria West

Victoria

BAY ST

QUADRA ST

Oak Bay

ESQUIMALT RD

GOVERNMENT RD

PANDORA AV

Inner Harbour

JOHNSON ST

FORT ST

BELLEVILLE ST

Parliament Buildings

Government House

SUPERIOR ST

FAIRFIELD RD

COOK ST

James Bay

MENZIES ST

Beacon Hill Park

DALLAS RD

BEACH DR

Ross Bay

Enterprise Channel

N

0 SCALE 0.5 KILOMETER 0.5 MILE

ROAD HIGHWAY
PARK AREA POINT OF INTEREST

Food

Ⓐ Barb's Fish and Chips

Ⓑ Blethering Place Restaurant

Ⓒ Deep Cove Chalet

Ⓓ Don Mee's Restaurant

Ⓔ Dutch Bakery and Coffee Shop

Ⓓ Herald Street Cafe

Ⓕ Jack Lee's Chinese Village

Ⓖ The Latch

Ⓗ Ming's

Ⓘ Oak Bay Marina

Ⓙ Pagliacci's

Ⓚ *Princess Mary* Restaurant

Ⓛ Sooke Harbour House

Ⓜ Spice Jammer

Lodging

Ⓝ Backpackers Hostel

Ⓞ Berry House

Ⓟ Cedarwood Motel

Ⓠ Empress Hotel

Lodging *(continued)*

Ⓡ Green Gables Inn

Ⓢ Hostelling International Victoria

Ⓣ Laurel Point Inn

Ⓤ Oak Bay Beach Hotel

Ⓥ Ocean Pointe Resort

Ⓦ Olde England Inn

Ⓧ Union Club of British Columbia

Ⓨ University of Victoria Housing and Conference Services

Ⓩ Victoria Regent Hotel

ⓐ YMCA-YWCA

Camping

ⓑ All Fun RV Park and Campground

ⓒ Fort Victoria RV Park

ⓓ Goldstream Provincial Park

ⓔ Thetis Lake Campground

Note: Items with the same letter are located in the same area.

drool over this Victorian institution's impeccable pastries. I'm told that the hamburgers that have been served at the tables in the rear of the store for the past 40 years are the best in Victoria, but I have yet to get past the pastries and chocolates. Speaking of chocolate, don't miss **Rogers Chocolates**, 913 Government Street, (250) 384-7021, and its turn-of-the-century architecture.

The **Blethering Place Tea Room and Restaurant**, 2250 Oak Bay Avenue, (250) 598-1413, is another Victorian institution, second only to the Empress for its ritual of afternoon tea and pastries, and equal perhaps to the **Oak Bay Beach Hotel**, 1175 Beach Drive,

(250) 598-4556. Dinner is also good at both places.

Herald Street Cafe, 546 Herald Street, (250) 381-1441, is wildly popular at the moment, and lines spill onto the street. The restaurant is small and the decor is diffident, but staff and patrons are passionate about its Pacific Northwest cuisine, health-conscious menu, and imaginative desserts. Dinners are in the $11–$20 range.

Another wildly popular restaurant is **Pagliacci's**, 1011 Broad Street, (250) 386-1662. Tables and customers are packed closely together, and celebrity photos line the walls. This was the first restaurant in Victoria to make its own focaccia bread and to bake cheesecake. It has live entertainment.

The *Princess Mary* **Restaurant**, 358 Harbour Road, just west of the Johnson Street Bridge, (250) 386-3456, is the top deck of an actual sailing ship, the *Princess Mary*, that sailed the local waters for 40 years. Residents don't rave about the food—burgers, sandwiches, soup, and seafood—but they do bring their out-of-town visitors to this popular Victorian institution.

If you're looking for Chinese food, three popular choices are **Ming's**, 1321 Quadra Street, (250) 385-4405; **Jack Lee's Chinese Village**, 755 Finlayson Street, (250) 384-8151; and **Don Mee's Restaurant**, 538 Fisgard Street, (250) 383-1032.

For more elegant dining (dinners start at $30), Victoria has several world-acclaimed restaurants. Lunch on the terrace of the **Deep Cove Chalet**, 11190 Chalet Drive, North Saanich, (250) 656-3541, and treat yourself to sweeping lawns, beautiful gardens, and exquisite food, especially the Sunday seafood buffet. Go for dinner (French cuisine) and you get sunset over Saanich Inlet for free. **The Latch**, 2328 Harbour Road, Sidney, on the east side of the Saanich Peninsula, (250) 656-6622, is another intimate and expensive location but with excellent food. The **Sooke Harbour House**, a country inn at 1528 Whiffen Spit Road, Sooke, on the southwest coast of the island, (250) 642-3421, hosts a restaurant known continent-wide for its local seafood served with fresh herbs and fresh flowers from its gardens. In Victoria itself, you can dine over the water at **Oak Bay Marina Restaurant**, 1327 Beach Drive, (250) 598-8555.

For East Indian food, visit Amin and his family at the **Spice Jammer**, 852 Fort Street, (250) 480-1055.

In June, plan to eat out nightly at Victoria's annual **Folk Fest**, in Centennial Square behind City Hall. You'll get almost nonstop free entertainment as well.

LODGING

Tourism Victoria's handy toll-free line for accommodation information and advance reservations, (800) 663-3883, offers lots of choices.

The first hotel on everyone's list is the historic, ivy-clad **Empress Hotel**, overlooking the Inner Harbor at 721 Government Street, right in the swing of things downtown, (800) 441-1414. Grand rooms, even grander lobbies, the renowned Bengal Room for curries and drinks, the daily afternoon tea ritual, arcades of expensive shops—the Empress is a tourist destination in itself. Celebrities hit the hotel regularly, including wild cougars on at least two occasions—once on the hotel steps and once recently in the parking lot.

In the high season (May through October), rates run $275–$345 and $335–$405 a night; low season (October through May), $140–$210 and $235–$305 a night. The B&B rate in low season is $169–$239; in high season, $225–$285. The hotel offers several package plans at particular times of the year, such as Christmas.

For less history and more razzamatazz, look across the Inner Harbor to modern, state-of-the-art hotels such as the **Laurel Point Inn**, 680 Montreal Street, (250) 386-8721, and the brand new **Ocean Pointe Resort**, 45 Songhees Road, (250) 360-2999, which arguably have better views of what's going on in Victoria than the venerable Empress. Rather than walking across the Johnson Street Bridge to the Ocean Pointe Resort, a fun way to get there is by water, on a little tug-like ferry. In addition to superlative views from its dining rooms (the Victorian and the Boardwalk), health-conscious menus, its own wine shop, and artwork from around the world, the Ocean Pointe is the only hotel in Western Canada with a complete European-style spa. The full treatment includes mud body wraps, hydrotherapy, aromatherapy, massage, fitness training, swimming, and a sauna. If you have money to burn, try the New Year's Delight for $360, an Ancient Roman Bathing Ritual for $95, or five computerized facial treatments for $250. But that's after whale-watching, squash, tennis, and golf. It's all at 45 Songhees Road, (800) 667-4677.

If you think Victoria is losing some of its highly touted English charm, stay at the **Olde England Inn**, 429 Lampson Street, (250) 388-4353. All rooms have seventeenth- and eighteenth-century antiques, some have open fireplaces, and family suites are available. Rooms range $80–$200 a night. This distinctive half-century-old inn is part of a reconstructed English village that includes copies of William

Shakespeare's birthplace and Anne Hathaway's thatched cottage. You'll enjoy roast beef, steak-and-kidney pie, sherry trifle, scones, and crumpets served by costumed wenches in the Shakespeare Dining Room. The **Oak Bay Beach Hotel**, 1175 Beach Drive, (800) 668-7758, is a Tudor-style establishment on the waterfront. Rates run $136–$226. The current home of the **Union Club of British Columbia** (est. 1879), 805 Gordon Street, (250) 384-1151, was built in 1911 and has a truly Victorian atmosphere. Rates range $73–$193 a night, including continental breakfast.

The **Victoria Regent Hotel**, a condo hotel at 1234 Wharf Street, (250) 386-2211 or (800) 663-7515, is as close to the Inner Harbor as you can get. From its balconies you look down on sailboats, tugs, and barges.

As a tourist mecca, Victoria has an abundance of bed and breakfast places. Being a romantic, I would choose a heritage building such as **Berry House** (built in 1907), 114 St. Andrews Street, (250) 744-9125. Rates run $45–$75.

For more ordinary lodgings but close to the airport, try **Cedarwood Motel**, 9522 Lochside Drive, Sidney, (250) 656-5551. **Green**

Saanich Inlet, Vancouver Island

Lyn Hancock

Gables Inn, 850 Blanshard, (250) 385-6787, is clean, pleasant, and conveniently downtown, with rates of $99–$150.

For the youthful or budget-conscious, Hostelling International Victoria is in a convenient heritage building at 516 Yates Street, (250) 385-4511; rates run $15–$19 a night. There's also a Backpackers Hostel at 1418 Fernwood Road, (250) 386-4471. University of Victoria Housing and Conference Services, at Sinclair and Finnerty Road, Box 1700, Victoria, (250) 721-8396, is a good choice between May 1 and August 31. Rates range $32–$65, with breakfast included. The YMCA/YWCA, 880 Courtenay Street at Quadra Street, (250) 386-7511, is basic but convenient and a good value, especially since all Y facilities are included.

CAMPING

Fort Victoria RV Park, 340 Island Highway 1A, (250) 479-8112, looks like a fort from its palisade and recalls the city's beginnings. It offers full services for $23–$25 a night, double occupancy. All Fun RV Park and Campground, 2207 Millstream Road, (250) 474-4546, entices families with its adventure golf and driving range, waterslides, go-karts, batting cages, bumper boats, and auto racetrack. Prices range $18–$24, based on four persons.

The Greater Victoria area has lots of day-camping areas and picnic sites that are exquisite in spring wildflower season. Use the regional and provincial parks for more natural camping. Thetis Lake Campground, #1-1938 Trans-Canada Highway, Thetis Lake, (250) 478-3845, is close to excellent boating, swimming, and hiking. Rates are $15 a night for two. Goldstream Provincial Park, 2930 Trans-Canada Highway, (250) 391-2300, offers old-growth forests, fall salmon-spawning, and the Freeman King Nature Centre.

NIGHTLIFE

No longer are the sidewalks rolled up at night in staid old Victoria. *Happenings*, Victoria's weekly entertainment calendar in the *Times-Colonist* newspaper, and the weekly *Monday Magazine* list current events. The McPherson, Royal, and Belfry Theatres offer live performances year-round, while the Fringe Theatre Festival is a popular citywide event in August. The Victoria Symphony performs a Symphony

Splash on a barge in the Inner Harbor each summer to an open-air audience of often more than 40,000 (if it doesn't rain).

Pubs and brewpubs are popular in Victoria. **Spinnakers Brewpub**, 308 Catherine Street, (250) 384-6613, and **Swans Pub**, 506 Pandora Avenue, (250) 361-3310, are two of the most popular and well-positioned. Swans is also a hotel, restaurant, and wine and beer shop. A rooftop patio with live entertainment, four multilevel cricket themed rooms, and the world's only rooftop sand volleyball court make the **Sticky Wicket Pub and Restaurant** in the Strathcona Hotel, 919 Douglas Street, (250) 383-7137, well worth visiting.

Nightclubs currently in vogue include **Legends**, 919 Douglas Street, in the Strathcona Hotel, (250) 383-7137; **Planet Harpo's**, 15 Bastion Square, (250) 385-2626; and the **Drawing Room**, 751 View Street, (250) 920-7797. For coffee, try the popular **Grabbajabba's** two locations: 1211 Douglas Street, (250) 381-6484, and 816 Government, (250) 388-3770. For ballroom dancing—very trendy right now—I like **McMorran's Beach Restaurant**, 5109 Cordova Bay Road, (250) 658-5527.

4

HIGHWAY LOOPS AND ISLANDS

The Island," as British Columbians affectionately call Vancouver Island, is larger than most people think (450 km/280 mi long). Much is inaccessible except by driving a maze of restricted logging roads. You still can't drive to the island's very tip, despite the new multi-lane paved highway under construction between Victoria and Campbell River and the already finished sections between Campbell River and Port Hardy.

Diversity is part of the Island's appeal. On the west coast, mountains and rainforest jungles sliced by fjords plunge into a reef-ridden, storm-tossed ocean. On the east side, a drier, gentler land is tamed south of Campbell River by homes, farms, and gardens that overlook placid, protected passages. In high places, forests and logging slash open out onto colorful alpine meadows and perpetually snowcapped peaks. Underground is a labyrinth of caves; around its edge, a necklace of islands and islets.

You can zip up or down to the island in a few hours on the new Island (or Inland) Highway, but take the backroad loops on the old Island Highway instead. Try the loop to Bamberton, Mill Bay, Yellow Point, Cedar, Lantzville, Nanoose Bay, Cowichan Bay, Maple Bay, and Crofton. Better still, take ferries to offshore islands wherever you can. Hop over to Saltspring, Thetis, Gabriola, Newcastle and Protection, Lasqueti, Denman and Hornby, Quadra and Cortes, and Malcolm and Cormorant Islands. You could spend a whole season island-hopping your way up and down the east coast of Vancouver Island. ◼

A PERFECT DAY ON THE ISLAND HIGHWAY

Go whaling from Telegraph Cove. This charming dockside community of a couple of dozen people, 438 km (270 mi) up-island from Victoria, was owned until 1985 by the late Fred Wastell, whose father chose it in 1912 for a telegraph station. Later a sawmill, fish-box factory, and saltery were established, and docks, post office, store, school, community hall, and houses were built on the rock or on wooden pilings over the cove. Fred's boat, *Gikumi*, is now used by Stubbs Island Charters to take people out on daily cruises (mid-June through mid-October) to Johnstone Strait, which is the most accessible and predictable location in the world for seeing orcas (killer whales). Perfection for me would be watching orcas rubbing themselves on the beaches of Robson Bight, an Ecological Reserve 20 km (12 mi) east of Telegraph Cove.

For orca-watching, contact Stubbs Island Charters, Box 7, Telegraph Cove, British Columbia V0N 3J0; (250) 928-3185 or (800) 665-3066. Cost: Adults $60; children to 12, seniors 65-plus, and groups of 10-plus, $54 per person. A variety of B&Bs and campgrounds are available close-by in Port McNeill, but I would book a cottage on stilts overlooking the boardwalk and marina right inside Telegraph Cove for $125 per night (minimum two-night stay).

SIGHTSEEING HIGHLIGHTS

★★★ **Chemainus**—This is the Little Town That Did—or, rather, did not die when its local sawmill closed down. Instead, it transformed itself into the world's largest outdoor art gallery. Each summer, artists gather to paint giant murals depicting local history on the walls of its buildings. It's now a popular and colorful destination for the whole family, with sidewalk cafes, ice-cream parlors, tea rooms, antiques stores, a dinner theater, and a horse-drawn carriage to more easily see them all. Details: Chemainus Festival of Murals Society, Box 1311, Chemainus, British Columbia V0R 1K0; (250) 246-4701. (2 hours)

★★★ **Denman and Hornby Islands**—You get these two neighboring rural islands practically for the price of one, they're so closely connected by ferry. From Buckley Bay, 20 km (13 mi) south of Courtenay, it's just a 15-minute ferry trip to Denman, where you can take a 15-minute drive to catch a connecting ferry to Hornby. Don't miss Fillongley Provincial Park and the many artisan studios on Denman. Take the 5-km

(3-mi) hike around Helliwell Provincial Park and be sure to swim at Tribune Bay Provincial Park, which has some of the warmest waters and finest white sandy beaches of any in the province. Hornby Island, dubbed "the undiscovered Hawaii of British Columbia," is fun for the whole family, whether you drive, cycle, or hike. Details: Denman/ Hornby Tourist Services; (250) 335-2293 or (250) 335-2731. (1 day)

★★★ **Nanaimo**—Nanaimo is also called The Hub or Harbor City. It's easy to get fed up with the snarl of traffic in the narrow, fan-like downtown streets or the endless humdrum malls of north Nanaimo, but be patient and stop to have some fun. The residents do. Take a walk along the waterfront or in one of Nanaimo's many parks. A Waterfront Walkway winds around a harbor crammed with boats, and passes two parks and Swy-A-Lana Tidal Lagoon, the only artificially created tidal pool in Canada. Browse the shops and restaurants, buy fresh seafood from Fisherman's Wharf, and listen to the noon cannon fired by costumed guards at the Hudson's Bay Company's Bastion, the oldest remaining structure of its type in North America. My favorite is Piper's Lagoon Park, once the site of a whaling station and a Japanese fishing village. If you're lucky, you'll

Lyn Hancock

Telegraph Cove

HIGHWAY LOOPS AND ISLANDS

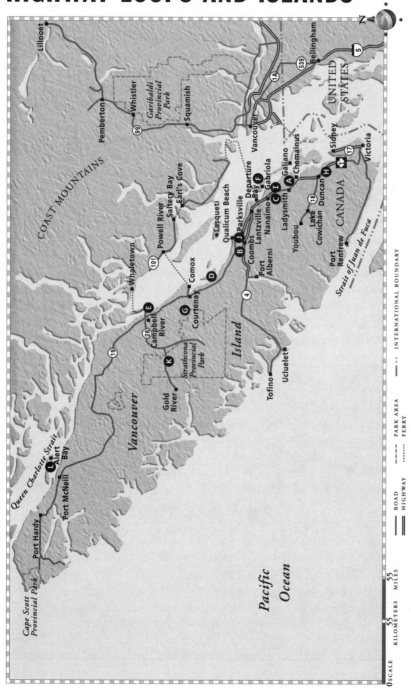

N

Lillooet

Pemberton

Whistler

Garibaldi
Provincial
Park

Squamish

COAST MOUNTAINS

Bellingham

UNITED
STATES

5

539

14

Vancouver

Sidney

17

Victoria

Galiano

Chemainus

Departure
Bay
Gabriola

A

Nanaimo

Duncan

Ladysmith

Lantzville

Lasqueti

Qualicum Beach

Parksville

Coombs

Powell
River

Saltery Bay

Earl's Cove

Port
Alberni

Youbou

Lake
Cowichan

18

Port
Renfrew

CANADA

Strait of Juan de Fuca

Whaletown

101

Comox

4

Island

Courtenay

Campbell
River

28

19

Gold
River

Strathcona
Provincial
Park

Ucluelet

Vancouver

Tofino

Alert
Bay

Port McNeill

Queen Charlotte Strait

Port Hardy

Cape Scott
Provincial Park

Pacific
Ocean

INTERNATIONAL BOUNDARY

PARK AREA

FERRY

ROAD

HIGHWAY

SCALE

55 MILES

55 KILOMETERS

Sights

Ⓐ Chemainus

Ⓑ Coombs Emporium

Ⓒ Cyber City Adventures

Ⓓ Denman and Hornby Islands

Ⓔ Discovery Pier, Campbell River

Ⓕ Gabriola Island

Ⓖ Mount Washington Ski Resort

Ⓒ Nanaimo

Ⓗ Native Heritage Centre

Ⓘ Newcastle Island Provincial Marine Park

Ⓙ Parksville and Qualicum Beach

Ⓚ Strathcona Provincial Park

Ⓛ U'mista Cultural Centre

Note: Items with the same letter are located in the same town or area.

see killer whales, which have been known to chase sea lions into the lagoon.

December through April, hundreds of California and Steller's sea lions spend their winter in Nanaimo, often on the log booms of local saw- and pulpmills, resting and feeding on spawning herring. Hundreds of bald eagles gather to feed or scavenge as well. In most years Nanaimo holds a wildlife festival to celebrate such gatherings, and, as in Chemainus, local artists paint murals. In July, contestants in the Great International Nanaimo Bathtub Race shoot 55 km (34 mi) across the Strait of Georgia to Vancouver in bathtubs fitted on flat planing boards and powered by 7.5-hp outboard motors. And in the Annual Silly Boat Race, locals are given a short time to concoct zany boats from a variety of fun materials, then race the boats in the harbor. At the Bungy Zone intrepid bungee jumpers plunge 43 meters (140 ft) into the Nanaimo River Gorge and, thanks to the elastic bungee, spring back from oblivion just before hitting the water. At least, they hope to. Finally, while in Nanaimo, do take in a Nanaimo Bar (no, it's not a local watering hole, it's a sweet, calorific concoction designed to please). Details: Contact Nanaimo Travel Info-Centre, 266 Bryden Street, Nanaimo; (250) 754-8474 or (800) 663-7337. (2 days)

★★★ **Newcastle Island Provincial Marine Park**—Funny that you can live for years in a place like Nanaimo and not get around to taking the five-minute ferry ride to this provincial park so close to the city. It's a marvelous destination for a day with the whole family. Take the people-only ferry from the waterfront walkway at Maffeo Sutton Park or take your own boat. Newcastle Island was once owned by the Canadian Pacific Railroad (CPR) as a pleasure resort, and the CPR Pavilion was a popular site for elegant big-band dances. Now it's an outdoor pleasure resort. Don't miss walking and swimming in Kanaka Bay (a shallow, warm-water lagoon) and hiking trails that circle the island. Details: B.C. Parks, 2930 Trans-Canada Highway, RR6, Victoria, British Columbia V9B 5T9; (250) 387-4363. (1 day)

★★★ **Parksville and Qualicum Beach**—These two seaside resort and retirement villages are famous for their sun and sandy beaches. At low tide, the sea recedes to leave the hard sand exposed for hundreds of yards (ideal for beachcombing and sandcastle-building); when the tide comes in over the warmed sands, it's perfect for swimming. Each summer Parksville hosts an annual Sandcastle Competition—well worth your participation. Each April a Brant Festival celebrates the arrival of thousands of Brant geese. There's plenty to keep you occupied in the Parksville-Qualicum area—and use its central position to explore the rest of the island. Don't miss the Big Qualicum River Fish Hatchery, Englishman River Falls, and Horne Lake Caves. Details: Parksville Chamber of Commerce, (250) 248-3613; Qualicum Beach Travel Info Centre, (250) 752-9532. (2 days)

★★★ **Strathcona Provincial Park**—This rugged mountain wilderness almost in the center of the island is the province's first provincial park. Many of the hikes are uphill, but the alpine scenery is worth the climb. Golden Hinde, at 2,200 meters (1875 ft), is the island's highest peak. Della Falls, one of the highest waterfalls in Canada, has an overall drop of 440 meters (275 ft) in three cascades. I recommend hiking to Paradise Meadows, Battleship Lake, and Forbidden Plateau (easy); and to Marble Meadows and Flower Ridge (more difficult).

A private resort, Strathcona Park Lodge and Outdoor Education Centre is a superb base for such outdoor activities as hiking, climbing, cross-country skiing, and canoeing; and indoor activities such as quilting, yoga, wellness strategies, and other year-round special-interest programs. Strathcona is both a scenic place to stay and an outdoor education center. Don't miss it. Details: Box 2160S, Campbell River, British Columbia V9W 5C9; (250) 286-8206. (1 day)

★★ **Coombs Emporium**—Before the new Inland Island Highway was constructed, this popular market in the village of Coombs was my first stop on Highway 4 West to the island's west coast. Now it's easier to visit as a side trip from Nanaimo, Parksville, or Qualicum Beach. Kids will love the goats who live on the grass-covered roof of the main market building. Other attractions with a "Wild West" atmosphere, such as funky shops, outdoor cafes, and street entertainment, have proliferated in Coombs. Details: Coombs Old Country Market, 2326 Alberni Highway, Parksville; (250) 248-6272. (2 hours)

★★ **Discovery Pier (Campbell River Fishing Pier)**—Campbell River is headquarters of the Tyee Club, whose members must catch a salmon of 30 pounds or more while fishing from a rowboat in the raging waters of Discovery Passage. A less thrilling but safer fishing hole is the 183-meter (600-foot) Discovery Pier, the first fully equipped saltwater fishing pier in Canada. It has shelters for dry fishing on rainy days, as well as fish-cleaning stations, seating, and night lights for fishing after dark. It's open 24 hours a day and has built-in rod holders and bait stands. It's also a favorite spot for watching the cruise ships pass by on their way to Alaska. Details: Next to the Government Wharf in downtown Campbell River. Concession stand: (250) 286-6199. (½ hour)

★★ **Mount Washington Ski Resort**—Now accessible from Courtenay by the 40-km (25-mi) paved Strathcona Parkway is this reasonably priced alpine ski destination for the whole family, with special programs and facilities for kids and disabled skiers. The area's alpine trails and wildflowers, and the possibility of seeing the rare Vancouver Island marmot, are also a delight in summer. Details: (250) 338-1386. Drive, bus, or take Via Rail's E and N Dayliner train from Victoria to Courtenay, (800) 561-8630. (1–2 days)

★★ **Native Heritage Centre**—This living history museum and art gallery dedicated to the culture of the Northwest Coast Indians offers demonstrations of carving, weaving, silversmithing, beadwork, and dancing; a midday salmon BBQ; and theatrical presentations. Details: 200 Cowichan Way, Duncan; (250) 746-8119; open daily mid-May through mid-October 9:30 a.m. to 5 p.m., and the rest of the year

10 a.m. to 4.30 p.m. Admission: Adults $7.25, families $19, seniors and students $6.50, ages 6–12 $3.25, and under 6 free. Midday show July through September Tuesday through Saturday at noon. Show admission is adults $23.60, children $16.82. (minimum 1 hour)

✶✶ U'mista Cultural Centre—Take the ferry from Port McNeill to the fishing village of Alert Bay on Cormorant Island to see this fine collection of elaborately carved masks and other artifacts that depict the Potlatch Ceremony of the Kwagu'l people. At a potlatch (ceremonial feast and dance), the host, perhaps an important chief, distributes gifts such as copper, masks, and blankets. The more gifts distributed, the higher the status of the giver becomes. Coppers, in particular, are a sign of wealth. Also in Alert Bay is a 53-meter (173-foot) totem pole featuring 22 carved figures, considered the world's tallest. Details: In Alert Bay, Cormorant Island; (250) 974-5403; open year-round Monday through Friday 9 a.m. to 5 p.m., extended summer hours include Saturday, Sunday, and holidays noon to 5 p.m. Admission: Adults $5, over 65 $4; under 12 $1. Guided tour $2. (1 hour)

✶ Gabriola Island (Island of Eagles)—The most northerly of the Gulf Islands, Gabriola is easily reached from Nanaimo by a 20-minute ferry ride. Ferries run hourly between 6 p.m. and 10:45 p.m., and Nanaimo workers take advantage of such easy access, living in greater serenity on Gabriola, an ideal car or bike circle tour. The main attraction is the Malaspina Galleries, a 12-foot-high weathered sandstone rock formation that looks like a petrified tidal wave. Also worth visiting are the ancient petroglyphs behind the United Church near Degnen Bay. Gabriola boardwalk's Folklife Village shopping center was recreated from the Folklife Pavilion at Vancouver's EXPO '86. Details: Gabriola Visitor Info Centre, (250) 247-9332. (1 day)

Cyber City Adventures—Let the kids (adults, too) try this adventure park fun with lasers, mountain bikes, go-karts, space balls, power balls, golf balls, and a virtual reality arcade. Details: 1815 Bowen Road, Nanaimo; (250) 755-1828. (2 hours)

FITNESS AND RECREATION

Vancouver Island has endless opportunities for recreation: bungee-jumping in Nanaimo, whale-watching in Tofino and Telegraph Cove, skiing at Mt. Washington, spelunking at Horne Lake and Little Hustan Regional Cave Park near Qualicum Beach, salmon-fishing in Port Alberni and Campbell River, kayaking in the Broken Group Islands in Barkley Sound, hiking in innumerable parks, swimming, sandcastle-building, sailing, windsurfing, fishing, canoeing, kayaking, cycling, mountain biking, and more. Choose any destination and you'll find a variety of pursuits. Use the well-developed logging roads that crisscross the island to get you off the beaten and not-so-beaten track, but remember: use of logging roads is limited to after-hours and weekends.

There's an indoor climbing center called **Romper Room** at 4385-B Boban Drive, Nanaimo; (250) 751-ROCK (7625).

FOOD

Vancouver Island still reveals much of its English heritage, so when asked for dining suggestions, Islanders are likely to suggest an English-style pub. A copy of *Island Pubbing*, by Robert Moyes, will help. One of my favorites is the **Crow and Gate**, 2313 Yellow Point Road, Nanaimo, (250) 722-3731. It's a "meat and potatoes" pub (no TV or loud music) set in the middle of a field, and its loyal local clientele enjoy its low ceilings, Tudor-style architecture, English specialties (bangers and mash, steak-and-kidney pie, and Melton Mowbray pie), and reasonable prices. The menu's most expensive dinner item is roast beef and Yorkshire pudding, at $12.35.

A really different kind of pub is the **Dinghy Dock Marine Pub and Bistro**, overhanging Nanaimo Harbor on Protection Island, (250) 753-2373 or (250) 753-8244. If you don't want to paddle your canoe or kayak, or tie your motorboat to the pub's "front door," then board the Protection Island ferry at the Waterfront Walkway. Cost is $4.25 round trip. If you bring a kid, you can get a seat right on the dock in the no-smoking area. Have a snack or dinner while you watch the action in the harbor and the striking sunsets over the mountains that surround the city. The best deal on the menu is a gargantuan dish of BBQ ribs, chicken, and smokie sausage with a giant stuffed spud and a Caesar salad on the side—all for about $13. Pub closes between November and March.

The best clam chowder I have eaten was at the **Fairwinds Golf and Country Club**, 3500 Fairwinds Drive, Nanoose Bay, (250) 468-9915. Deer and geese graze on the course in front of you, competing with the golfers for your attention. I like the innovative healthy food

HIGHWAY LOOPS AND ISLANDS

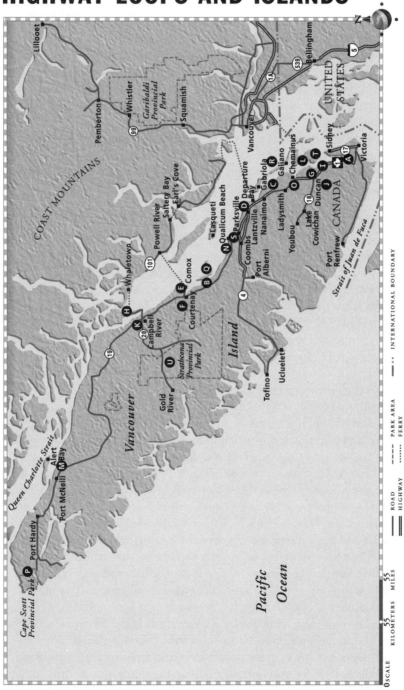

N

UNITED STATES

CANADA

Bellingham

5

539

1A

Vancouver

Lillooet

Whistler

Garibaldi
Provincial
Park

Pemberton

Squamish

99

COAST MOUNTAINS

Saltery Bay

Earl's Cove

Powell River

Lasqueti

Qualicum Beach

Parksville

Coombs

Port
Alberni

Whaletown

Comox

Courtenay

Campbell
River

28

Strathcona
Provincial
Park

Gold
River

Vancouver

Island

4

101

19

Youbou

Lake
Cowichan

Port
Renfrew

Ladysmith

Nanaimo

Departure
Bay

Lantzville

Gabriola

Galiano

Chemainus

Duncan

18

Sidney

Victoria

17

Strait of Juan de Fuca

Tofino

Ucluelet

Pacific
Ocean

Alert
Bay

Port McNeill

Port Hardy

Cape Scott
Provincial Park

Queen Charlotte Strait

C
D
N
S
B
Q
E
F
H
K
U
M
P
G
O
R
I
L
T
J
A

O SCALE

55
KILOMETERS

55
MILES

ROAD
HIGHWAY

PARK AREA
FERRY

INTERNATIONAL BOUNDARY

Food

Ⓐ Aerie Inn

Ⓑ *Brico*

Ⓒ Crow and Gate Pub

Ⓒ Dinghy Dock Marine Pub and Bistro

Ⓒ Earl's

Ⓓ Fairwinds Golf and Country Club

Ⓔ Filberg Heritage Lodge

Ⓒ Grotto

Ⓕ Old House Restaurant

Ⓒ Pounders Dining and Gathering Place

Ⓖ Vinoteca

Lodging

Ⓐ Aerie Inn

Ⓗ April Point Lodge

Ⓘ Deer Lodge Motel

Ⓕ Economy Inn

Ⓙ Fairburn Farm Country Manor

Ⓚ Haig-Brown House

Lodging *(continued)*

Ⓛ Hastings House

Ⓜ Pacific Hostelry

Ⓚ Painter's Lodge

Ⓕ Paradise Seashell Motel

Ⓝ Qualicum College Inn

Ⓞ Yellow Point Lodge

Camping

Ⓟ Cape Scott

Ⓠ Helliwell

Ⓕ Miracle Beach

Ⓕ Mitlenatch Island Nature Park

Ⓡ Montague Harbor Provincial Park

Ⓢ Paradise Adventures Mini Golf and RV Park

Ⓢ Rathtrevor Beach Provincial Park

Ⓣ Ruckle Provincial Park

Ⓤ Strathcona Provincial Park

Ⓠ Tribune Bay Campsite

Note: Items with the same letter are located in the same town or area.

served at **Pounders Dining and Gathering Place**, an increasingly popular Mongolian stir-fry restaurant, at 18 Commercial Street, Nanaimo. The chef cooks your choice of meat, seafood, vegetables, and sauces as you watch. You pay $7.49 for a pound of cooked lunch and $10.99 for a pound of cooked dinner—thus the name. Rice is complimentary, and dinner add-ons include such exotics as wild boar and alligator. Also distinctive is **Vinoteca**, an Italian farm winery lounge set romantically in a vineyard, at 5039 Marshall Road, RR#, Duncan, (250) 748-2338. Try the frittata with chorizo sausage, peppers, zucchini, and mozzarella cheese served on a homemade potato latke. Tapas dishes have been recently added to the otherwise simple rustic Italian menu.

If you have only one splurge on the island, make it the **Aerie Inn**, Spectacle Lake turnoff, (250) 743-7115. Intimate, formal, seven-course dinners are about $55.

The delightfully decorated **Grotto**, 1151 Stewart Avenue, Nanaimo, (250) 753-3303, is now expanding its West Coast menu to include a sushi bar and other Asian enticements. For family meals, **Earl's** is a popular chain of quality restaurants.

You can't beat the reasonable prices and charming ambiance of the **Old House Restaurant**, 1760 Riverside Lane, downtown Courtenay, (250) 338-5406. Kids will enjoy eating their burgers in the hold or on the top deck of the *Brico*, a derelict cable-laying ship grounded on the oyster beds by the highway at Fanny Bay. Enjoy specialty teas and homemade meals served in beautifully landscaped gardens at the **Filberg Heritage Lodge and Park Tea House** in Comox. Go during the first week of August for the Filberg Festival, when hundreds of artisans demonstrate and sell their wares.

LODGING

The island has lots of charming character lodgings, but let's start with the opulent. The **Aerie Inn**, (250) 743-7115, is a great splurge for lodging as well as dining. A magnificent multitiered castle in the mountains above Malahat Drive, 20 minutes north of Victoria, it over-looks a misty scene of fjords and islands. Touted as one of North America's twelve best country inns, it has been featured on the American TV program *Run Away with the Rich and Famous*. Some suites have fireplaces and Jacuzzis, all have a touch of class. Rates range $145–$365 a person.

Like The Aerie, **Hastings House**, 160 Upper Ganges Road, Saltspring Island, (250) 537-2362 or (800) 661-9255, is part of the Relaix and Chateaux chain. This elegant Tudor-style manor house built in 1939 was fashioned after the owner's eleventh-century ancestral home in Sussex, England. Barns and farmhouses have been reconstructed as charming garden cottages. Single or double occupancy is $230–$440, with breakfast and afternoon tea included. Formal table d'hote dinners are about $65. For a fun alternative to the dining room, sit in the kitchen with the chef for a behind-the-scenes experience.

Fairburn Farm Country Manor, (250) 746-4637, once a millionaire's country estate, is a working farm 5 miles southwest of Duncan, in the peaceful Cowichan Valley. The Archer family offers cottage or B&B accommodations. Guests may help with chores, and most of the food served is home-grown. Rates range $80–$140.

Deer Lodge Motel, behind the fence at 2529 on the Island Highway in Mill Bay, (250) 743-2423 or (800) 668-5011, is a charming, downplayed version of Hastings House. With its flower gardens and gorgeous views over Saanich Inlet to Mount Baker, it scarcely should be called a motel. Rates are $45–$145 a person.

Yellow Point Lodge, 3700 Yellow Point Road near Ladysmith, (250) 245-7422, is a popular log retreat on the ocean that appeals to romantics and outdoors types. Rates range from $58–$109. That ivy-clad, Tudor-style **Qualicum College Inn**, 427 College Road, Qualicum Beach, (250) 752-9262 or (800) 663-7306, was once a private boys' boarding school only adds to its charm. The Inn hosts regular Murder Mystery Weekends. Rates are a reasonable $79–$109.

Campbell River appeals to anglers. A special B&B right on its banks is **Haig-Brown House**, (250) 286-6646, the former home of British Columbia's favorite fisherman-author-philosopher, Roderick Haig-Brown. Rates are $65–$85. **Painter's Lodge**, in Campbell River, (800) 663-7090, and more secluded **April Point Lodge**, on nearby Quadra Island, (250) 285-2222, are world-famous salmon-fishing resorts.

For a less famous and more economical change of pace, try the **Economy Inn** in Courtenay, (250) 334-4491, or the **Pacific Hostelry** in Alert Bay, (250) 974-2026. Alternatively, the reasonably priced **Paradise Seashell Motel**, (250) 248-6171, is nearby. Rates range from $38 for a single to $109 for a suite (for six).

CAMPING

Vancouver Island and the Gulf Islands have an abundance of camp-spots, both public and private, to match the diversity of the area. I suggest using the provincial parks first. Some of my favorites are **Strathcona** near Campbell River, **Rathtrevor Beach** near Parksville, **Ruckle** on Saltspring Island, **Montague Harbor** on Galiano Island,

Miracle Beach and Mitlenatch Island Nature Park near Courtenay, Tribune Bay and Helliwell on Hornby Island, and way up north at the end of the island, the remote and incomparable Cape Scott. Most are located near scenic areas, and rates are reasonable (i.e., less than $20 a night for two to four people) or free for day use.

You can't miss Paradise Adventures Mini Golf and RV Park on the Island Highway in Parksville, (250) 248-6612. Kids will be fascinated by its Disneyland look. They can play around the giant-sized Big Shoe, Castle, Water Wheel, and Old Sailing Ships on Treasure Island, while their parents play minigolf or fix supper on the BBQ before everybody troops off to the adjacent beach.

WEST COAST OF VANCOUVER ISLAND

G od's Country" is how British Columbia's coast was described when I landed here as an immigrant in 1962. It rained for six straight weeks, but when the sun finally shone through the fog, I knew I had truly reached paradise.

At that time I was fortunate enough to explore this magnificent meeting of land and sea—its graveyard reefs, surf-pounded beaches, wind-lashed forests—by floatplane and rubber boat. Since then, only the west coast of Vancouver Island has become easily accessible by any other means. You can now drive to this rugged wilderness coast, by a paved Pacific Marine Highway, from Port Alberni to the villages of Ucluelet and Tofino and the Pacific Rim National Park, in about 90 minutes. You can also navigate a maze of logging roads from Port Alberni to the boardwalk village of Bamfield, or cruise to Bamfield and Ucluelet through Barkley Sound by small freighter. Ironically, at the time of writing, the magic words "west coast" are still not signposted on the new Inland Island Highway. You have to remember that Port Alberni is your signal to turn west, or else you'll barrel northward on the blacktop into Courtenay or Campbell River. ◼

WEST COAST OF VANCOUVER ISLAND

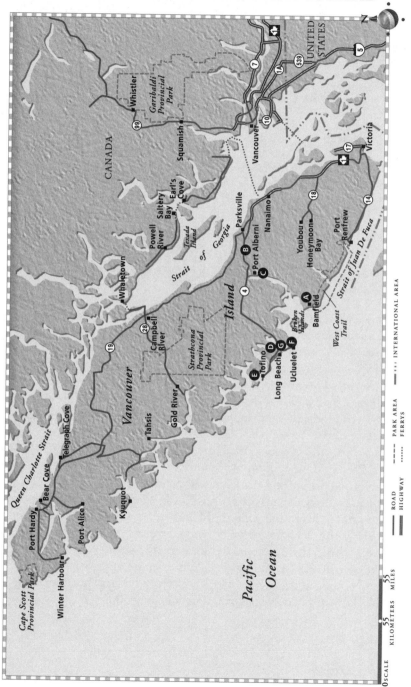

Sights

Ⓐ Bamfield

Ⓑ Cathedral Grove

Ⓒ *Lady Rose*

Ⓓ Pacific Rim National Park Reserve

Ⓔ Tofino

Ⓕ Ucluelet

Food

Ⓒ Blue Door Cafe

Ⓒ *Canadian Princess* Restaurant

Ⓔ Common Loaf Bake Shop and Cafe

Ⓔ Crab Bar

Ⓒ Little Bavaria

Ⓔ Pointe Restaurant, Chesterman Beach

Ⓔ Schooner Restaurant

Ⓖ Wickaninnish Restaurant

Lodging

Ⓐ Aguilar House Resort

Ⓑ Cable Cove Inn B&B

Ⓒ *Canadian Princess* Resort

Ⓔ Himwitsa Lodge

Ⓔ Middle Beach Lodge

Ⓔ Pacific Sands Beach Resort

Ⓔ Paddlers' Inn B&B

Ⓒ Riverside B&B

Ⓔ Vargas Island Inn and Hostel

Ⓖ Wickaninnish Inn

Ⓔ Wilp Gybuu (Wolf House) B&B

Camping

Ⓔ Bella Pacifica Resort and Campground

Ⓓ Green Point Campground

Ⓕ Ucluelet Campground

Note: Items with the same letter are located in the same town or area.

A PERFECT DAY ON THE WEST COAST OF VANCOUVER ISLAND

Pick a sunny one, and at 8 a.m. board the MV *Lady Rose* or MV *Frances Barkley* at the Harbour Quay in Port Alberni for a trip down the Alberni Canal into Barkley Sound and through the Broken Group Islands to arrive in Ucluelet, at 1 p.m. Arrange for a rental vehicle or a partner with a car to meet you in Ucluelet, and let the partner board the boat at 2 p.m. for the return journey to Port Alberni while you go back by the Pacific Rim Highway. If you were me, you'd rush off to Tofino at the end of the road, stopping where the highway meets the ocean at Long Beach for a quick walk on the sand, and again at the newly built Wickaninnish Inn for a cup of clam chowder. I'd choose a long summer day so I could complete the drive back east along the Pacific Rim Highway in daylight, at least as far as Cathedral Grove. That's if I had only one day. Preferably, I'd stay for weeks and have the *Lady Rose* drop me off in Bamfield and Barkley Sound for other adventures.

SIGHTSEEING HIGHLIGHTS

★★★ **Cathedral Grove**—A violent storm felled some of the trees in this park during the winter of 1996–1997, but it is still worth stopping along Highway 4 west of Parksville to stroll one of the looped trails in this awe-inspiring forest of 800-year-old Douglas firs. The largest tree measures 3 meters (10 ft) in diameter, over 9 meters (30 ft) around, and 75 meters (240 ft) high. Douglas firs dominate the south side of the road, and western red cedars, the north. Forest baron H. R. MacMillan donated these trees to the province in 1944. A new visitors' center opens in 1997. Details: In MacMillan Provincial Park. (minimum ½ hour)

★★★ **The *Lady Rose***—A west coast legend, for more than 50 years the *Lady Rose* has delivered mail, cargo, and passengers to isolated villages, fishing resorts, and logging camps. Another legend, Salal Joe, who lived on a float of logs roped to Turtle Island before his home became a national park, used to flag down the *Lady Rose* to send out the salal (a small, berry-producing shrub) he picked for florist shops. Now the historic freighter picks up and drops off kayakers bent on paddling in Barkley Sound or hikers tackling the West Coast Trail from Bamfield. Details: Alberni Marine Transportation, Box 188, Port Alberni, British Columbia V9Y 7M7; (250) 723-8313, or April through September (800) 663-7192. Full-day round trip to Ucluelet costs $44, children 8–15 half-fare. In summer, reservations are required. (1 day)

★★★ **Pacific Rim National Park Reserve**—Almost half a million people visit this park each year, mostly between late May and early October. It stretches 125 km (80 mi) from near Tofino in the north to Port Renfrew in the south, although not continuously, and contains sandy beaches, dense rainforests, rugged headlands, and rocky islands. There are three separate areas in the park: the popular Long Beach

unit along the highway between Ucluelet and Tofino, the Broken
Group Islands unit between Ucluelet and Bamfield in Barkley Sound,
and the West Coast Trail unit between Bamfield and Port Renfrew.
You have lots of different ways to enjoy this wild west coast—hiking,
beachcombing, boating, surfing, driving, and storm-watching from a
cozy window—but the very best way is hiking, and in all weather. The
park is open all year, although many facilities such as park interpre-
tation and dining at the Wickaninnish Centre are seasonal.

Long Beach should be your choice if your time is limited. It is
named for an 11-km (7-mi) curve of smooth, hard, surf-swept sand
exposed to the open Pacific Ocean. Next stop into the sunset is Japan.
The Wickaninnish Centre, at the beginning of Long Beach, was once a
famous inn. Now it's the park's headquarters, containing a restaurant
overlooking the beach, exhibits, and a theater; it's also the starting point
for self-guided and guided tours. Of the eight main marked trails in the
park, which vary in length from 1 to 5 km (.5 to 3 mi), my favorite is the
half-mile trail to Schooner Cove. The Shorepine Bog and South Beach
Trails are wheelchair accessible. Travelers with a yen for learning can
join adventures in education from the Heritage Learning Program, (250)
726-7721, on such topics as Rainforest Gardens, Marine Wonders,
Night Walks, and Legends of the Lighthouses.

The Broken Group Islands consist of about 100 islands and
rocks in the middle of Barkley Sound that have recently become very
popular destinations for canoeists and kayakers. The easiest access is by
having the *Lady Rose* drop you off at Sechart, the site of a former
whaling station. There are eight designated campsites (maximum stay is
four days at any one), and fees are $5 per person per night May 1
through September 30.

The West Coast Trail is for hikers and those with extra time to
spend. It follows the coast for 72 km (45 mi) between Bamfield and
Port Renfrew. Built along the route of a former telegraph line hung
from tree to tree in the 1890s to help survivors of ships wrecked in this
Graveyard of the Pacific, it was known as the Lifesaving Trail or the
Shipwrecked Mariners' Trail. Two of its prettiest sections are Tsusiat
Falls and Nitinat Lake and Narrows.

The West Coast Trail is open only from April 15 through
September 30, and access is limited to 8,000 hikers a season. A quota
system governs the number of hikers permitted to start each day at any
one of the three access centers (Pachena Bay, Gordon River, and Diti-
daht First Nations Nitinat Lake Visitor Centre). The permit fee in

1996 was $60. If you don't want to tackle the whole trail, choose one of the three access centers and do day hikes or part of the trail. For reservations after April 1, phone (800) 663-6000. A convenient way to get from Victoria, Duncan, or Nanaimo to the Bamfield starting point (295 km/177 mi) is by West Coast Trail Express, (250) 477-8700, at a cost of $46.73.

Details: Contact the Superintendent, Pacific Rim National Park Reserve, Box 280, Ucluelet, British Columbia V0R 3A0; (250) 726-7721. Park Information Centre, (250) 726-4212, at the Wickaninnish Centre on Wickaninnish Beach, is open daily mid-March through September 9:30 a.m. to 5 p.m. (I also recommend picking up a copy of the *Official Guide to Pacific Rim National Park Reserve*, $14.95.) Admission for private vehicles is by daily permit ($5) March through October, or by annual permit ($35), which also allows you access to other western national parks. Under Canada's recent austerity program, there are extra fees for camping, guided tours, theater, and day-use facilities. Parking lots sell parking permits at vending machines that accept Visa, MasterCard, coins, or bills. There is no fee to drive through the park without stopping. (1–3 days)

★★★ **Tofino**—From mid-March to mid-April, Tofino, the western terminus of the Pacific Rim Marine Highway (Highway. 4) joins the adjacent national park to celebrate the Pacific Rim Whale Festival. This is when thousands of Pacific gray whales migrating north from the Baja Peninsula in Mexico to feeding grounds in Alaska are seen close to shore. Each whale travels up to 15,000 km (9,500 mi) annually, the longest migration of any mammal in the world. Tofino, once a sleepy fishing village, is now a thriving tourist destination with several companies eager to take you closer to the whales. Some of the gray whales, and occasionally, humpback whales have been known to remain in the area until fall, when they rejoin the migration back to Mexico. Meares Island provides a dramatic backdrop to Tofino and an excellent paddling destination for kayakers. Details: Tofino Chamber of Commerce, Box 476, 380 Campbell Street, Tofino, British Columbia V0R 2Z0; (250) 725-3414. For whale-watching tours, try Remote Passages, (250) 725-3330 or (800) 666-9833; or Jamie's Whaling Station, (250) 725-3919 or (800) 667-9913. (2 hours)

★★ **Bamfield**—In this charming little fishing village, called by some "the Venice of Vancouver Island," the main street is an inlet leading to

Barkley Sound, and the pavement is a boardwalk linking the buildings. Walk to picturesque Brady's Beach, Cape Beale Lighthouse, or Pachena Bay, which is the beginning of the West Coast Trail. Tour the Marine Biological Station, which was once the TransCable Station, or use Bamfield as a base for fabulous fishing. Details: Bamfield Chamber of Commerce, Box 5, Bamfield, British Columbia V0R 1B0. (½ day)

★★ Ucluelet—Also surrounded by water, it's another handy base for whale-watching tours. The best way to appreciate Ucluelet is to explore its coves and beaches by foot, wander along its waterfront, and browse its arts and crafts shops. Amphitrite Point Lighthouse is now automated but is a good destination for a short hike. Details: Ucluelet Chamber of Commerce, Box 428, 227 Main Street, Ucluelet, British Columbia V0R 3A0; (250) 726-4641. (½ hour)

FITNESS AND RECREATION

Hiking, kayaking, canoeing, surfing, swimming—the possibilities are endless in this ocean and forest playground. You can be as organized (or not) as you like. Hike the many trails in **Pacific Rim National Park Reserve**, kayak the islands in **Clayoquot Sound** off Tofino, surf the waves off Long Beach, fish for salmon in **Barkley Sound**, dig for clams and oysters in **Toquart Bay**, dive for wrecked ships in the **Graveyard of the Pacific**, or soak in the natural hot springs of **Hot Springs Cove**, now part of Maquinna Marine Park. One of my favorite strolls is to walk the boardwalks and beaches of **He-tin-kis Park** in Ucluelet, a miniature version of Pacific Rim National Park.

The **Sea Kayaking Company**, 320 Main Street, Tofino, (250) 725-4222 or (800) TOFINO-4, has lots of ideas for exploring the local areas by kayak. One of its trips is a guided paddle to Vargas Island for an overnight stay.

FOOD

Wherever you eat on the west coast, try to get a window seat overlooking the surf. One such place is the newly opened **Pointe Restaurant and On-the-Rocks Bar** in the Wickaninnish Inn at Chesterman Beach, (250) 725-3100 or (800) 333-4604. You get a 240-degree view from a dining room that features soaring ceilings, cedar post-and-beam construction, and a circular wood-burning fireplace. The menu specializes in west coast seafood. Main-course prices range $12–$26. Less expensive and with a panoramic view of Long Beach is the **Wickaninnish Restaurant**, in the Wickaninnish Centre at the Pacific Rim National Park headquarters, (250) 726-7706. Be prepared to wait, since this restaurant advertises "seafood, sunsets, and romance."

An appropriate place for seafood dining is the *Canadian Princess* **Restaurant**, on a 236-foot ship in Ucluelet's Boat Basin overlooking the fishing fleet, (250) 726-7771. **Schooner Restaurant**, 331 Campbell Street, Tofino, (250) 725-3444, also specializes in seafood and is popular with local residents, who praise its clam chowder. Just as good is the **Crab Bar**, in a cozy cottage at 601 Campbell Street, (250) 725-3733; locals rave about the freshness of its crab.

For less elegant dining, hobnob with the locals at the **Common Loaf Bake Shop and Cafe**, 131 First Street, Tofino, (250) 725-3915. It's a popular lunch stop for wholesome soups, breads, and pizzas. In Port Alberni, try **Little Bavaria**, 3035 4th Avenue, (250) 724-4242, for great German food and a lively atmosphere. And for terrific breakfasts, check out the **Blue Door Cafe**, 5415 Argyle Street, (250) 723-8811.

LODGING

Two brand-new resort hotels overlook the wild west coast in Tofino. They're expensive but worth it. **Middle Beach Lodge**, (250) 725-2900, on a private peninsula in the middle of a forest, offers rooms, suites, and self-contained cabins ranging $65–$210 a night per person. The hotel actually has two lodges on the site, one adult-oriented and the other for families. Ask for winter specials and enjoy storm-watching, which is fast becoming a growth industry on the west coast. You'll love the wraparound boardwalk and cedar plank decks for ocean-viewing.

Not so private, but still with water and a forest backdrop, is the new **Wickaninnish Inn**, (250) 725-3100, at the northern end of Chesterman, my favorite Tofino beach. A local resident, his family, and friends have recreated the rustic elegance of Long Beach's old Wickaninnish Inn, now the park interpretive center. Guest rooms feature floor-to-ceiling picture windows, private balconies with soaker tubs inches away from surf-lashed rocks, and furniture fashioned from recycled old-growth timber and driftwood. Handicapped-equipped rooms are available. The Inn specializes in winter storm-watching between November 1 and February 27. Rates vary from $80 (winter) to $300 (summer) per person.

Locals like the older **Cable Cove Inn B&B**, 201 Main Street, (250) 725-4236 or (800) 663-6449, on a pristine bay near downtown Tofino. It has just six rooms, each with a fireplace, queen-size four-poster bed, and private marble Jacuzzi tub. Prices are $105–$190 peak season, $75–$145 off-season. **Himwitsa Lodge**, 300 Main Street, (250) 725-3319 or (800) 899-1947, is less private but overlooks the bay and has a First Nations art gallery attached. Prices range $95–$235.

I like the oceanfront cottages and suites with kitchens or kitchenettes at the **Pacific Sands Beach Resort**, (250) 725-3322 or (800) 565-2322. Its back door is 1421 Pacific Rim Highway, Tofino, but its front door is at the south end of magnificent Chesterman Beach, where waves crash under your window, and rock pinnacles beg for your camera. Prices range $75–$190.

Kinder on the budget is **Wilp Gybuu (Wolf House) B&B**, 311 Leighton Way, Tofino, (250) 725-2330, which offers a full home-cooked breakfast. **Paddlers' Inn B&B**, 320 Main Street, Tofino, (250) 725-4222, is basic but comfortable and convenient to sea-kayaking tours; rates including breakfast are a reasonable $58 for two people, $80 for a suite. Island lovers will head for yet another: **Vargas Island Inn and Hostel**, (250) 725-3309, a wilderness resort 20 minutes by boat from Tofino. Rooms start at $60 for the inn (including boat transportation and meals), but prices vary according to time of year, length of stay, number of people, and type of lodging. Kayakers pay $30 per night at the hostel, including meals, $40 per night if you are picked up by boat.

There's less choice in Ucluelet, but the nostalgic me would stay at the *Canadian Princess* Resort, (250) 726-7771, a historic west coast steamship permanently moored in Ucluelet Harbor. It's open from March 10 through September 30 and specializes in whale-watching, fishing packages, and nature cruises. Rates run $49–$129 per person. In Bamfield, I'd stay at historic and exclusive **Aguilar House Resort**, (800) 665-2533. Port Alberni locals suggest the **Riverside B&B**, 6150 Ferguson Road, (250) 723-3474; rates are $60 single or double.

CAMPING

Your first choice should be **Green Point Campground**, a shell's throw from Long Beach in Pacific Rim National Park Reserve, (800) 689-9025. It has 94 year-round sites for tents, trailers, and RV units, with heated washrooms. Additional tent camping is available at 33 walk-in beach sites and 20 walk-in forest sites nearby. This campground is highly popular between Easter and Thanksgiving, so book ahead or face a long wait. Rates are $20 in low season, $22 in high season, plus a $6.42 nonrefundable reservation fee per night up to a maximum of $19.26. From late June through early September, illustrated lectures, films, and audiovisual presentations are given nightly; free for registered campers, $2 for non-registrants, parking included. There's also a more primitive walk-in campsite on the beach at the end of the Schooner Trail.

If you can't find space in the park, try **Bella Pacifica Resort and Campground**, on the Pacific Rim Highway 3 km (2 mi) south of Tofino on sandy Mackenzie Beach, with private nature trails to Templar Beach; (250) 725-3400. Cost for two persons is $19–$26.50 in season, electricity included. In Ucluelet, try the **Ucluelet Campground** at Seaplane Base Road, overlooking Ucluelet Harbor and adjacent to a boat launch, (250) 726-4355. Cost is $16–$24 per vehicle, electricity included.

Now here's something different: camp in a tree tent! **Vancouver Wilderness Adventures** flies you by helicopter to a rainforest tree camp, where you sleep on a unique, 175-square-foot, fully enclosed sleeping platform built tipi-style around an ancient tree. Activities at this previously unexplored mountaintop destination include alpine hiking, mountain-climbing, bird-watching, trout-fishing, ice fishing, cross-country skiing, and snowshoeing. Contact Philip Jarman, 5840 Compton Road West, Port Alberni, British Columbia V9Y 7V2, (250) 723-1622, fax (250) 723-9413. Internet: pjarman@port.island.net

PORT HARDY TO THE CARIBOO

Cariboo Country reminds me of old California—British Columbia's Wild West cow and cowboy country. Situated in the center of the province, it extends from the fjords and rainforests of the central coast, to the mountains and canyons of the Chilcotin, to the lakes, grasslands, and rolling sagebrush hills of Cariboo proper. This part of Western Canada is for hunters and anglers, hikers and horseback-riders, paddlers and gold-panners.

Traditionally coastal aboriginal tribes accessed the area by way of the Grease Trail, a native trading route between Bella Coola and the Fraser River (Quesnel). In 1793 Sir Alexander Mackenzie, the first person to cross continental North America, reached the Pacific Coast by the same trail. Following the 1859 gold discovery near Horsefly, gold-seekers rushed into the area on the arduous Cariboo Wagon Road (now the Gold Rush Trail and part of Highway 97). Lillooet marks Mile 0 of the original wagon road to Barkerville, and communities along the way (70 Mile House, 100 Mile House, and 108 Mile Ranch) still bear the old names.

The most recent (1996) and innovative way to get to the Cariboo is by B.C. Ferries' Discovery Coast ferry from Port Hardy on Vancouver Island to Bella Coola on the northern mainland, then east on Highway 20 through the Chilcotin Country to Williams Lake. Highway 20, called "the Freedom Road," was built by local entrepreneurial residents who demanded access to the rest of the province. ∎

PORT HARDY TO THE CARIBOO

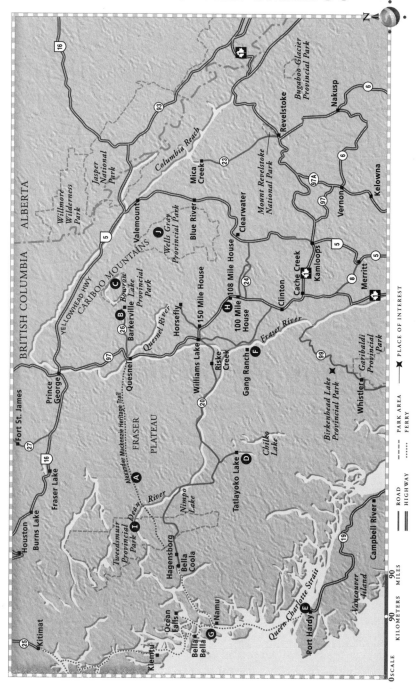

N

Legend

ROAD
HIGHWAY
PARK AREA
FERRY
PLACE OF INTEREST

SCALE
0   90
KILOMETERS   MILES
0   90

Map labels

BRITISH COLUMBIA
ALBERTA

Willmore Wilderness Park
Jasper National Park
Bugaboo Glacier Provincial Park
Nakusp
Revelstoke
Columbia Reach
Mica Creek
Mount Revelstoke National Park
Kelowna
Vernon
YELLOWHEAD HWY
Valemount
Wells Gray Provincial Park
Blue River
Clearwater
CARIBOO MOUNTAINS
Bowron Lake Provincial Park
Barkerville
Cache Creek
Kamloops
Merritt
108 Mile House
Clinton
Quesnel River
Horsefly
150 Mile House
100 Mile House
Fraser River
Quesnel
FRASER PLATEAU
Williams Lake
Riske Creek
Gang Ranch
Birkenhead Lake Provincial Park
Garibaldi Provincial Park
Whistler
Fort St. James
Prince George
Fraser Lake
Alexander Mackenzie Heritage Trail
Dean River
Nimpo Lake
Tattayoko Lake
Chilko Lake
Houston
Burns Lake
Kitimat
Tweedsmuir Provincial Park
Hagensborg
Bella Coola
Ocean Falls
Namu
Bella Bella
Klemtu
Queen Charlotte Strait
Port Hardy
Vancouver Island
Campbell River

Sights

Ⓐ Alexander Mackenzie Heritage Trail

Ⓑ Barkerville

Ⓒ Bowron Lake Provincial Park

Ⓓ Bracewell's Alpine
Wilderness Adventures

Ⓔ Discovery Coast Passage

Ⓕ Gang Ranch

Ⓖ Hakai Recreation Area

Ⓗ 108 Resort and
108 Heritage Site

Ⓘ Tweedsmuir Provincial Park

Ⓙ Wells Gray Provincial Park

A PERFECT DAY IN THE CARIBOO

Where to start? A day re-living Barkerville history? Canoeing the Bowron Lakes? Paddling Lava Canyon in Chilko Lake? Hiking the Rainbow Range Trail? Fly-in fishing from Nimpo Lake? Driving the Gold Rush Trail? Watching the Williams Lake Stampede?

I'd prefer chartering a plane for a personalized aerial tour of Mt. Waddington, British Columbia's highest mountain, and nearby Homathko Ice Fields, but my budget would probably settle for a day (or week) of horseback-riding or a flight through Tweedsmuir Provincial Park out of Nimpo Lake.

The Cariboo is chock-full of guest ranches and working ranches where you can ride with cowboys, fish- or bird-watch at one of the many lakes, go for a hayride, and sing around the campfire. If visiting the Hills Health and Guest Ranch or the 108 Ranch near 100 Mile House, add a swim and Jacuzzi soak—or maybe a massage, wrap, or facial.

SIGHTSEEING HIGHLIGHTS

★★★ **Alexander Mackenzie Heritage Trail**—This is a 420-km (250-mi) recreation trail between the confluence of the Blackwater and

Fraser Rivers, near Quesnel and Sir Alexander Mackenzie Provincial Park in Dean Channel, and near Bella Bella, where a monument recalls the end of the fur trader's historic 1793 journey across Canada. Mackenzie was the first person to record such a journey (more than ten years before the similar Lewis and Clark expedition across the United States). The Alexander Mackenzie Heritage Trail takes you from British Columbia's interior plateau country through mountainous Tweedsmuir Provincial Park, along the Bella Coola Valley, to coastal fjords and the Pacific Ocean. The 80-km (50-mi) trail section inside the park takes about five to seven days to travel and is perhaps the most scenic part of the route.

Hikers can walk the entire trail in about 18 days, although three weeks is more relaxing. Day-trippers can do shorter walks from several road-accessible trailheads. Local outfitters offer guided pack trips. Details: For a variety of trail guides, contact the Alexander Mackenzie Trail Association, Box 425, Stn. A, Kelowna, British Columbia V1Y 7P1. For other trail information, phone the Ministry of Forests, (250) 982-2000. (5 days–3 weeks)

★★★ **Barkerville**—The Gold Rush to the Cariboo comes to life again in this restored ghost town. When Billy Barker struck gold here in 1862, Barkerville quickly became the most populated city west of Chicago and north of San Francisco. The town is open year-round, but the full interpretive program of historical characters dressed in period costume, guided tours of some of its 125 original and restored buildings, live theater, displays, shows, and demonstrations operates only in summer. It's educational and entertaining for the whole family. Details: 8 km (5 mi) from Wells; Barkerville Historic Town, Barkerville Post Office, Barkerville, British Columbia V0K 1B0; or Barkerville/Wells Visitors Infocentre, (250) 994-3302 or 994-3332. Admission: Late June through Labor Day (good for two days) adults $5.50, over 65 and ages 13–17 $3.25, ages 6–12 $1. (1 day)

★★★ **Bowron Lake Provincial Park**—The 115-km (72-mi) canoe circuit of lakes, streams, and portages through this park, set amid the 2,425-meter (8,000-ft) peaks of the Cariboo Mountains, is one of the most beautiful canoe trips in the world. It's unique in that canoeists can return to the starting point without backtracking. Most people take eight days to travel the full circuit, but it can be completed in six days if necessary. Peak use occurs the last week of June through the first week of September, but avoid crowds by traveling at the end of May or the first week of October. Be prepared for rain and cold weather in any case. Details: 29 km (18 mi) northwest of Wells. Reserve with D.J. Park Contractors, 358 Vaughan Street, Quesnel, British Columbia V2J 2T2; (250) 992-3111 or fax (250) 992-6624. Only ten to 18 positions are reserved for people who walk in without reservations. To maintain the wilderness experience, only 50 people are allowed onto the circuit per day. Contact B.C. Parks, (250) 398-4414, for further information.

Fees for the full circuit are $60 per two-person canoe/kayak. Personal checks must be drawn on a Canadian account. An informational pretrip video is available upon request with a deposit of $20, refunded when the video is returned. Paddlers *must* see this video at the Registration Centre prior to traveling. (6–8 days)

★★★ **Discovery Coast Passage**—In the early 1960s I had the good fortune to travel up and down British Columbia's forested fjord-cut coast by floatplane and small rubber boat. In those days native and sawmill communities, fishing villages, and boardwalk canneries were alive with far more people and activities than they are today. In 1996, in an attempt to begin a new era in tourism, the British Columbian government launched a new ferry, the *Queen of Chilliwack*, to cruise what it dubbed the Discovery Coast Passage, between Port Hardy and Bella Coola. The new ferry loads and unloads freight and passengers at or near each of its milk-run stops: Finn Bay, known coast-wide for its huge chinook salmon; Namu, with a former cannery and a 10,000-year-old archeological site; Bella Bella, home to about 1,500 aboriginal people; Shearwater fishing resort; Ocean Falls, a former mill town; and Klemtu, once a cannery, now a small community of 200. The new ferry allows kayaks to be loaded and unloaded at all stops, opening up another vast area for kayakers to explore.

The Discovery Coast ferry is more like a miniature cruise boat, with deck golf, Bingo, showers, engine-room tours, and on-board entertainment. Although onshore facilities are still being built, passengers are offered walking tours, salmon barbecues, fishing trips, dance demonstrations, and visits to aboriginal longhouses. You can sail right through to Bella Coola on a 15-hour day cruise, or you can extend the voyage all summer by getting on and off the ferry as many times as you want. If you can afford only one stopover activity, paddle in a canoe across Lama Passage with Heiltsuk native Frank Brown and pick up the ferry again at Shearwater. The trip can be booked on the ferry. Campgrounds and accommodations along the route are limited, so reservations and prior planning are advisable. It is possible to sleep on the reclining chairs on board or to set up tents in the solarium.

The only road out of Bella Coola is the infamous "Hill," which switchbacks up a narrow 20-km (12-mi) gravel road with up to 18 percent grades to reach its highest point at 1524 meters (5,000 ft). Highway 20 then goes 285 miles through the lake country of the Chilcotin to the town of Williams Lake on Hwy. 97.

Details: Cost of car and driver between Port Hardy and Bella Coola is $330 one way and $110 for each additional passenger. RVs cost more. Tent rental, including bedding, is $25 for two nights. (I like sleeping on the benches in the cafeteria—they're narrow but quiet and uncrowded.) Season runs May through September. Routes, schedules, and cruise lengths vary, so contact B.C. Ferries, 1112 Fort Street, Victoria, British Columbia V8V 4V2; (888) BCFERRY/(888) 223-3779 (toll-free) for up-to-the-minute information. (2–3 days)

★★★ **Tweedsmuir Provincial Park**—This is the second-largest provincial park in British Columbia after Tatshenshini. When the Kenney Dam was built to power the hydroelectric plant at Kemano and the aluminum smelter at Kitimat, the water levels of the park's northernmost lakes rose, resulting in an eyesore of drowned trees and floating debris hazardous to boaters. However, the central and southern areas offer a variety of wilderness attractions: the colorful Rainbow Mountains, an ancient volcanic area composed of lava and other rock that have eroded to expose vivid hues; the Dean River, one of British Columbia's best fly-fishing areas; the Atnarko River, which supports the largest population of chinook salmon on the central coast and where visitors to Stuie can view spawning fish; and an arduous nine-hour hiking trail leading to Hunlen Falls. I would recommend flying to Tweedsmuir Wilderness Camp with Tweedsmuir Air Services from Nimpo Lake, (800) 668-4335, and spending a few days canoeing the Hunlen Valley chain of lakes. Hunlen Falls is more comfortable seen from the air. Nearby is the village of Hagensborg, established in the late 1890s by Norwegians, who chose the area because it reminded them of their homeland. Tweedsmuir is a wilderness park with few amenities. Details: B.C. Parks, Bag 5000, Smithers, British Columbia V0J 2N0; (250) 847-7320; or B.C. Parks, 301-640 Borland Street, Williams Lake, British Columbia V2G 4T1; (250) 398-4414. (minimum 1-hour drive through park or 2-hour trail hike)

★★★ **Wells Gray Provincial Park**—Nicknamed "the Waterfalls Park" for the beauty and abundance of its waterfalls and waterways, Wells Gray's best-known cascade is Helmcken Falls. Like Tweedsmuir, it offers an infinite variety of superb scenery: in the north, a multitude of unnamed peaks and glaciers; in the south, extinct volcanoes, lava beds, and mineral springs. Wells Gray has an extensive trail system leading to its main attractions. Details: Access park from Clearwater or Blue River. Contact B.C. Parks, 1210 McGill Road, Kamloops, British Columbia V2C 6N6; (250) 828-4494. (Hiking trails range from half-hour nature walks to weeklong backpacking trips.)

★★ **Bracewell's Alpine Wilderness Adventures**—Four generations of Bracewells have been taking customers on guided packhorse trips around the Cariboo—hunting, fishing, wildlife-viewing, glacier-touring, prospecting, bird-watching, practicing survival skills. The family also includes guests in seasonal activities on their working ranch and flies them around the Cariboo, sightseeing by bush plane or heli-copter. The Bracewells have plenty of stories to tell around the camp-fire at night or back at their 10,000-square-foot log ranch house. Details: Bracewell's Alpine Wilderness Adventures, Box 1, Tatlayoko Lake, British Columbia V0L 1W0. Phone November through June: (250) 476-1169, (250) 476-1165, or Chilanko JJ Channel H492-430. (minimum 4 days)

★★ **Hakai Recreation Area**—This extensive and scenic archipelago is the largest marine park on British Columbia's west coast. Accessible only by boat or plane and blessed with spectacular white-sand beaches and sheltered inlets, it's an ideal playground for boaters, fishers, kay-akers, and divers. Hakai Pass is world-famous for salmon-fishing and is home to a number of floating fish camps and resorts, including the 136-foot *Marabell* (Oak Bay Marine Group, 800-663-7090). Details: 43 km (27 mi) south of Bella Bella. (4- or 5-day organized trips)

★ **Gang Ranch**—This historic, million-acre working ranch near Clinton offers a small guest house and unguided activities such as horseback-riding (bring your own horse), hiking, photography, and viewing of the world's second-largest herd of California bighorn sheep. Details: Gang Ranch Post Office, Gang Ranch, British Columbia V0K 1N0; (250) 459-2624. Cost is $85–$150 per person per day, depending on room and meals requested. (1–2 days)

✵ **108 Resort and 108 Heritage Site**—Located on Highway 97, this former cattle ranch is now a 263-hectare (650-acre) recreational community and a roadside reconstruction of the original log buildings from the 108 Ranch. Accommodations amd dining, plus year-round activities that include cross-country skiing, golf, horseback-riding, hiking, canoeing, and swimming are offered. It's interesting to note the number of ginseng farms beside Highway 97 near Ashcroft. The world's supply of North American ginseng, an Asian medicinal root crop, is grown in the Cariboo. Details: Box 2, 108 Mile Ranch, British Columbia V0K 2Z0; (250) 791-5211 or (800) 667-5233. (minimum 1 day)

FITNESS AND RECREATION

The Cariboo is a recreational paradise—from boating and saltwater fishing on the coast; to hiking, freshwater fishing, rafting, and horseback-riding in the interior; to my favorite heli-hiking in **Bugaboo Glacier Provincial Park** further east. Try a guest ranch vacation with **Chilcotin Holidays** (the Cariboo has more guest ranches than any other area in British Columbia) or fly-in fishing at **Stewarts' Lodge** on Nimpo Lake, or hang-gliding around **Lime Mountain** near Clinton. There are excellent wildlife-viewing areas in the Cariboo: California bighorn sheep in the **Junction Wildlife Management Area** on Farwell Canyon Road south of Riske Creek, white pelicans at **Stum** and **Puntzi Lakes**, and all kinds of birds at **Chilanko Marsh**.

FOOD

In the Cariboo, eat your steaks or fish at a floating fish resort, working guest ranch, or around the campfire by a secluded lake or park trail. Locals like to eat at the **Alpine Inn Restaurant**, 496-A Anderson Drive, West Quesnel, (250) 992-2220, which features Chinese cuisine and specializes in a weekend smorgasbord. Also popular in Quesnel is **Ulysses Restaurant**, 122 Barlow Avenue, (250) 992-6606, which serves Greek food as well as steak, seafood, and pasta. In 100 Mile House, locals recommend **Happy Landing** on Hwy. 97 at 99 Mile Hill, (250) 395-5359; **Olde English Fish and Chips Shoppe**, 378-C, Hwy. 97, (250) 395-1944; and the **Red Coach Inn**, 170 Cariboo Hwy. N., also on Hwy. 97, (250) 395-2266. In Williams Lake, the **Fraser Inn Hotel**, 285 Donald Road, (250) 398-7055, has good views, food and service.

Hat Creek Heritage Ranch restaurant near Cache Creek, half a mile west of Highway 97 on Highway 99, (250) 457-9722, is a restored Cariboo Trail roadhouse and farm that offers history, tours, and trail rides with your food. Open daily mid-May through mid-October 10 a.m. to 6 p.m. Wake Up Jake's, in an authentic saloon on Barkerville's main street, serves plain but wholesome food. Try their caribou stew and sourdough bread. Open May through September.

LODGING

If sleeping under the stars in the warm summer desert air of the Cariboo is not your choice, try the popular Overlander Motor Inn, 1118 Lakeview Crescent, Williams Lake, (250) 392-3321 or (800) 663-6898. It has three restaurants, fitness facilities, complimentary coffee, and a panoramic view over the lake and the town. Rates range $79–$135 per person, with seniors' discounts available. Jamboree Motel, 845 Carson Drive, Williams Lake, (250) 398-8208, is centrally located and economical with rates of $45–$58.

Calling itself the "Guest Ranch Capital of North America," Clinton offers a variety of guest ranches—from a tent or tipi on the trail, to chalets, cabins, lodges, or ranch houses. Some welcome families, others are adult-oriented. Some include guests in their working operations, others don't. Meals feature cowboy breakfast rides, trail lunches, and BBQ dinners. Activities are many and varied. The Hills Health and Guest Ranch, C-26, 108 Ranch at 100 Mile House, British Columbia V0K 2E0, (250) 791-5225, offers a world-class health spa. Rates range $69–$150 per person, with kitchenettes $20 extra. The Best Western 108 Resort, 4816 Telqua Drive, Box 2, 108 Mile Ranch, British Columbia V0K 2Z0, (250) 791-5211 or (800) 667-5233, or e-mail 108rst&netshop.net, is a lakeside golf and Nordic ski resort that offers a multitude of amenities. Rates range $135–$180 per person.

Beckers Lodge on Bowron Lake, Box 129, Wells, British Columbia V0K 2R0, (250) 992-8864 or (800) 808-4761, is a good choice for some luxury before—or after—attacking the Bowron Lake Canoe Circuit. It has a restored main lodge, a general store, canoe rentals, log cabins and chalets in a wilderness setting with a lakeview restaurant and RV sites. Open January through March, and May through October. Rates range from $46 per person for Trapper Cabins, which are quite rustic, to $100 for one to two people ($150 for three to four people) for the newer cabins, which have their own private bathrooms.

PORT HARDY TO THE CARIBOO

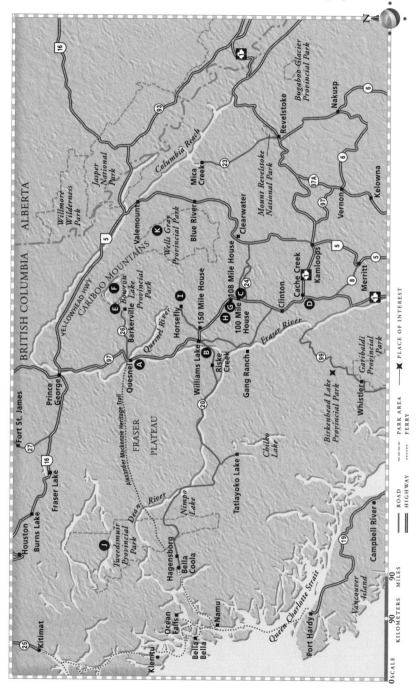

N

Z

16

16

ALBERTA

BRITISH COLUMBIA

Fort St. James

27

Prince George

16

Houston

Burns Lake

Fraser Lake

Kitimat

25

Klemtu

Bella Bella

Bella Coola

Ocean Falls

Namu

Hagensborg

Tweedsmuir Provincial Park

J

Dean River

Nimpo Lake

Tatlayoko Lake

Chilko Lake

Alexander Mackenzie Heritage Trail

FRASER PLATEAU

Quesnel

A

26

Barkerville Provincial Park

Bowron Lake

Cariboo Lake

E F

CARIBOO MOUNTAINS

YELLOWHEAD HWY

5

Valemount

K

Wells Gray Provincial Park

Blue River

Clearwater

Mount Revelstoke National Park

Mica Creek

23

Columbia Reach

Jasper National Park

Willmore Wilderness Park

93

Bugaboo Glacier Provincial Park

Nakusp

6

Revelstoke

6

97A

Kelowna

Vernon

97

Kamloops

5

Merritt

5

8

Cache Creek

Clinton

24

C

108 Mile House

G

H

100 Mile House

I

150 Mile House

Horsefly

Quesnel River

97

Williams Lake

20

B

Riske Creek

Gang Ranch

Fraser River

99

Birkenhead Lake Provincial Park

Whistler

Garibaldi Provincial Park

19

Campbell River

Vancouver Island

Queen Charlotte Strait

Port Hardy

D

PLACE OF INTEREST

PARK AREA

FERRY

ROAD

HIGHWAY

0 SCALE

90 KILOMETERS

90 MILES

Food

A Alpine Inn Restaurant

B Fraser Inn Hotel

C Happy Landing

D Hat Creek Heritage Ranch Restaurant

C Olde English Fish and Chips Shoppe

C Red Coach Inn

A Ulysses Restaurant

E Wake Up Jake's

Lodging

F Becker Lodge

G Best Western 108 Resort

C Hills Health and Guest Ranch

B Jamboree Motel

B Overlander Motor Inn

Camping

E Barkerville Provincial Park's Forest Rose Camp

H Crystal Springs Campsite (Historical) Resort

I Tatanka Ranch

J Tweedsmuir Provincial Park

K Wells Gray Provincial Park

Note: Items with the same letter are located in the same town or area.

CAMPING

The Cariboo offers comfortable camping—summers are usually dry and warm. Find a lake to yourself, put up a tent, and throw in your fishing line. **Wells Gray Provincial Park** has four main campgrounds as well as numerous wilderness camping areas and wheelchair access. **Tweedsmuir Provincial Park** has only two campgrounds and few tenting areas. Campers need to be self-sufficient and experienced, but the scenery is worth the effort. Fees must be paid in cash. **Barkerville Provincial Park's Forest Rose Camp** has three campgrounds adjacent to Barkerville, open May through October. Reserve at 181 First Avenue North, Williams Lake, British Columbia V2G 1Y8; (250)

398-4414. Fees are charged in provincial parks between May and September and average $9.50–$12 for four persons.

Crystal Springs Campsite (Historical) Resort on Hwy. 97, 12.8 km (8 mi) north of Lac La Hache, (250) 396-4497, is open April 1 through October 31 and offers fully equipped log chalets as well as RV sites. Units vary from $65 single to $90 triple; campsites are $11 per vehicle, with utilities $5 extra. This is a Good Neighbor Park that gives Good Sam discounts.

Tatanka Ranch on Stanchfield Road, Box 654, 150 Mile House, British Columbia V0K 2G0, (250) 296-4155, has sunny, grassy sites overlooking twin lakes in a peaceful wilderness setting. Open May through October 15, $15 per vehicle.

7

QUEEN CHARLOTTE ISLANDS

The Misty Isles. The Canadian Galapagos. *Gwaii Haanas*, or "place of wonder," to the Haida First Nations people. The Charlottes to everyone else. This archipelago of some 200 storm-swept islands, 90 km (56 mi) off the British Columbia coast and inhabited by some 6,000 people, is one of the richest biological and cultural areas in North America. Despite its reputation for fog and rain (it rains an average of 213 days a year), the Charlottes have become an international tourist destination. The islands offer remarkable trees and unique plants; an overwhelming abundance of nesting bald eagles and colorful seabirds, an incredibly rich intertidal life, excellent year-round fishing and hunting, unparalleled wilderness cruising for boaters, a bountiful paradise for scuba divers, long, sandy, deserted beaches for hikers, and the dramatic totem poles of the seafaring and artistic Haida.

Of the two main islands, Graham Island is the largest, most accessible, and most populated. Its communities include Skidegate Landing (the B.C. Ferries terminal), Skidegate, Queen Charlotte City, Port Clements, and Massett. To the south of Graham is Moresby Island, whose main community is Sandspit and whose most outstanding feature is South Moresby (Gwaii Haanas) National Park Reserve. ◨

QUEEN CHARLOTTE ISLANDS

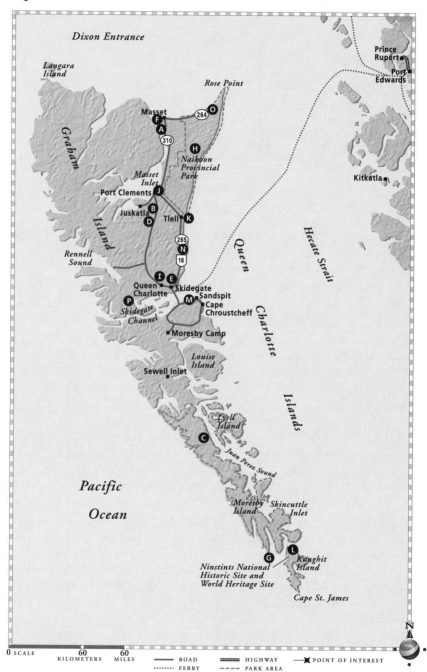

Dixon Entrance

Prince Rupert

Langara Island

Port Edwards

Rose Point

Masset
F
A
264
O
310
H

Naikoon Provincial Park

Kitkatla

Graham

Masset Inlet

Port Clements
J
B
Juskatla
D
Tlell
K

Hecate Strait

Island

Rennell Sound

265
N
16

Queen

Queen Charlotte
I
E
Skidegate
Sandspit
M
Cape Chroustcheff

P
Skidegate Channel

Moresby Camp

Charlotte

Louise Island
Sewell Inlet

Islands

Lyell Island
C

Juan Perez Sound

Pacific

Ocean

Moresby Island
Skincuttle Inlet

G
L
Kunghit Island
Ninstints National Historic Site and World Heritage Site

Cape St. James

N

0 SCALE   60   60
KILOMETERS   MILES   ——— ROAD   ▬▬▬ HIGHWAY   ➤ POINT OF INTEREST
·········· FERRY   ▬ ▬ ▬ PARK AREA

Sights

(A) Delkatla Wildlife Sanctuary

(B) Golden Spruce

(C) Gwaii Haanas National Park Reserve

(D) Haida Canoe

(E) Haida Gwaii Museum

(F) Naikoon Provincial Park

(G) Ninstints

(H) Old Masset

Food

(I) Humming Bird Cafe

(J) Margaret's Cafe

(J) Meeting Place Restaurant

Lodging

(K) Cecilia's B&B

(H) Copper Beach House

(L) Gracie's Place

Lodging *(continued)*

(I) Hecate Inn

(H) Naikoon Park Motel and Hostel

(I) Premier Creek Lodging

(L) Rose Harbour Guest House

(J) Sea Raven Resort Motel

(M) Seaport B&B

(N) Tlell River House

Camping

(O) Agate Beach Campground

(M) Gray Bay

(H) Masset RV Park

(K) Misty Meadows Campground

(P) Rennell Sound Wilderness Campsites

Note: Items with the same letter are located in the same town or area.

A PERFECT DAY IN THE CHARLOTTES

Sail to special places in the Gwaii Haanas wilderness of South Moresby Island on a tour boat such as the 68-foot ketch *Island Roamer*. Anchor in secluded bays, walk pristine sandy beaches, look for Japanese glass fishing floats, explore tide pools, photograph nesting puffins, and gaze at weather-worn cedar totem poles in deserted Haida villages. Exult in the colorful sea stars, urchins, cucumbers, anemones, and nudibranchs; feast your eyes on Old Masset reflected in the clear waters of Burnaby

Narrows at low tide; enjoy the roar of Steller's sea lions swimming in the surf off Cape St. James; and glide into the old Haida village of Ninstints on Anthony Island to imagine what life was like when dozens of Haida prepared their salmon, carved their canoes, and lived in longhouses on this very beach. At day's end, soak in an outdoor tub on Hotspring Island.

Be sure to listen to Haida Gwaii Watchmen tell stories of their ancestral way of life, and to long-time residents tell of boating and homesteading in these islands of enchantment. For *Island Roamer* information, contact Randy Burke, #3-252 E. 1st Street, North Vancouver, British Columbia V7L 1B3, (604) 980-3800.

GETTING TO AND AROUND THE CHARLOTTES

The Charlottes can be reached daily by jet aircraft from Vancouver to Sandspit on Moresby Island; by amphibian planes daily from Prince Rupert to Sandspit, Masset, and Queen Charlotte; and by ferry (three times a week in winter, six times a week in summer) from Prince Rupert to Skidegate on Graham Island. Be prepared for rough seas on

Cape St. James Lighthouse on Queen Charlotte Island

the six-hour, 93-nautical-mile crossing of Hecate Strait. The ferry has facilities for the disabled.

A smaller ferry joins Graham Island (at Skidegate) to Moresby Island (at Alliford Bay). There are few roads on the Charlottes, but on Graham Island you can drive from Queen Charlotte and Skidegate through Tlell and Point Clements to Masset, Old Masset, and Tow Hill. You must get around Moresby by boat, plane, or helicopter, since the only public road goes from the ferry terminal at Alliford Bay to the small settlement of Sandspit (a private logging road continues to Copper Bay).

Useful information: Queen Charlotte Islands Travel Infocentre, 3922 Hwy. 33, Box 337, Queen Charlotte, British Columbia V0T 1S0; (250) 559-4742. Sandspit Airport Terminal Building, (250) 637-5362.

SIGHTSEEING HIGHLIGHTS

★★★ **Gwaii Haanas National Park Reserve (Moresby Island)**—It's hard to get to on your own, but do try to see some of South Moresby Island's Gwaii Haanas National Park Reserve, which is managed jointly by Parks Canada and the Council of the Haida Nation. The closest you can drive to the park's boundaries 48 km (30 mi) is the abandoned Moresby logging camp on Cumshewa Inlet. From there, you need a boat or kayak. A comfortable way to see Gwaii Haanas is to join a packaged tour; weather is unpredictable, and only experienced out-doorspeople should travel alone. As many as 50 commercial operators offer ways to enjoy Gwaii Haanas.

Highlights on Moresby Island include crumbling totem poles and longhouses in old Haida villages. A million or more seabirds nest along the shoreline in summer, migratory birds pass through in spring and fall, and most of British Columbia's Peales peregrine falcon population lives here. Moresby also boasts the largest sea-lion rookery in the province (the Kerouard Islands); innumerable coves, narrows, and islands for anchorages, beachcombing, and intertidal exploring on the east coast; dramatic fjords and photogenic rockscapes on the west coast; and remains of old canneries and logging and mining camps. Try to see the sea lions at the now-automated lighthouse at Cape St. James, the puffins of Flatrock Island, and the marine life in Skincuttle Inlet. Details: Information is available at Parks Canada offices in Queen Charlotte City, (250) 559-6319, and Sandspit, (250) 637-5362. If you want to visit any of the beautifully located Haida villages (and you should) register with either Parks Canada or the Haida Gwaii Watch-men office in Skidegate, (250) 559-4496 or (250) 559-8225. In summer the Haida maintain base camps at the ancient villages of Skedans, Ta-nu, and Ninstints, and on Hotspring Island. (1 week)

★★★ **Haida Gwaii/Queen Charlotte Islands Regional Museum (Graham Island)**—This distinctive cedar and glass building over-looking the waterfront contains totem poles from abandoned Haida villages, argillite (soft slate) carvings, and other native artifacts. Natural history displays accompany equipment used by early settlers who tried unsuccessfully to establish farms on the eastern side of the island. Watch as Haida carve new poles in longhouse-style workshops nearby. Details: At Second Beach on the western edge of the Skidegate Reserve. Box 1373, Skidegate, British Columbia; (250) 559-4643. (1 hour)

★★★ **Naikoon Provincial Park (Graham Island)**—It's largely bog-land with stunted trees, but its wild, unspoiled, sandy beaches are mag-nificent. You can drive on the North and South Beaches below the driftwood zone, but don't get stuck in the sand or caught by the tide (four-wheel drive is recommended). A variety of hiking trails lead to interesting features such as the sand dunes at Rose Spit, the basalt rock column of Tow Hill, and the Blow Hole. Details: Trails start from points along Trumpeter Drive and from gates along Cemetery Road; (250) 557-4390 or (250) 847-7320. (1 hour to drive by or 1 day to walk its beaches and trails)

★★★ **Ninstints (Anthony Island)**—This Haida village was aban-doned after 1884. At that time, there were 20 houses, 25 carved poles, 20 mortuary poles, and 20 people on this secluded island at the southwest tip of the Charlottes. Ninstints has been declared a UNE-SCO World Heritage Site because it has the world's largest collection of Haida mortuary poles still standing in their original positions (all more than 100 years old). While the weather continues to erode the dozen or so that remain, efforts are being made to extend their life. Helicopters are not allowed to land, but tours by boat and fixed-wing plane (to within 24 km/15 mi) may be arranged in Sandspit or Queen Charlotte, weather permitting. Details: For flight informa-tion, try South Moresby Air Charters, (250) 559-4222, or Moresby Explorers, (250) 637-2215 or (800) 806-7633, for a one- to four-day Zodiac boat trip that includes Ninstints. Air charters land at Rose

Harbour on Kunghit Island, from which skiffs take you the rest of the way. (1 hour)

★★ **Delkatla Wildlife Sanctuary (Graham Island)**—This is a good place to see birds, especially sandhill cranes, on their spring and fall migration. The park has trails, boardwalks, and viewing platforms to assist bird-watchers. Details: At the head of Delkatla Inlet, Masset. (1 hour)

★★ **The Golden Spruce (Graham Island)**—This tree, which owes its color to a lack of the pigment carotenoid (a sun damage protectant), has long been a tourist attraction on the Charlottes. To the Haida, it was a member of their band and a guardian of the Yakoun River. However, to the horror of almost everyone who has visited or lived on these islands, the tree was chopped down in January 1997, an act of vandalism that received national media attention. The Haida conducted funeral ceremonies. In efforts to grow more golden spruce, hundreds of cuttings were taken from the downed tree and grafted on a new rootstock. Secret cuttings—which were taken from the old golden spruce 30 years ago and have grown into trees—were resurrected and, at this writing, will be planted on the old tree site. Details: The trail to the Golden Spruce landmark is clearly marked about 5.6 km (3.5 mi) south of Port Clements, along Juskatla Road. It winds among giant trees to the Yakoun River, on whose banks only a stump marks the site, though young golden spruce trees should by now have been planted. (10-minute walk from road)

★★ **Old Masset (Graham Island)**—The Haida village of Old Masset is worth visiting to see its artisans at work. At the Ed Jones Haida Museum (open weekends in summer) and in various gift shops and private homes, you can watch Haida craftspeople as they fashion silver and gold jewelry or cedar canoes and totem poles. Details: 3 km (2 mi) north of Masset, at the northwest end of Masset Inlet. For information on Haida artists, consult the Old Masset Village Office; (250) 626-3337; open Monday through Friday 8:30 a.m. to noon and 1 p.m. to 4 p.m. (2 hours)

★★ **Trail to the Haida Canoe (Graham Island)**—8 km (5 mi) up Juskatla Road, south of the Golden Spruce turnoff is another well-signposted short trail that leads to the Haida Canoe. It is a western red cedar dugout canoe left unfinished by its carvers in the forest after being cut, chiselled, and probed to its very heart by the Haida—a mammoth task and a mammoth heartbreak. (10-minute walk from road)

FITNESS AND RECREATION

You won't have to look for an aerobics class when the great outdoors of the Charlottes awaits. Fishing is the most popular sport. In summer the hot spot is Langara Island, at the northernmost tip of Graham Island, and adjacent Hecate Strait because this is the first place the salmon stop on their migration back to the rivers from the open ocean. Some say these are the best ocean salmon-fishing grounds in the world and the most popular fishing spot in British Columbia. Sportfishing facilities abound, such as **Langara Fishing Lodge**, where you can stay in a refurbished 120-foot paddle-wheeler; or **Langara Island Lodge**, a cedar post-and-beam building in the treetops from which you ride to your boat in an aerial tram. Prices range $2,500–$4,200 for four- to eight-day packages that include round-trip air charter from Vancouver to Sandspit and floatplane to Langara Island. Bonuses here are nesting peregrine falcons and a triple mortuary pole in the nearby abandoned Haida village of Kiusta, the only pole of its kind still standing on the west coast. For either of these lodges, call (800) 668-7544. Less isolated is **Kumdis River Lodge** near Port Clements, (800) 668-7544.

You can charter or rent a boat, or just fish by a roadside stream. In winter steelhead trout flourish in the **Yakoun River**. The **Tlell River** is famous for its coho salmon and steelhead trout runs. Huge halibut and lingcod also abound.

Try some beach-walking in **Naikoon Provincial Park**, but watch the tides and undertow. A 16-km (10-mi) round-trip hike begins at Tlell River bridge and leads to the Pesuta Shipwreck. Continue up the coast to Rose Spit, North Beach, Agate Beach, and Tow Hill for an 88-km (55-mi) hike. Hiking south to north puts the wind at your back.

FOOD

Fresh salmon and halibut steaks on an open fire, a giant crab boil on the beach, a big bowl of steaming mussels, a huge seafood stew, roast venison—this is the Queen Charlotte Islands' cuisine. Do what the islanders do. Gather 'round and shoot the breeze at the local cafes, hangouts with good plain food, plenty of talk, and perhaps some souvenirs, the owner's arts and crafts, or the neighbor's jewelry for sale.

The **Humming Bird Cafe**, above Howler's Pub in the Misty Harbour Inn in Queen Charlotte, (250) 559-8583, is a family restaurant for lunch and dinner. **Margaret's Cafe**, Queen Charlotte, (250) 559-4204, is open Monday through Saturday for breakfast and lunch. In Port Clements, try the **Meeting Place Restaurant**, (250) 557-4505, for lunch and dinner. It features vegetarian dishes. Locals rave about the mobile summertime **Bun Wagon** in Sandspit, (250) 637-5722. It's known for its great fish and chips and burgers.

LODGING

The Charlottes offer varied accommodations, from luxury fishing lodges to B&Bs and a motel/hostel. (In winter kitchenettes are important because some hotel and restaurant owners take off for drier climes to the south.)

Premier Creek Lodging in Queen Charlotte, (250) 559-8415 or (888) 322-3388 (toll-free), is one of the island's oldest buildings (1910). Fully modernized, it offers large view rooms, rooms with kitchenettes, and small budget sleeping rooms. Rates range $30–$75. **Gracie's Place**, 8-3113 3rd Avenue, Queen Charlotte, (250) 559-4262 or (888) 244-4262 (toll-free), is a renovated house with four antiques-furnished rooms, Tiffany lamps, and down quilts. It has self-contained suites with kitchens and budget sleeping units. Gracie advertises herself as "a nutty landlady" and is one of the island's characters. **Hecate Inn**, Box 124, 3 blocks west of the post office in Queen Charlotte, (250) 559-4543 or (800) 665-3350, offers "great beds and goose-down duvets," according to one satisfied customer. The **Sea Raven Resort Motel**, 3301 3rd Avenue, Queen Charlotte, (800) 665-9606, is 2 miles from the Skidegate ferry terminal. Rates range $60–$90.

The **Tlell River House**, a mile off the main highway in Naikoon Provincial Park, (250) 557-4211 or (800) 667-8906, is centrally located for day-tripping. It overlooks the Tlell River and extends to the wind-swept beaches of Hecate Strait. It offers cooking facilities for those wishing to prepare their own meals. Rates range $60–$90, and it's close to year-round trout- and salmon-fishing. The **Seaport B&B**, 371 Alliford Bay, Sandspit, (250) 637-5698, was the first bed and breakfast to open on the Charlottes. The owner, Bonnie Wasyleski, is well loved, and the rates are a reasonable $30–$40 for a single or double bed in one or the other separate rooms found in each of three small water-front houses nestled beside the main house. Breakfast is self-serve. You may, however, prefer to tent right on the beach.

Another unusual place on the beach is **Cecilia's B&B**, a newly renovated log house on Highway 61 in Tlell, (250) 557-4664. Rooms range from $15 per night for a common area to $80 for a double room. If you're looking for antiques, a heritage house, and a flamboyant host who smothers you with food, try the **Copper Beach House**, 1590 Delkatla Street, Masset, (250) 626-5441. Room rates range $50–$100 per night.

The only private commercial facilities within Gwaii Haanas Park Reserve are at **Rose Harbour Guest House** in Rose Harbour, (250) 559-8455, or radiophone N159057 Channel 24 Cape St. James. In 1978 a group of island residents bought a former 150-man whaling station site and built imaginative homes amid the ruins. In Masset, try **Naikoon Park Motel and Hostel**, (250) 626-5187.

CAMPING

Despite the ruggedness of the mostly roadless terrain, especially along the west coast, the Charlottes is a friendly place for camping. You can pretty well camp anywhere you can get to, and most of the land is publicly owned. There are few, if any, rules—except in the Gwaii Haanas National Park Reserve and, to a lesser extent, Naikoon Provincial Park. Camping is not allowed in some of the Haida villages and it is discouraged in some ecologically sensitive sites. The two most popular camping spots are **Agate Beach**, (250) 847-7320, near Tow Hill, and **Misty Meadows Campground**, (250) 847-7320, south of the Tlell River. **Masset RV Park** has 22 sites overlooking the Delkatla Wildlife Sanctuary, some with power and TV hookups, flush toilets, and showers. Fees are collected; no reservations or phone.

Although there are few paved roads on the Charlottes, the Ministry of Forests and private logging companies maintain hundreds of miles of logging roads that may be accessed by campers and boaters. Pick up the Recreation Map of the Queen Charlotte Islands Forest District for a description of camping spots maintained by the B.C. Forest Service. Some favorites are **Rennell Sound Wilderness Campsites**, on the west coast of Graham Island (be careful on the hill leading down to the beach), and **Gray Bay**, on a beautiful sandy beach south of Sandspit. Phone B.C. Forest Service at (250) 559-6200 or (250) 559-8447 for campsite information.

8

NORTHERN BRITISH COLUMBIA

Few but hunters, trappers, and fly-in fishers know the breathtaking beauty of British Columbia's northern wilderness—its jumble of rugged mountains, spectacular glaciers and volcanoes, colorful lakes and rivers, and abundant and varied wildlife. It has been called North America's Serengeti, a global treasure. Only three main roads traverse this vast sweep of almost roadless wilderness north of Prince George. This meeting of the Coast Mountains and the Northern Rocky Mountains is the most mountainous area of Canada's most mountainous province. With such a tortured topography and an area larger than England and Scotland combined, it can be overwhelming. However, local guides and outfitters know where the best spots are, and they have the horses, boats, planes, and all-terrain vehicles to get there.

Hundreds of pristine provincial parks and protected areas exist in Northern British Columbia. My favorites are Tatshenshini-Alsek, Atlin, Mount Edziza, Spatsizi Plateau Wilderness, Tatlatui, and Kwadacha Wilderness in the west; and Muncho Lake, Stone Mountain, and Wokkpash Recreational Area in the east. These are the Northern Rockies, with fewer cars and no crowds.

By car you can access Northern British Columbia by driving the Alaska Highway north from Dawson Creek to the Yukon border; Highway 37 (the Cassiar) north from the Skeena River to Stewart and the Alaska Highway; and Highway 16 (the Yellowhead) from Prince Rupert east to Prince George and the Alberta border. These are roads to adventure, "the last frontier" of Western Canada. ◨

NORTHERN BRITISH COLUMBIA

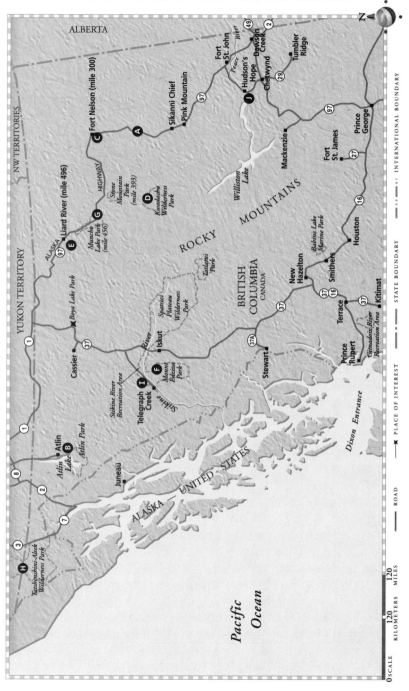

Sights

A Alaska Highway, Dawson Creek to Yukon Border

B Atlin

B Atlin Provincial Park

C Fort Nelson Heritage Museum

D Kwadacha Wilderness Provincial Park

E Liard River Hotsprings Provincial Park

F Mount Edziza Provincial Park

G Muncho Lake Provincial Park

H Tatshenshini-Alsek Provincial Park

I Telegraph Creek and the Grand Canyon of the Stikine

J W.A.C. Bennett Dam and Peace Canyon Dam

Note: Items with the same letter are located in the same town or area.

A PERFECT DAY IN NORTHERN BRITISH COLUMBIA

For a true wilderness experience in the most remote part of the Northern Rockies, I would fly to Chesterfield Lake in Kwadacha Provincial Park (see Photo Safari Tour, below). On my perfect day I would soar over the Lloyd George Icefield (the centerpiece of Kwadacha Park), drop down to catch a trout or grayling on some unnamed wilderness lake, make a campfire to cook my catch and enjoy a shore lunch on a sandy beach, watch a grizzly with her cubs near Fern Lake, then land for supper on clear, deep, turquoise Chesterfield Lake. I would return to Northern Rockies/Highland Glen Lodge for a boat ride on Muncho Lake. I would fall asleep that night thinking of all the photos I had snapped that perfect day.

PHOTO SAFARI TOUR OF NORTHERN BRITISH COLUMBIA

Urs and Marianne Schildknecht of Liard Tours, out of Muncho Lake, Historical Mile 462 of the Alaska Highway, offer a ten-day guided photo safari that covers the high spots. The photo safari begins with a flight from Vancouver to Fort Nelson and a drive on the Alaska Highway to the new Northern Rockies/Highland Glen Lodge on magnificent, 11-km-long (7-mi) Muncho Lake. Each day, guests are flown over ice-capped mountain peaks, remote valleys, and secluded lakes in this little-known region—Tuchodi Lakes, South Nahanni River, Wokkpash Gorge, Kechika and Gataga River Valleys, Stone Mountain and

Kwadacha Provincial Parks. Each night, guests relax in the Liard River Hot Springs, fish from a lakefront wilderness cabin under the midnight sun, or watch bush pilot films back at the log lodge on Muncho Lake. For more information, contact Liard Tours, Box 8, Muncho Lake, British Columbia VOC 120 (800) 663-5269 or (250) 776-3481.

SIGHTSEEING HIGHLIGHTS

★★★ **The Alaska Highway**—This road, sometimes called the "Alcan," was not created for tourists. It was built in 1942 out of anger and fear that the Japanese would invade Alaska. A speedy military supply line, not scenery, was the prime motivation. The road went wherever a bulldozer could go, rammed through a remote wilderness of mountains, muskeg, and mud, through British Columbia, the Yukon, and Alaska. In just eight months and 23 days, 16,000 American and Canadian soldiers and civilians did backbreaking work 24 hours a day, seven days a week, in temperatures that ranged from –68°C to –57°C (–90°F to –70°F). It was called "the premier engineering feat of the century." Upgrading has continued since the war's end: most of the loops and wiggles have been straightened, 90 percent is equivalent to paved, and it's now more of a road through wilderness than a wilderness road. (Take care at Steamboat Mountain, Kilometer 516/Mile 322, where ongoing construction can make for an adventure.) Distance markers along the road in Canada are shown in kilometers, but the historic mileposts are still used as mailing addresses and reference points. If you drive this road, make sure you take along *The Milepost* (Vernon Publications), "the bible of northern travel." Take a week to drive this 909-km (568-mi) highway from British Columbia to the Yukon. The most scenic section of the Alaska Highway is north of Fort Nelson (Kilometer 454/Mile 300). Highlights are Stone Mountain Provincial Park, Summit Lake, Muncho Lake, and Liard River Hotsprings Provincial Park.

The first 160 km (100 mi) or so start at the famous Mile Zero Cairn in Dawson Creek and roll through fertile Peace River Country farmlands. Stop in Dawson Creek to photograph the sign letting the folks back home know that you are "doing" the Alaska Highway, then visit—1 block north—the **Northern Alberta Railway Park**, which houses the tourist information bureau, a museum in a restored railway station, and an art gallery in a refurbished wooden grain elevator. Details: Information center and museum are open daily in summer 8 a.m. to 7 p.m., (250) 782-9595. The art gallery is open daily in summer 9 a.m. to 6 p.m. Winter hours are restricted. Also worth seeing is the **Walter Wright Pioneer Village**, at the junction of Hart and Alaska Highways, (250) 782-7144, which displays the buildings and equipment used by pioneers to homestead the area before the highway was constructed. (2–4 hours)

★★★ **Atlin**—Atlin is the most northwesterly town in British Columbia, but, ironically, it must be accessed by driving through the Yukon. Turn south from "Jake's Corner," Kilometer 1392/Mile 870 of the Alaska Highway, and drive 93 km (5 mi) to the town that's been called "the Switzerland of Canada" for its stunning beauty. Atlin overlooks the crystal-clear glacial meltwaters of Atlin Lake, the largest natural body of water in British Columbia, a lake as colorful as the Canadian Rockies' Lake Louise. This town of just 500 people is surrounded by dramatic mountains and backdropped by dozens of glaciers that sweep down from the Juneau Ice Field at the boundary of Canada (British Columbia and the Yukon) with the United States (Alaska). Atlin was founded in 1898 with the discovery of gold in the lake area, and gold is still mined here. Try some fishing for lake and Dolly Varden trout, arctic grayling, and whitefish. Swim in the Warm Bay Hotsprings. View the MV *Tarahne*, one of the White Pass and Yukon Route ships that once plied local waters with freight and passengers. It now sits on the lakeshore downtown. Details: Atlin Visitors' Association, Box 365-NW, Atlin, V0W 1A0; (250) 651-7522. (minimum 1 day)

★★★ **Liard River Hotsprings Provincial Park**—You'll appreciate stopping for a soak, chatting with other travelers, enjoying the lush greenery, or watching wildlife (such as moose) here. Known as the "Liard Tropical Valley," these hot springs are the second largest in Canada. Two bathing pools are linked by a boardwalk trail that leads you to viewpoints overlooking the Hanging Gardens, wildflowers that bloom on natural terraces created by the hot springs. Join in the Visitor Program, which is held five days a week during the summer season. Watch out for bears. Details: At Kilometer 800/Mile 497; (250) 787-3407; open 6.00 a.m. to 11.00 p.m. (minimum 1 hour)

★★★ **Muncho Lake Provincial Park**—Muncho Lake is best known for its beautiful jade waters, colors that are due to the leaching of copper oxide into the lake. The Alaska Highway edges the lake for several miles. Look out for the Stone sheep and mountain caribou that walk down the gravel trails and alluvial river fans to lick the salt left from winter road maintenance. They're most likely to congregate between Kilometer 278 and 284/Miles 445 and 455, more often in the early morning or early evening. In its mineral licks and hoodoos, its extensive alluvial fans, and its folded mountains with thrust faults and dips of limestone bedding, this park is very typical of the Northern Rockies landscape. Stay at Northern Rockies/ Highland Glen Lodge, (250) 776-3481 or (800) 663-5269. A good guide outfitter for this region is Spatsizi Wilderness Vacations, Box 3070, Smithers, V0J 2N0, (250) 847-9692.

Access the route from the now abandoned Churchill Mines Road trail at Kilometer 613/Mile 382. Wait until low water early in the day to make your stream crossings. Use Maps 94K/10 and 94K/7, a variably marked trail, and available cairns to climb from Wokkpash Creek into high alpine valleys and then back down again via braided Macdonald Creek and well-defined horse trails to the Alaska Highway near Kilometer 616/Mile 385 and 115 Creek. Take at least four days for this 70-km (42-mi) circular hike. Weather can be hot—I've done this trip in a bikini. Details: Lake is at Kilometer 698/Mile 436 of the Alaska Highway (Historical Milepost 456) in Muncho Lake Provincial Park. Toad River Office of B.C. Parks, (250) 232-5460. (4 days)

★★★ **Tatshenshini-Alsek Provincial Park**—This park protects what has been called the most magnificent river system on Earth and a step back in time to the last ice age. The Alsek and Tatshenshini Rivers are a World Heritage Site for their exceptional scenery, plants, and animals, so try not to miss them. Best to leave the paddling to the experts and book a canoe or inflatable raft trip with a reputable operator such as Whitewolf Adventure Expeditions, #44-1355 Citadel Drive, Port Coquitlam, V3C 5X6, (250) 944-5500 or (800) 661-6659; or Ecosummer Expeditions, 1516 Duranleau Street, Vancouver, V6H 3S4, (604) 669-7741, in Canada (800) 465-8884, in U.S.A. (800) 688-8605. The river is so popular that private canoe and kayak trips may wait years for the necessary permits. Most tours begin at Dalton Post, Kilometer 164/Mile 99 of the Haines Highway, which is partly in the Yukon, partly in British Columbia, and partly in Alaska. Highlights on the river include exciting white-water (class III–IV) rapids, flower-strewn meadows, glacier-capped peaks, hikes on the Walker Glacier, a float amid icebergs calved from glaciers, and probable grizzly bears. (most tours take 12 days)

★★★ **Telegraph Creek and the Grand Canyon of the Stikine**—
Historic Telegraph Creek Road, which leads into this area, is switchbacks and gravel all the way but worth driving for its panoramic views
of the Grand Canyon of the Stikine and the Tahltan Canyon. The town
of Telegraph Creek, home of the Tahltan First Nations, was once a
telegraph communication terminal but is now a jumping-off point for
wilderness hikers and river rats. Its main street is scarcely changed from
Gold Rush days. Many residents make their living by fishing for
salmon. The Grand Canyon of the Stikine is a landform unparalleled
elsewhere in Canada: 80 km (50 mi) long, and from 300 meters (985 ft)
to as little as 2.4 meters (8 ft) wide. Experienced canoeists do paddle the
Stikine River, but the wild Grand Canyon section is almost impassable.
Details: Area may be accessed from Dease Lake off Highway 37 (the
Cassiar) by the 113-km (70-mi) Telegraph Creek Road. Phone Stikine
Riversong Cafe, Lodge and General Store May through September for
local information, (250) 235-3196. (minimum 1 day)

★★ **Atlin Provincial Park**—The park shimmers with glaciers, ice
fields (fully one-third of the park's area), and the waters of Atlin Lake,
and can be reached by boat or floatplane from the townsite. Canoes or
boats may be rented, but strong winds on the lake make boating
hazardous. I'd get closer to the scenery by splurging on a plane. The
park has two undeveloped hiking trails: the Llewellyn Glacier Trail,
which leads from the head of Llewellyn Inlet to the foot of the glacier;
and the Cathedral Glacier Trail from Torres Channel to the smaller
Cathedral Glacier. Details: Contact B.C. Parks, 3790 Alfred Avenue,
Bag 5000, Smithers, V0J 2N0, (250) 847-7320. No park staff in Atlin,
but you can get local information from the Conservation Officer there,
(250) 651-7501. (1 day by plane, a week or more on foot)

★★ **Fort Nelson Heritage Museum**—Stop here to talk to Marl
Brown. Marl's long, flowing beard makes him look like Mr. Yukon, but
he's actually Mr. Alaska Highway. His wife made him clear out the
Alcan memorabilia (old trucks and construction equipment) that
cluttered his home, which led to creation of the museum. Also in Fort
Nelson, you can join in the town's **"Welcome Visitors Program,"**
held in the Phoenix Theatre on the impressive town square on summer
evenings (Monday through Thursday 6:45 p.m. between June and
September). Listen to a talk by a Mountie, a forester, a trapper, or a
dogsled racer, or see a bush pilot's slide show—they bring the Alaska

Highway to life. Contact the Fort Nelson Travel Info-centre at Bag 399, Fort Nelson, V0C 1R0, (250) 774-2541. Details: The museum is at Historical Mile 300, across from the travel infocenter on the Alaska Highway. Fort Nelson Historical Society, Box 716, Fort Nelson, V0C 1R0; (250) 774-3536; open mid-May to mid-September 8:30 a.m. to 7:30 a.m. Admission: $2. (1 hour)

★★ **Kwadacha Wilderness Provincial Park**—If you really want to get off the beaten track, fly or ride with guides into Kwadacha Wilderness Provincial Park and Recreational Area in the Northern Rockies. The nearest highway is the Alaska Highway, about 80 km (50 mi) to the north (Summit Lake) and 130 km (78 mi) to the east (Trutch). The Lloyd George Icefield, one of the largest glaciers in the north, is the source of four northern rivers: the Tuchodi, Muskwa, Warnford, and North Kwadacha. Few people ever get into this remote area, but those who do likely land at Fern and Chesterfield Lakes. Fern Lake has rainbow trout and the only developed campsite in Kwadacha. In June and July the area between these lakes is used by a number of female grizzlies with cubs. Details: Ministry of Forests, Fort Nelson, (250) 774-3936 or (250) 787-3407. Don't forget to bring the appropriate topographic maps. (1 day)

★★ **Mount Edziza Provincial Park**—You can see the park if you look west from Kinaskan Lake on Highway 37 (the Cassiar), but to get close you must fly in to one of the park's main lakes—Mowdade or Buckley—from one of the nearest points on the highway—Telegraph Creek, Tatogga Lake, or Dease Lake. The closest connection is to get a ride with a fisherman or boater at Kinaskan Lake Park to the head of Mowdade Lake Trail. This 24-km (14.4-mi) trail takes you to the central area of Edziza Park, which is largely an alpine plateau.

From then on, use the routes indicated on park and topographic maps to help you explore the cones, craters, and glaciers of this isolated and fantastic recreational treasure. The most popular route is to hike from Mowdade Lake to Buckley Lake, hike the west side of Mount Edziza, and exit via the Buckley Lake Route to Telegraph Creek.

This is one of the best places to realize how volcanic action gave birth to British Columbia's staggering landscapes. Eve Cone, one of several volcanoes on the flanks of Mount Edziza, appeared as recently as 1,300 years ago. The riotously colored Spectrum Range in the south end of the park was formed from lava flows through which hot sulfurous mineral waters percolated to the surface and stained the mountainsides with red, yellow, purple, and white stripes, making what looks like a vast watercolor. Details: Before you go, check with B.C. Parks, Area Supervisor, Box 118, Dease Lake, V0C 1L0; (250) 771-4591. Buy map 104G (1:250,000 scale) and be sure to take a compass. (1 day if you fly, 1 week or more if you hike)

W.A.C. Bennett Dam and Peace Canyon Dam are major hydroelectric projects on the Peace River. Backup water from the dam forms Williston Lake, the province's largest. Details: 24 km (15 mi) west of Hudson's Hope; (250) 783-5211. Free underground tours into the powerhouse and manifold chambers are available daily Victoria Day in May through Thanksgiving in October 9:30 a.m. to 4:30 p.m., the rest of the year Monday through Friday 9 a.m. to 6 p.m. Reservations are required. (2 hours)

FITNESS AND RECREATION

For fitness and recreation, you don't have to look any farther than leaving your car and trying some of the sightseeing highlights outlined for this region, especially the hiking, canoeing, and horseback-riding activities in the provincial parks. I like the idea of having someone else carry my stuff in these areas; try a llama with **Near Heaven Llama Treks**, Box 1452-TG96, Mackenzie, British Columbia V0J 2C0, (250) 997-6713. For a different kind of recreation, the less energetic and their children appreciate **Troy's Family Amusement Park** in Fort St. John, (250) 785-8655; or horseback-riding at **Crystal Springs Ranch**, at Charlie Lake near Fort St. John, (250) 787-4960. The very best way to experience the Northern Rockies (if you don't have your own personal floatplane) is by booking an organized expedition with a local guide or outfitter. In addition to the ones already mentioned, try these: **Canadian Explorer**, Hudson's Hope, (250) 783-5396; **Canadian River Expeditions**, Whistler, (604) 938-6651 or (800) 898-7238; **Nahanni River Adventures**, Whitehorse, Yukon, (403) 668-3180; **Walkabouts** at Redfern Lake, Fort Nelson, (250) 774-6457; or **High and Wild Wilderness Safaris**, Fort St. John, (250) 787-8431 or (250) 262-3287.

FOOD

To get anywhere in Northern British Columbia you'll probably pass through Prince George, and, regardless of where you're going, head for **Esther's Inn** in Prince George, dubbed a "Tropical Oasis in Northern B.C.," at 1151 NW Commercial Drive, (250) 562-4131 or (800) 663-6844. Sunday brunch between 10 a.m. and 2 p.m. is best—a roasted pig, a hip of beef, a lavishly decorated salmon, and a smorgasbord of everything else you can think of—served in a beautiful setting of flowing water and tropical plants for a reasonable $10.99.

Prince Rupert is another entry point into Northern British Columbia, but before you take off into the wilderness, dine at Prince Rupert's elegant **Waterfront Cafe**, in the Crest Motor Hotel, 222 First Avenue West, (250) 624-6771 or (800) 663-8150. Order the cafe's big halibut and salmon plate for $21.95, or any of the other fresh seafood specialties. Reserve a window table so you can look out at the mountains, the busy harbor, and in fall, the eagles congregating to eat the spawning salmon.

As you start your journey up the Alaska Highway, don't miss the colorful **Alaska Hotel Cafe and Dew Drop Inn Pub**, located 55 paces south of the Mile Zero Post in the center of Dawson Creek, (250) 782-7040. It's one of Canada's top 500 restaurants and a member of World Famous Restaurants International. The atmosphere is casual, the decor is reminiscent of the prewar days of highway construction, and you can get almost anything you want to eat. Entrees range $11–$20.

Despite the humble facades and ho-hum decor of most restaurants along northern wilderness highways, some are intriguing because of their local color, their history, or their ma and pa home cooking. Be sure to strike up a conversation with local residents at roadside cafes to enrich your experience. Locals and visitors like eating at the sidewalk cafe of the **North Peace Cultural Centre**, 10015 100th Avenue, Fort St. John, (250) 827-3676. Further up the Alaska Highway at Kilometer 45/Mile 72 is the **Shepherd's Inn**, known for its quality home-cooked meals and gourmet coffees. The owners specialize in making travelers feel at home. **Mae's Kitchen**, by Pink Mountain at Kilometer 92/Mile 147 on the Alaska Highway, is proud of its homemade soups, breads, pies, and pastries. You may want to buy their souvenir cookbook.

In Fort Nelson, **Dan's Neighbourhood Pub and Bistro**, on the Alaska Highway at the south end of town, is a popular gathering place open daily. The **Fort Nelson Motor Hotel** dining room, (250) 774-6971 or (800) 663-5225, is unexpectedly luxurious. You walk in from a muddy or dusty street to dine in a tropical courtyard by a pool. When I lived there in the 1970s, the owner was a big-game hunter; his trophies—huge elephants, giraffes, and buffalo—hung on the walls.

LODGING

En route to the Alaska Highway is the **Stagecoach Inn**, in the western-style, chainsaw-sculpture town of Chetwynd, (250) 788-9666 or (800) 663-2744 (Alberta and British Columbia only), which prides itself on being a motel with "a billion-dollar view" over the Sukunka Valley. It has a good restaurant, hot tubs, and coffeepots and alarm clocks in the rooms. Rates vary from $58 (single) to $64 (double). Mailing address is Box 927-SM, 5413 South Access Road, Chetwynd, V0C 1J0.

Lodge names along the Alaska Highway might conjure up images of southern luxury resorts, but they're not. Names on the map are often little more than service stations with cafes and rooms attached, some with campgrounds and stores. Even so, the rooms are generally clean, the food good and amply portioned, and the people friendly. Northern hospitality is special. Some places leave a note for late night travelers: "Rooms with doors open are vacant. Please help yourself and register in the morning." Talk to the locals and you'll learn about the land and the people along the way.

Don't miss staying—or as the name says, dropping in—at the **Alaska Hotel Cafe and Dew Drop Inn**, 10213 10th Street, Dawson Creek, (250) 782-7040. This historic building places itself "just 55 paces from the Mile Zero Post." It's the oldest continuously occupied building in Dawson Creek and displays antiques and works of art. Accommodations are basic but dandy for those with a sense of history and place. And the price is right: rooms start at $25.

Further up the Alaska Highway, at Kilometer 45/Mile 72 near Fort St. John, is **Shepherd's Inn**, which is open 24 hours, has a restaurant attached, and is ideal for families. Rates range $34 (single) to $50 (double) a night for units; $12–$16 per vehicle for RV sites. Write Box 6425, Fort St. John, V1J 4H8, (250) 827-3676.

Don't miss the **Fort Nelson Motor Hotel**, at Mile 300, for its modern rooms overlooking a tree-lined indoor courtyard, pool, and the Tiki dining room. Rates vary from $51.75 single in the old section to $80 a night double in the new courtyard section. Contact the hotel at Box 240-TG96, Fort Nelson, V0C 1R0, (250) 774-6971 or (800) 663-5225.

The other "don't miss" is **Northern Rockies/Highland Glen Lodge**, at Mile 462, Alaska Highway, (250) 776-3481 or (800) 663-5869, or by mail at Box 8, Muncho Lake, V0C 1Z0. Complementing the long-standing log chalets and motel units, the lodge's newly built main building is said to be British Columbia's largest log structure,

NORTHERN BRITISH COLUMBIA

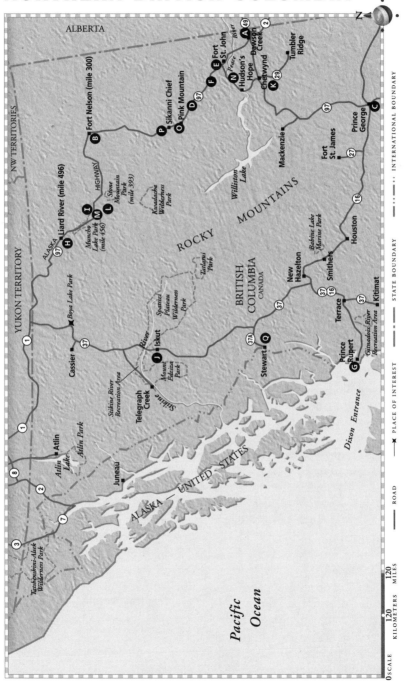

ALBERTA

NW TERRITORIES

YUKON TERRITORY

ALASKA

Fort Nelson (mile 300)

Liard River (mile 496)

HIGHWAY

Stone Mountain Park (mile 393)

Muncho Lake Park (mile 456)

Kwadacha Wilderness Park

ROCKY MOUNTAINS

Williston Lake

Mackenzie

Fort St. James

Prince George

Sikanni Chief

Pink Mountain

Fort St. John

Hudson's Hope

Peace River Tower

Dawson Creek

Tumbler Ridge

Chetwynd

Boya Lake Park

Cassier

Stikine River Recreation Area

Telegraph Creek

Iskut

Mount Edziza Park

Spatsizi Plateau Wilderness Park

Tatlatui Park

Stikine River

BRITISH COLUMBIA
CANADA

New Hazelton

Babine Lake Marine Park

Smithers

Houston

Terrace

Kitimat

Gitnadoix River Recreation Area

Stewart

Prince Rupert

Atlin

Atlin Lake

Atlin Park

Juneau

Tatshenshini-Alsek Wilderness Park

ALASKA — UNITED STATES

Dixon Entrance

Pacific Ocean

INTERNATIONAL BOUNDARY

STATE BOUNDARY

PLACE OF INTEREST

ROAD

SCALE
120 KILOMETERS
120 MILES
0

Food

- Ⓐ Alaska Hotel Cafe and Dew Drop Inn Pub
- Ⓑ Dan's Neighborhood Pub
- Ⓒ Esther's Inn
- Ⓒ Fort Nelson Motor Hotel Dining Room
- Ⓓ Mae's Kitchen
- Ⓔ North Peace Cultural Centre Cafe
- Ⓔ Rupert
- Ⓕ Shepherd's Inn
- Ⓖ Waterfront Cafe

Lodging

- Ⓐ Alaska Hotel Cafe and Dew Drop Inn
- Ⓑ Fort Nelson Motor Hotel
- Ⓗ Liard Hotsprings Lodge
- Ⓘ Northen Rockies/Highland Glen Lodge

Lodging *(continued)*

- Ⓙ Red Goat Lodge
- Ⓕ Shepherd's Inn
- Ⓚ Stagecoach Inn
- Ⓙ Tatogga Lake Resort
- Ⓛ Toad River Lodge

Camping

- Ⓜ J&H Wilderness Resort
- Ⓐ Northern Lights RV
- Ⓝ Pine Ridge Campgrounds
- Ⓞ Pink Mountain Campsite
- Ⓟ Sikanni River RV Park
- Ⓔ Sourdough Pete's Tent and RV Park
- Ⓠ Stewart Lions Campground and RV Park
- Ⓑ Westend Campground

Note: Items with the same letter are located in the same town or area.

featuring a 13.5-meter-high (45-ft) fireplace in an open-ceiling dining room. This is an all-in-one holiday resort. The owner-operator, Urs Schildknecht of Liard Air, will fly you to any of the parks and fishing lakes in the largely undiscovered hinterland. Rates range from $52 single to $86 triple; RV sites are $16–$25 for two persons.

Toad River Lodge, at Mile 422 of the Alaska Highway, (250) 232-5401, is a modern motel whose slogan is "Hang Your Hat Where It's At." The lodge is known for its collection of almost 4,000 hats. Good sheep and caribou wildlife-viewing are nearby.

Trapper Ray's **Liard Hotsprings Lodge**, just across the highway from Liard Hotsprings Provincial Park at Kilometer 801/Mile 497, is an inviting, European-style log structure with all modern conveniences, including a handicapped-accessible suite and diamond willow staircase. Open year-round. Contact the lodge at Mile 497-TG96, Alaska Highway, British Columbia V1G 4J8, (250) 776-7349.

On Highway 37 (the Cassiar), between Kitwanga and Watson Lake, are several wilderness lodges clustered around the small Tahltan Indian community of Iskut, on Eddontenajon and Tatogga Lakes. They offer the usual highway-lodge amenities plus guided tours into the neighboring wilderness parks. Noteworthy is **Red Goat Lodge**, (250) 234-3261, a superior B&B inn and a lakeshore camp for RVs and tenters, in the shadow of Loon's Beak Mountain, open May 25 through September 15. Rates are $65 single to $85 triple for rooms with a gourmet breakfast; $9.35 for RV vehicles, and $15 for hostel accommodations in the basement of the owner's chalet. Mailing address is Highway 37, Box 101, Iskut, V0J 1K0, (250) 234-3261 or (888) 733-4628. Ask new owners Mitch and Jacquie Cunningham about reasonably priced ways to access the neighboring wilderness parks. Another is **Tatogga Lake Resort**, Kilometer 387.4/Mile J 240.7, Box 59, Iskut, V0J 1K0, (250) 234-3526. Be sure to stop for a bowl of homemade soup at this cozy and colorful log cabin.

CAMPING

Camping is the way to go in these wilderness areas, either on a guided trip or on your own at a private or provincial campground. Overnight camping is prohibited at highway turnouts, despite the temptation. In July or August, it's always best to get to a campsite by midafternoon or to reserve in advance. Of the hundreds available, try these. I opt for the provincial parks first.

Northern Lights RV, Box 2476, Dawson Creek, V1G 4T9, (250) 782-9433, e-mail NLRV@pris.bc.ca, on Highway 97 South, .9 km (1.5 mi) south of the junction with Alaska Highway, is open 24 hours from mid-April through mid-October. It has hot showers and does minor vehicle repairs. Cost is $10–$15 for two persons.

Pine Ridge Campgrounds, General Delivery, Fort St. John, V1J 4H5, (250) 262-3229, on the 114-acre Bentley Ranch halfway between Hudson's Hope and Fort St. John, has attractive sites, a cookhouse, horseshoe pits, Ping-Pong tables, a childproof fence, and plenty for kids to do. It's open May 15 through September 15. Cost is $8 per vehicle (no credit cards).

At Kilometer 28/Mile 45 of the Alaska Highway near Fort St. John is **Sourdough Pete's Tent and RV Park**, 7704 Alaska Road, Box 6911, Fort St. John, V1J 4J3, (250) 785-7664 or (800) 227-8388, adjacent to an amusement park and helpful for families. Cost is $10–$18 per vehicle. **Pink Mountain Campsite**, Kilometer 89/Mile 143, Alaska Highway, (250) 774-1033, is an all-encompassing place to stay, with cabins, campground, RV park, gas station, post office, store, and liquor store.

Sikanni River RV Park, Kilometer 101/Mile 162 of the Alaska Highway, is scenically situated at the bottom of Sikanni River Hill, (250) 774-7628. Rates for cabins are $35 single, $45 double; for RV vehicles it's $10–$14. If you want an alternative to a hotel in Fort Nelson—and you should spend a night in this town if driving the highway—try the **Westend Campground**, Box 398, Fort Nelson, V0C 1R0, (250) 774-2340, next to the museum. It offers free firewood and a free car wash, minigolf, native crafts and hides, a wildlife display, and a playground for the kids. Open April 1 through November 1; $12–$17 per vehicle.

If you can't manage a night of luxury at the Northern Rockies/Highland Glen Lodge at Muncho Lake, try camping at **J&H Wilderness Resort**, Box 38, Muncho Lake, V0C 1Z0, at Alaska Highway Kilometer 289/Mile 463, (250) 776-3453. Cost is $12–$17 per vehicle. It has a convenience store, a floatplane dock, and common-sense dining.

Stewart Lions Campground and RV Park, Box 431, Stewart, V0T 1W0, (250) 636-2537, has the usual amenities plus tennis courts, a nature walk, and a trout stream. Cost is $12–$15 for two people. It also arranges tours to the nearby Bear Salmon Glaciers.

NIGHTLIFE

The bars in the ghost town of **Hyder**, Alaska (which are accessed from Stewart, British Columbia), are world-famous for "Hyderizing" their patrons, who must gulp down a lot of hard liquor to earn a certificate. Hyder's nightlife has earned it the title "The Friendliest Little Ghost Town in Alaska." You'll find plenty of smoke-filled, hearty local atmosphere in the bars along the wilderness roads of the north, but as an alternative, you might prefer the sound of a crackling fire by a rushing stream under the northern lights instead.

Scenic Route: Glacier Highway to Stewart and Hyder

So many detours, so many circles—but I'd definitely take off from **Meziadin Lake** on Highway 37A, and drive the 66-km (41-mi) Glacier Highway to Stewart and Hyder. The highlights of this stunningly scenic road are **Bear Glacier** and **Strohn Lake** (into which the glacier calves its icebergs), all of which can be easily seen from your vehicle. From Stewart, you can drive up a narrow, winding, 48-km (30-mi) road to the abandoned **Granduc minesite** and **Salmon Glacier.** In August, watch chum and pink salmon spawning in nearby Fish Creek, and the bald eagles and black bears who feast on them. Stewart is a popular location for film-making. Contact the Stewart-Hyder International Chamber of Commerce, Box 306 NW, Stewart, British Columbia V0T 1W0, (250) 636-9224. ◼

GLACIER HIGHWAY TO STEWART AND HYDER

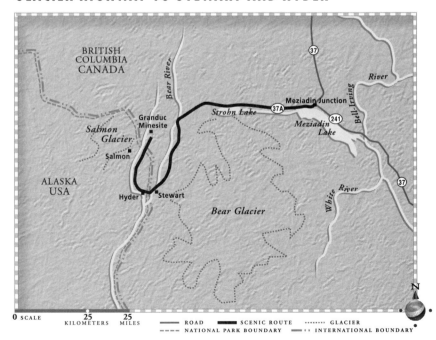

9
JASPER NATIONAL PARK

One of the four Canadian Rocky Mountain National Parks that make up a UNESCO World Heritage Site, Jasper National Park is as spectacular as Banff—but fortunately less crowded. Jasper is spectacularly beautiful, with glistening glaciers glissading down the valleys, rivers rushing to meet the seas, and serene lakes.

In 1911 the Grand Trunk Pacific Railway wound slowly along the Athabasca River valley toward Yellowhead Pass, and a tiny town took shape where Jasper sits today; yet this was no new community. Back in 1811 mapmaking explorer David Thompson had already established a route through that pass, giving the early voyageurs new territory for their ventures a century before the railroad arrived. The area's value was recognized again in 1907, when Jasper National Park was created—largely because of Sir George Simpson, the indefatigable traveler and British governor of the Hudson's Bay Company's sizeable northern section. His 1841 "rave reviews" were regarded very highly, and following these reports, the well-to-do in England came, saw, and were conquered by the extravaganza of the overwhelming scenery.

The town was named for Jasper Hawkes, who established a trading post nearby in the early 1800s. Later it became, and still is, a railway town with a third of its residents employed by the Canadian National Railway. The population swells in the summer from 3,000 to over 10,000. The small town sits in a wide, well-forested valley below Pyramid Mountain's rich red cliffs. The wildlife is diverse, including mountain goats and bighorn sheep in the highlands. ■

JASPER NATIONAL PARK

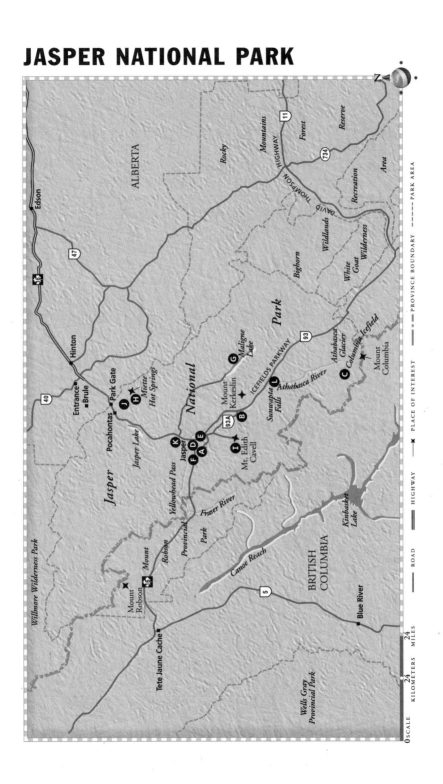

Sights

Ⓐ Aerial Tramway

Ⓑ Athabasca Falls

Ⓒ Columbia Icefield

Ⓓ Jasper Park Lodge

Ⓔ Jasper Yellowhead Museum

Ⓕ Lakes Annette and Edith

Ⓖ Maligne Lake and Canyon

Ⓗ Miette Hot Springs

Ⓘ Mount Edith Cavell

Ⓙ Old Fort Point

Ⓚ Pyramid and Patricia Lakes

Ⓛ Sunwapta Falls

A PERFECT DAY IN JASPER NATIONAL PARK

Get up early to drive from south to north along the Icefields Parkway (Highway 93), the 230-km (144-mi) scenic mountain drive that some say is the world's most beautiful road. I would start at the Columbia Icefield before other tourists arrived en masse and book my seat on the first possible Snocoach for a tour of the Athabasca Glacier. There's something awesome about walking on ice that's heaven knows how thick, or straddling crevasses so deep they appear to be bottomless. Then I'd drive north slowly—hoping to glimpse elk, moose, bear, bighorn sheep, or mountain goat. The Icefields Parkway is a naturalist's dream, especially in spring and fall, and I'd have my camera at the ready, if not for wildlife, then for landscapes such as Sunwapta Canyon, Mount Edith Cavell, Sunwapta Falls, and Athabasca Falls.

Once in Jasper, I'd book into the Jasper Park Lodge (remember, this is a perfect day!) and hurry out to photogenic Maligne Lake for a hike, horseback ride, or boat tour. I'd end the day with a soak in Miette Hot Springs and a late night dinner back at one of the many restaurants in Jasper Park Lodge.

PARKS ADMISSION

For further information on Jasper National Park, contact the Super-intendent, Box 10, Jasper, Alberta T0E IE0, (403) 852-6161. There are two infocenters: one in Jasper on Connaught Drive across from the CNR station, and the other at Columbia Icefield, Highway 93. Admission charge to all Rocky Mountain Parks: one day adults $8, seniors $6; three days adults $16, seniors $12; annual adults $50, seniors $38.

JASPER WILDLIFE

The slopes, and particularly the surrounding meadows, are the grazing grounds of deer and elk whose disdain for motorists frequently causes lines, not necessarily because people are watching them, but because the animals are in no hurry to clear the way!

Do take care as you drive. Too many animals are killed or maimed on these roads. Moose and bear are fairly common visitors—great to photograph, but potential dangers to others even if you aren't chased or harmed. Never be the cause of someone else's injuries (or death) because you fed or approached the animals. Infrequent but distinctly possible are views of coyotes, lynx, and other predators.

Jays, magpies, eagles, and a variety of birdlife frequent the sur-rounding lodgepole and other pines, spruce, fir, and poplar. Although the park is open year-round, some areas are inaccessible in winter except to cross-country skiers or snowmobilers. Some businesses open only from May through October, or even September. Hunting is illegal, which is why the animals generally have little fear of humans.

SIGHTSEEING HIGHLIGHTS

☆☆☆ **Aerial Tramway**—Just 7 km (4.2 mi) south of Jasper is the longest aerial tramway in Canada. It takes just seven minutes to travel up 2,500 meters (8,100 ft) to reach the upper terminal atop Whistler Mountain, some 2,227 meters (7,500 ft) above sea level. Here you can look full-circle at five mountain ranges, two river systems, and many lakes from the glass-enclosed Sunset Dining Room (your lift ticket is included when you purchase a low-cost three-course meal). There are boardwalks, barbecue decks, and a 45-minute hike to the summit.

Details: (403) 852-3093, fax (403) 852-5779; open daily March 28 through October 31. (minimum 1 hour)

★★★ **Columbia Icefield**—This is one of the largest glacial fields outside the Arctic, 389 square km (150 square mi) in area and up to 385 meters (1,270 ft) thick. It's actually three conjoined glaciers—the Athabasca, Stutfield, and Dome. Their meltwaters feed four major river systems—the Columbia and Fraser, which flow to the Pacific Ocean; the Mackenzie, which flows to the Arctic; and the Saskatchewan, which eventually flows to the Atlantic via Hudson's Bay.

If you walk to the icefield's "toe," you'll notice markers showing the rapid receding action. (It's strange that some glaciers recede while others are growing.) Touch this ancient body of ice—walking on the ice may be dangerous—or take one of two available tours onto the glacier.

The three-hour guided walk with Athabasca Ice-Walks, (800) 565-7547, leaves from the Toe of the Glacier car park June 8 through September 22 at 11 a.m. and costs $27 adults, $12 under 18. On Thursday and Sunday is a five-hour walk ($31 adults, $14 under 18). Reservations are a must.

The other tour, Brewster's, (403) 762-6700, leaves in special Snocoaches every 15 minutes May through October 15 from 9 a.m. to 5 p.m. ($20.50 adults, $5 ages 6–15). Once "up," you alight to walk on the ancient ice surface and peer into the depths of blue crevasses. It is a strange thrill to walk on such a phenomenon.

Back in the new Icefield Centre, (403) 852-6650, you'll find a dining room, cafeteria, snack bar, interpretive center, and accommodations. Details: 105 km (67 mi) south of Jasper, along the Icefield Parkway. (2 hours)

★★★ **Jasper Park Lodge**—Located on Lac Beauvert, this world-class resort was built in the 1920s by Canadian National Railway (CN) as an exclusive mountain resort to compete with Canadian Pacific Railway's (CP) resort hotel, Banff Springs. Ironically, CN recently sold Jasper Park Lodge to CP, who spent $25 million to develop and renovate it. It has an 18-hole golf course; riding stables; tennis courts; cycle and boat rentals; fishing facilities; a walking path around the lake; cross-country ski trails; and many restaurants, boutiques, nightclubs, lounges, and meeting rooms. Details: 7 km (4.4 mi) east of Jasper on Highway 16; (403) 852-3301. (1 hour)

★★★ **Maligne Lake**—This second-largest, and perhaps prettiest, glacial lake in the world is one of Jasper National Park's biggest attractions, and the view of Spirit Island is world-famous. The lake offers canoes, rowboats (electric motors can also be rented), tackle, and even fishing guides. Trail rides and white-water rafting can be arranged. Cruises depart daily May 18 through June 5 and September 5 through October at 10 a.m., noon, 2, and 3 p.m.; June 6–24 hourly to 4 p.m.; June 25 through September 4 hourly to 5 p.m. A day lodge and cafe offer respite. Details: 48 km (30 mi) southeast on Highway 16 and Maligne Road; (403) 852-3370. (1 hour)

★★ **Lakes Edith and Annette**—You can enjoy a really bracing swim in either (or both) of these lovely lakes, set close to Jasper but up in the mountains. There's a picnic and play area, hiking trails, a bicycle trail around Lake Edith, and a paved wheelchair path round Lake Annette. Details: 5 km (3 mi) east of town on Highway 16 and Lodge Road. (1 hour)

★★ **Maligne Canyon**—The longest, deepest, and most impressive canyon in Jasper National Park was carved by river action. Footbridges along self-guided trails provide stunning views down into the 55-meter (165-ft) depths, which are little more than 1 meter wide in places. One trail leads down the canyon to the valley floor. Details: 11 km (6.8 mi) east of town via Highway 16 and Maligne Road; (403) 852-3370. (1 hour)

★★ **Miette Hot Springs**—Very hot water feeds into two outdoor pools here, where an interpretive center explains the reasons for such hot water and the geology of the area. The water is cooled to 40°C (104°F), and one of the pools is wheelchair accessible. Details: 60 km (37.5 mi) east of Jasper on Highway 16, then south 17 km (10.6 mi) on Miette Road; (403) 866-3750; open daily mid-May through mid-June 12:30 to 8 p.m., mid-June through September 2, 8:30 a.m. to 10:30 p.m. Admission: Adults $4; seniors and children $3.50; bathing suit rental $1.50, towel $1. (1 hour)

★★ **Mount Edith Cavell**—This 3,363-meter (10,200-ft) mountain was named to honor a British nurse who was executed by the Germans for helping Allied troops escape during World War I. On the northeast slope is Angel Glacier. The road leading here snakes along the Whirlpool River Valley and is open June through October only. It's twisty but like most roads in similar areas, virtually every curve brings a fantastic view, hence its reason for being. Details: 29 km (11.8 mi) from Jasper on Hwys. 93 and then 93A (which virtually parallels Highway 93), then along an access road—it's a worthwhile drive! (1 hour)

✪✪ **Pyramid and Patricia Lakes**—You can enjoy a really bracing swim in either or both lakes, which are set in the serene, beautiful, and exciting region of the Pyramid Mountains. Boat rentals, fishing, swimming, hiking, horseback-riding, and picnicking are available here, as well as accommodations. Details: 8 km (5 mi) northwest of Jasper. Turn from Connaught Drive onto Cedar Avenue, then onto Pyramid Lake Road. (½ hour)

✪ **Jasper Yellowhead Museum**—This museum displays the history of the area's early explorers, the fur trade, and the development of the early railroad. Also featured is a gallery dedicated to local artists. Details: 400 Pyramid Lake Road; (403) 852-3013. (½ hour)

✪ **Old Fort Point**—Near the site on which an early fur brigade post stood, from here a number of hiking trails branch out, and a mountain creek cascades in a most unusual shape over a cliff to create a narrow, irregular crevice in the rock. Details: 48 km (30 mi) east of Jasper on Highway 16, then 1 km (.6 mile) along Miette Road. (minimum ½ hour)

FITNESS AND RECREATION

Hiking is the most popular activity for those visiting. In the Jasper area, day hikes alone would make up a whole book! Here are just a few possibilities:

From the foot of **Mount Edith Cavell**, a trail takes you through a spectacular alpine meadow, then onto the north face of the mountain and **Angel Glacier**. Allow half a day for this.

From Miette Hot Springs, there's a fabulous half-day hike through subalpine forests and meadows to a great view from **Sulphur Ridge**—and the hot springs await your return!

The **Wilcox Pass Trail** begins in subalpine forest and ascends quickly to an alpine meadow and the ridge that provides superb views of the Athabasca and Dome Glaciers. There's a good chance that you'll see mountain sheep or goats in the pass area. This can be a full- or half-day hike.

The **Maligne Canyon Trail** is quite short but makes up for it with a good chance of seeing a 300-million-year-old fossil among the peculiar glacial deposits and karst features. In winter, it's an impressive ice walk.

A 6-km (2-mi) trail from **Old Fort Point** takes you through several microclimates in a boreal mixed forest where pileated woodpecker holes, squirrel middens, and bear scratchings are readily visible. This is a comfortable two-plus-hour hike. **Mystery** and **Jacques Lakes** each offer a two-day hike.

The **Tonquin Valley, Skyline**, and **Fryatt Hut Trails** each offer three-day hikes, but there are longer hikes to be enjoyed.

Rocky Mountain Hiking, Box 2623, Jasper, Alberta T0E 1E0, (403) 852-5015, will provide information on such guided hikes and also on caving. An exciting one-day trip into an ancient drainage system takes you deep into a mountain in one of Canada's largest caves. This trip is well-suited to children and adults in good health.

Rocky Mountain Hiking also offers an interpretive guiding service, providing outdoor activities or natural-history programs that include walks, hikes, and overnight pack trips as well as caving. Programs are adaptable for groups, individuals, tours, or even conventions.

All Things Wild, based in Jasper, (403) 852-5193, offers knowledgeable Parks Canada–certified guides for their hikes. A half-day costs $25; a full day, $35.

Golfers will enjoy the **Jasper Park Lodge Golf Course**. There's cross-country and downhill skiing at **Marmot Basin** and **Maligne** and **Pyramid Lakes**; and white-water rafting on the **Maligne** and **Athabasca Rivers**. Dogsled tours, horseback trips, boat and bike rentals, fishing, and tennis are all possible here.

FOOD

Jasper Park Lodge is the place to go in Jasper, whether you eat or not, but I suggest you do—the $18.95 Sunday brunch in the Beauvert Dining Room. Of course, if you can afford fine French cuisine, then dress up and go to the Edith Cavell Dining Room, where you'll also be treated to the romantic sounds of a harp and the ceiling-to-floor window views of Lac Beauvert and the Rocky Mountains. Like most of these grand CP hotel resorts, Jasper Park Lodge offers a variety of restaurants to suit your taste buds and pocketbook. Food will be more expensive than downtown, but what price can you put on the view and the ambiance? I haven't tried the Moose's Nook, but the Lodge describes it as "world-famous Canadiana cuisine," which I hope doesn't mean hamburgers and maple syrup, but I think might. Anyway, music is included, and anything served at Jasper Park Lodge is good. If you manage to stay in one of the cottages, order something by room service just for the experience of having it delivered by bicycle. Jasper Lake Lodge is situated just west of Athabasca River Bridge and accessed from the Maligne Lake Road, (403) 852-3301.

Popular with Jasper residents when they want a night out is **Becker's Gourmet Restaurant**, five minutes south of Jasper on the Icefields Parkway at Becker's Chalets, (403) 852-3535. It serves classic continental food—wild mushroom paté, B.C. salmon, cognac flambéed venison, and turtle pie—in a country setting overlooking the Athabasca River and Mt. Kerkeslin. Entrees range from $12–$20.

Another high-end place to eat is the **Jasper Tramway**, (403) 852-3093. It is literally high in terms of its location atop Whistlers Mountain and its glass-enclosed 270-degree view overlooking six mountains, including the highest mountain in the Canadian Rockies, Mt. Robson. It's the longest and highest tramway in Canada. Take it to the top for the restaurant's Sunset Dinner Package.

You also get a harpist at **Chateau Jasper**'s award-winning Beauvallon Dining Room, 96 Geikie Street, (403) 852-5644. It's not likely you'll be eating rabbit sausage, ostrich crepes, guinea fowl, and deer ragout back home, so try them here. The Chateau specializes in wild game cuisine. The fixed-price menu, including dessert, is about $30; there is a weekend buffet and a spectacular Sunday brunch with 25 selections for about $14. Seniors and children 6 to 12 pay less.

You can probably watch the real thing (wild game in the wild, that is) from other restaurants with good views, such as the woodsy **Maligne Canyon Chalet**, (403) 852-3583, and the lakeside **Maligne Lake Chalet**, (403) 852-3370. And you can add a sunset over Pyramid Mountain from the terrace at **Grizzly's Restaurant** at Pyramid Lake, (403) 852-2143. The carved grizzly bears at this restaurant are recommended over the real thing.

At the other end of the monetary scale, join the locals at the **A&W Walk-in Jasper**, 624 Connaught Drive, (403) 852-4930; the **Jasper Pizza Place**, at 402 Connaught Drive, (403) 852-3225, where

JASPER

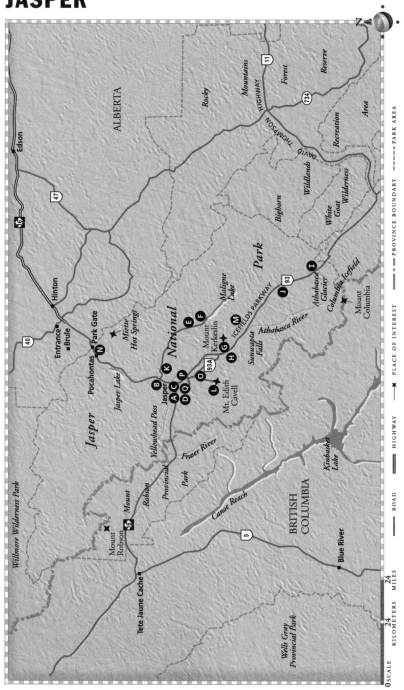

N

ALBERTA

Edson

Rocky

Mountains

Forest

Reserve

HIGHWAY

47

16

DAVID THOMPSON

11

734

Recreation

Area

Hinton

Wildlands

Bighorn

White
Goat
Wilderness

Entrance

Brule

40

Park Gate

Miette
Hot Springs

National

Park

Pocahontas

N

Jasper Lake

K

E

F

Maligne
Lake

M

Athabasca River

I

93

Columbia Icefield

Athabasca
Glacier

Jasper

B

A C

Mount
Kerkeslin

93A

G

H

Sunwapta
Falls

J

Mount
Columbia

Yellowhead Pass

D Q

O

L

Mt. Edith
Cavell

ICEFIELDS PARKWAY

Willmore Wilderness Park

Fraser River

Mount

Robson

Provincial

Park

Kinbasket
Lake

BRITISH
COLUMBIA

Mount
Robson

16

Canoe Reach

5

Blue River

Tete Jaune Cache

Wells Gray
Provincial Park

0 SCALE

24
KILOMETERS

24
MILES

ROAD ••••• HIGHWAY •—★ PLACE OF INTEREST

••• PROVINCE BOUNDARY ••••• PARK AREA

Food

- Ⓐ A&W Walk-Inn Jasper
- Ⓐ Becker's Gourmet Restaurant
- Ⓐ Bright Spot
- Ⓐ Chateau Jasper
- Ⓐ Dead Dog Bar and Grill
- Ⓑ Grizzly's Restaurant
- Ⓒ Jasper Park Lodge
- Ⓐ Jasper Pizza Place
- Ⓓ Jasper Tramway
- Ⓔ Maligne Canyon Chalet
- Ⓕ Maligne Lake Chalet
- Ⓐ Papa George's Restaurant
- Ⓐ Spooners

Lodging

- Ⓖ Athabasca Falls Hostel
- Ⓐ Athabasca Hotel
- Ⓗ Beauty Creek Hostel
- Ⓐ Bonhomme Bungalows

Lodging *(continued)*

- Ⓐ Chateau Jasper
- Ⓘ Columbia Icefields Chalet
- Ⓙ Hilda Creek Hostel
- Ⓐ Jasper International Hostel
- Ⓒ Jasper Park Lodge
- Ⓚ Maligne Canyon Hostel
- Ⓛ Mount Edith Cavell Hostel
- Ⓐ Whistler's Inn

Camping

- Ⓘ Columbia Icefield Campground
- Ⓜ Honeymoon Lake Campground
- Ⓝ Pocahontas Campground
- Ⓞ Wabasso
- Ⓟ Wapiti Campground
- Ⓠ Whistler's Campground

Note: Items with the same letter are located in the same town or area.

you can get such exotic toppings as smoked salmon, artichoke hearts, capers, scallops, and asparagus; **Spooners**, at 610 Patricia Street, (403) 852-4046, popular for quick inexpensive lunches (try the veggie lasagna or spanakopita); the **Bright Spot** at 701 Connaught Drive, (403) 852-3094, a clean and friendly family restaurant; and the sometimes rowdy **Dead Dog Bar and Grill**, 404 Connaught Drive, (403) 852-3351, where you char-broil your own steak.

Papa George's Restaurant, in the Astoria Hotel at 404 Connaught Drive, (403) 852-3351, is the traditional, tried-and-true Jasper standby, the kind of place to take Aunt Gertrude when she comes to town. Classic menu, generous portions, and cheesebread "to die for," says one of the locals. Like many of Jasper's restaurants that cater to hikers, Papa George's offers filling breakfasts and boxed lunches to go.

LODGING

If you've got a lot of cash or a lot of friends and relatives, then splurge for a night or more at Jasper's best—the newly renovated **Jasper Park Lodge**, (800) 441-1414. It is a park in itself—backdropped by mountains spread artistically around a lake and an 18-hole golf course, beautifully landscaped—with a variety of units that include a main lodge, bungalows, and guest houses. It has seven types of specialty "cabins"— perhaps cabin's the wrong word considering the $3,800 a night price tag for Milligan Manor—but then you can fit a lot of friends and relatives into its eight bedrooms. It's precisely $401 a night for a room in the main lodge building.

If you want deluxe accommodations in the heart of Jasper, try the **Chateau Jasper**, 96 Geikie Street, (800) 611-9323. You get downtown convenience, facilities such as heated indoor pools, extra-long beds, and the award-winning Beauvallon Dining Room, but you have to share the mountain views. Rates are $250–$275 in summer.

Another downtown hotel in a more moderate price category is **Whistler's Inn**, at 105 Miette Avenue, (800) 661-1315 (W. Canada) or (403) 852-3361. Distinctive features are the roof hottub, The Den (a wildlife museum displaying more than 100 species of native wildlife), exterior wall murals, and a European alpine lodge atmosphere. Rates range from $77–$156 a night.

A favorite hangout for the locals on weekends is the **Athabasca Hotel**, at 510 Patricia Street, (800) 563-9859 (W. Canada) or (403) 852-3386. This could be a disadvantage or an advantage, depending on your point of view. Rates vary from $75 for a room with shared bath over the popular tavern to $250 "on the quiet side." Built in 1929, the Atha B, as it is called locally, has recently been renovated in the Victorian style. There are two bars, the live entertainment side and the DA Room, short for the "Dead Animal Room," featuring the heads of stuffed animals. There are more in the lobby—elk, caribou, sheep, goats, moose— all road kills, the receptionist assures me.

If you want privacy downtown, try the **Bonhomme Bungalows**, (403) 852-3209, in a quiet forest setting 2 blocks off Connaught Drive on Bonhomme Street, yet within walking distance of the main shopping area. Accommodations range from original log cabins to contemporary chalets, many with wood-burning fireplaces and kitchenettes. Rates from $95–$270.

For out-of-town views, albeit slightly colder ones, stay at the **Columbia Icefields Chalet**, on Highway 93 between Lake Louise and Jasper. It overlooks the Athabasca Glacier, and its bright red roof brings extra color to a much-photographed spot. Rates are between $150–$170 a night, open only May to October, (403) 852-6550 in season, (403) 762-6735 off-season.

A lot of private homes advertise B&B accommodations. Check to see if they are members of Jasper's Private Home Accommodation Association before you book. For even more affordable accommodations, six hostels are in the Jasper area: **Athabasca Falls, Beauty Creek, Maligne Canyon, Mount Edith Cavell, Jasper International Hostel**, all at (403) 852-5560, and **Hilda Creek**, (403) 762-3441.

CAMPING

There are a dozen or so campgrounds in the Jasper National Park area; most are fairly small and basic and located along the Icefields Parkway. All can be reached at (403) 852-6161. As in Banff, accommodations are first come, first served. Costs range between $10–$22.

Columbia Icefield Campground brings back intriguing memories. A couple of decades ago, I spent the night in a pup tent there with my glamorous model of an Aussie sister in nightgown, makeup, and curlers—a girl who had never been tenting before—and a pet raccoon. The raccoon wandered off to find more room and compatible company. When I found him later, he was in a tent trailer, revelling in the rapt attention of a family feeding him sardines mouth-to-mouth. Me? Pets in the park? No, I told the warden, I don't have any cats or dogs!

Each campground has its advantages. Families like the **Pocahontas Campground**, open mid-May through early September, east of Jasper on Highway 16, then 1 km (.6 mi) south on Miette Road. It is large, with flush toilets, hiking trails, and facilities for the handicapped. **Honeymoon Lake Campground** has a nice lake. It has 35 sites, pump water, swimming, and good hikes, and is open mid-May to snowfall. It's 52 km (33 mi) south of Jasper.

Wabasso gives you wilderness privacy. It offers 238 sites, tap

water, flush toilets, hiking trails, and a kids' play area, and it's
wheelchair accessible. Open late June through Labor Day.

Wapiti Campground has 366 sites, tap water, flush toilets,
showers, sewage disposal, and a telephone, along with wheelchair-
accessible sites and washrooms, power, and winter camping. It's open
on Victoria Day (the Monday preceding May 25), then closes through
mid-June, when it opens again until early September. Just 5 km (3 mi)
south of Jasper on Highway 93.

Whistler's Campground, with 781 sites, has power, water, and
sewer for 77 sites and power alone for 100. With tap water, phone,
washrooms and showers, a play area, hiking trails, and wheelchair-
accessible sites, it's open mid-May through mid-October. Find it 3 km
(2 mi) south of Jasper on Highway 93.

NIGHTLIFE

Most visitors have probably seen, walked, or done enough to be
contentedly tired, but there are a few noteworthy nightspots. **Buckle's
Saloon**, (403) 852-7074, in Maligne Lodge at the west end of
Connaught Drive, has a cowboy decor, country-and-western music and
dancing, and cowboy-style food such as beans, buffalo burgers, and
beer margaritas.

Nick's Bar, in a glass-enclosed atrium, offers sports and ski movies
on a big screen, piano music, and food. It's on Juniper Street, between
Connaught and Geikie, (403) 852-4966. Two of the most popular
nightspots are **Pete's on Patricia**, (403) 852-6262, for those for whom
the hiking trails and ski slopes haven't worked off enough steam; and
the historic **Atha B Hotel**, 510 Patricia Street, (403) 852-3386.

10

EDMONTON

Edmonton, situated on the high bluffs of the North Saskatchewan River, has many attractions that are the largest of their kind—at least in Canada. Nearly everyone knows about the West Edmonton Mall, the world's largest shopping and entertainment complex, but few may realize that Edmonton also has more green space and parks per capita than any other Canadian city. Edmonton exists because of abundant natural resources—furs, gold, oil—which sparked three major booms. In 1795 Hudson's Bay Company founded Fort Edmonton; traders bartered with Cree and Blackfoot for prized animal pelts. The growing settlement quickly became central to routes north and west.

From here, the first prospectors raced for Klondike gold. Realizing they'd not get rich quick (or at all), many returned for slower but surer lifestyles. Edmonton grew sixfold, becoming a natural choice as the capital when Alberta, "Gateway to the North," was created in 1905. (Thereafter, the Edmonton-Calgary rivalry intensified.) Today's Klondike Days are becoming as famous as Calgary's Stampede.

In 1915 Edmonton became the Canadian Pacific Railway's north-south/east-west crossroad. In the 1930s, bush pilots flew vital supplies to northern outposts. When Alaska Highway construction began in 1942, Edmonton was a pivotal supply center. In 1947 Leduc #1 Well, southwest of Edmonton, gushed black gold, and over 2,250 nearby wells have been pumping oil ever since. Today only one airport remains, but with a transcontinental train station and major highways, Edmonton is an important travel center. ◥

EDMONTON

Northlands Park

106TH AV
98TH AV
90TH AV
84TH ST
83RD ST
ARGYLE RD

112TH AV
CONNORS RD
82ND AV
Mill Creek
63RD AV

FORT RD
JASPER AV
STADIUM RD
95TH ST
NORWOOD BLVD
107TH AV
HARBIN RD
99TH ST
100TH ST
101ST ST
SCONA RD
SASKATCHEWAN DR
99TH ST

E

B

111TH AV
102ND ST
QUEEN ELIZABETH PARK RD
103RD ST
104TH ST →

106TH ST
KINGSWAY
105TH ST
97TH
WHITEMUD HILL
104TH ST
PRINCESS ELIZABETH AV

A
109TH ST
104TH AV
109TH ST
99TH AV
WHYTE AV (82ND AV)
109TH ST

116TH ST
100TH AV
RIVER VALLEY RD
River
SASKATCHEWAN DR
113TH ST
114TH ST
UNIVERSITY AV
BELGRAVIA RD

119TH ST
108TH AV
117TH ST
102ND AV
JASPER AV
VICTORIA PARK RD
EMILY MURPHY PARK RD
University of Alberta
8TH AV

124TH ST
RD
PLAIN RD
GROAT RD
F
GROAT RD
SASKATCHEWAN DR
122ND ST

132ND ST
STONY
Saskatchewan
North
D
G
Whitemud Creek

111TH AV
C
142ND ST

149TH ST
107TH AV
95TH AV
87TH AV
76TH AV

156TH ST

STONY PLAIN RD
100TH AV
170TH ST
WHITEMUD DR
H
69TH AV

MAYFIELD RD

178TH ST

N

SCALE
0
2 KILOMETERS
2 MILES
ROAD
PARK BOUNDARY

Sights

- Ⓐ **Alberta Aviation Museum**
- Ⓑ **Edmonton Art Gallery**
- Ⓒ **Edmonton Space and Science Centre**
- Ⓓ **Fort Edmonton Park**
- Ⓔ **Muttart Conservancy**
- Ⓕ **Provincial Museum of Alberta**
- Ⓖ **Valley Zoo**
- Ⓗ **West Edmonton Mall**

A PERFECT DAY IN EDMONTON

Just one day? That's not nearly enough, since the West Edmonton Mall (the biggest in the world) alone will absorb much of one day—it's a vacation center in itself. I would contain my urge to shop (well, maybe I'd window-shop) and sample some of the city's many other attractions. Food outlets are everywhere, but tempt me not. I'd rather spend time at the Waterpark, swimming, riding the waves, thrilling to the many slides, and basking in some of Alberta's almost constant sunshine that pours through the glass roof. Next I would sharpen my golf strokes on the mall's two minicourses, venture underwater in a submarine, watch the sharks and penguins in Sea Life Caverns, then spend an hour of leisurely ice-skating in the Ice Palace. That evening I'd be off to the revolving restaurant at the top of the Château Lacombe.

SIGHTSEEING HIGHLIGHTS

★★★ **Edmonton Space and Science Centre**—This multipurpose facility houses state-of-the-art theaters and sound systems, an observatory, exhibit galleries, and live demonstrations. It contains the largest planetarium in Canada; an IMAX Theatre; the Margaret Zeidler Theatre, which presents musical laser light shows on a 23-meter (75-ft) domed ceiling; and a "Missions Centre," where you can

participate in simulated space missions. The Missions Centre explains unique phenomena even as it challenges and informs you. Details: 142nd Street at 112th Avenue; (403) 451-3344; open Tuesday through Sunday 10 a.m. to 10 p.m., with the observatory open Saturday and Sunday 10 a.m. to 10 p.m. Admission: Adults $7, seniors $6, ages 4–12 $5, families $26. IMAX and Zeidler Theatres are priced as above. (minimum 1½ hours)

★★★ **Muttart Conservancy**—Imagine four sheer glass pyramids, their reflections shimmering in a huge pool. Muttart Conservancy is just that from the outside, but on the inside each is a world within a world—a Tropical, an Arid, and a Temperate Pavilion (all with temperatures to match) and a Show Pavilion with changing seasonal exhibits. The floral displays are colorful, to say the least. Orchids, African violets, bonsai, and other shows are held throughout the year. Details: 9626 96A Street; (403) 496-8755; open Monday through Wednesday 9 a.m. to 9 p.m., Thursday and Friday 9 a.m. to 6 p.m., Saturday 11 a.m. to 6 p.m., Sunday 11 a.m. to 9 p.m.; closed December 25. Admission: Adults $4.25, seniors and ages 13–18 $3.25, ages 2–12 $2, families $12.50. (minimum 1 hour)

★★★ **West Edmonton Mall**—The number-one attraction on almost every visitor's list is the West Edmonton Mall, often described as the Eighth Wonder of the World. It's the world's best-known and largest shopping and entertainment complex, with more than 800 stores, 100 restaurants, cafes, and fast-food outlets, 19 movie theaters, and five major attractions. Probably the most outstanding is the 2-hectare (5-acre) World Waterpark, with the world's largest wave pool, 16 breathtaking waterslides as high as 136 meters (85 ft), a bungee jump, family picnic areas, and an artificial beach.

The 23 rides and attractions of the Mall's Amusement Park include the thrills of the Mindbender (a 14-story triple-loop roller coaster) and the Drop of Doom (a 13-story free-fall). Also interesting is the Deep-Sea Adventure, which features a submarine trip, five dolphin shows, and a life-sized replica of Columbus' *Santa Maria*. The mall also has aviaries, aquariums, wildlife exhibits, minigolf courses, an intriguing Fantasyland Hotel, and, of course, shops. If you don't have all the fun you expect, you may still find it if you forget which exit to use, where your car is parked, or where/when to catch the bus.

Details: 170th Street and 87th Avenue; (403) 444-5200, (800) 661-

8890, fax (403) 444-5223; open daily Monday through Friday 10 a.m. to
9 p.m., Saturday 10 a.m. to 6 p.m., Sunday and most holidays noon to 5
p.m.; attractions, theaters, and restaurants stay open later. Admission:
All-day pass $29.95 (includes all rides in the Amusement Park), those
under 1.2 meters (4 ft) tall $21.95, seniors $11.25, physically challenged
$9.95, each additional family member $12.50, and five immediate family
members $69.95. Entry to the amusement park itself is free, but rides
are 12 for $11.50, up to 100 for $70. Entry to the World Waterpark is
adults $29.95, ages 3–10 $21.95, seniors $11.25, physically challenged
$9.95, five immediate family members $69.95. The Ice Palace (skating)
is $5.50, 3–10 and seniors, $3; five immediate family members $16.95,
$4 for each additional member. (Time–incalculable!)

★★ **Fort Edmonton Park**—Here at Canada's largest living history
museum, you'll enter a world of the past where four periods of
Edmonton's development are re-created: an 1846 Hudson's Bay Company fur trading post, an 1885 settlement, and the city as it was in 1920
and in 1985. Costumed characters mingle with you to bring history
alive. You can ride in a 1908 streetcar and on a 1919 steam train
(included in admission). Details: Whitemud and Fox Drives; (403) 496-
8787; open daily May 18 through September 1. Admission: Adults
$6.75, seniors and youths $5, children $3.25, families $20. (3 hours)

★★ **Provincial Museum of Alberta**—A 1967 Centennial project
became the Provincial Museum of Alberta—a natural- and human-
history museum surrounded by a park of sculptures overlooking the
North Saskatchewan River Valley. Inside, dynamic displays illustrate
Canada's plains, sand dunes, hoodoos, and mountains. There are four
galleries: Habitat shows birds and animals in natural settings; Natural
History has specimens of animals and plants, past and present; Aboriginal People shows artifacts from earliest life on the prairies; and
Human History, the settlement of Europeans in Alberta. Facilities
include guided tours, a shop, and a restaurant. Details: 12845 102nd
Avenue; open daily May 16 through September 1 9 a.m. to 5 p.m.;
September 2 through May 15 Tuesday through Sunday 9 a.m. to
5 p.m. Admission: Adults $5.50, ages 7–17 $3, families $15, seniors
$4.50, under 7 free. (1 hour)

★★ **Valley Zoo**—This 70-acre (28-hectare) park has over 300 animals,
a children's area with a storybook theme, and daily elephant and sea

lion demonstrations. Details: 134th Street and Buena Vista Road; (403) 496-6911; open year-round, but hours vary depending on conditions. Both admission and time to allow vary, depending on weather and season. (1½ hours)

✸ **Alberta Aviation Museum**—The museum houses a collection of original aircraft showing the history of aviation in Alberta, particularly in Edmonton. The bush pilots of those days (like H. A. "Doc" Oaks, whose methods of engine heating and maintenance in extreme winter conditions became standards; Punch Dickens; and Wop May) created legends that thrill young and old alike. Details: City Centre Airport; (403) 453-1078; open year-round. Small admission fee. (minimum 1 hour)

✸ **Edmonton Art Gallery**—The emphasis here is on Canadian historical and Western Canadian contemporary art. Details: 2 Sir Winston Churchill Square; (403) 422-6223; open Monday through Wednesday 10:30 a.m. to 5 p.m., Thursday and Friday 10.30 a.m. to 8 p.m., Saturday, Sunday, and holidays 11 a.m. to 5 p.m.; closed December 25 and January 1. Admission: Adults $3, seniors and students $1.50, under 12 free; free to all Thursday 4 to 8 p.m. (1 hour)

FITNESS AND RECREATION

City parks offer baseball, softball, tennis, cycling, walking, hiking, and golfing in summer; cross-country and downhill skiing, tobogganing, and skating in winter. Multipurpose **Leisure Centres** offer swimming, diving, racquetball, and squash, with exercise and weight rooms galore.

There's indoor bungee jumping at the **West Edmonton Mall,** and flights in open-cockpit biplanes at the **Villeneuve Airport,** 5736 103A Street, T6H 2J5, (403) 460-8693. **Blue Rock Tours,** 9743 67th Avenue, T6E 0P1, (403) 448-9206, can arrange mountain-bike tours. For a one-hour tour of the river valley in a Hamilton-powered jet-boat, see **Klondike Jet Boats,** 10565 163rd Street, T5P 3P2, (403) 486-0896. For the more leisurely, **Double J Riding Centre,** 52468 Range Road 210, Ardrossan, T8G 2E3, (403) 922-2344, and **Keno Hills Stable,** 52165 Range Road 210, Sherwood Park, T8G 1A1, (403) 922-3067, both just east of the city, offer trail rides in the Cooking Lake area or the Blackfoot Recreation, Wildlife and Grazing Area.

FOOD

There are some 2,000 restaurants in Edmonton, serving more than 30 types of cuisine. To help you decide which to sample, take a stroll along the Avenue of Nations surrounding 107 Avenue from 95th Street to 116th Street. Or in summer, ride a rickshaw around this multicultural showcase as you decide between Chinese, Vietnamese, Italian, Ukrainian, Polish, Japanese, and Latin American cuisine. **Buffet World**, 13062 50th Street, (403) 478-8889, receives mixed reports but nonetheless is a popular spot for a medley of Chinese, Western, and Ukrainian dishes. **Between Friends**, 8615 54th Avenue, (403) 468-1919, is more upscale but serves a variety of innovative international menus with something for everyone. Its less formal section, **Sierras Cafe,** provides gourmet pizzas and deli sandwiches, and has extended hours.

A Central European menu of steak tartare, fish, or hearty portions of Wiener schnitzel ensures a good meal at **Bistro Praha,** 10168 100A Street, (403) 424-4218. It's closed on major holidays. Dinner is $11–$20; reservations are suggested.

You can enjoy cocktails and an a la carte menu of original creations in a casually elegant atmosphere at the **Chef's Table,** 11121 156th Street, (403) 453-3532. It's closed December 24 and 25. Dinner is $21–$30. Reservations suggested.

Everybody's favorite, though it doesn't match everyone's pocketbook, is **La Ronde,** 10111 Bellamy Hill, T5J 1N7, (403) 428-6611, (more commonly known by its former name, the Château Lacombe), a revolving rooftop restaurant at the Holiday Inn Crowne Plaza. It features excellent views over the North Saskatchewan River and the rest of the city. Dinners range $21–$30 and reservations are suggested.

For casual dining in a warm and quiet atmosphere, try **Von's Steak and Fish House,** 10309 81st Avenue, (403) 439-0041, specializing in Mediterranean and Louisiana-style menus. The **Xian Szechuan Restaurant,** 10080 178th St., right on Highway 16, (403) 484-8883, is a great spot for Chinese food. Dinners vary from $11–$20.

For panoramic views in elegant surroundings, try **Claude's on the River,** at 9797 Jasper Avenue, adjacent to the Edmonton Convention Center, (403) 429-2900. The **Harvest Room** in the historic Hotel MacDonald, 10065 100th Street, (403) 424-5181, faces a large terraced garden. A little less expensive than Claude's and La Ronde, this restaurant at "The Mac" offers a children's menu, health-conscious meals,

EDMONTON

Northlands Park
To D
To X g
112TH AV
106TH AV
84TH ST
98TH AV
To b c
90TH AV
83RD ST
ARGYLE RD

CONNORS RD
82ND AV
Mill Creek
63RD AV
To V
JASPER AV
FORT RD
STADIUM RD
95TH ST
98TH AV
NORWOOD BLVD
107TH AV
95TH ST
99TH ST
HARBIN RD
99TH ST
SCONA RD
99TH ST
To A
95TH ST
100TH ST
101ST ST
B I K F H
102ND ST
103RD ST
To N
105TH ST
104TH ST
To J M L P Y e
111TH AV
106TH ST
KINGSWAY
109TH ST
109TH AV
109TH AV
104TH AV
99TH AV
97TH ST
QUEEN ELIZABETH PARK RD
SASKATCHEWAN DR
WHYTE AV (82ND AV)
109TH ST
PRINCESS ELIZABETH AV
Q
116TH ST
100TH AV
JASPER AV
RIVER VALLEY RD
River
WATERDALE HILL
8TH AV
114TH ST
UNIVERSITY AV
113TH ST
T
119TH ST
108TH AV
117TH ST
118TH
102ND AV
VICTORIA PARK RD
EMILY MURPHY PARK RD
University of Alberta
GROAT RD
BELGRAVIA RD
SASKATCHEWAN DR
124TH ST
RD
PLAIN RD
GROAT RD
122ND ST
132ND ST
STONY PLAIN RD
Saskatchewan
North
Whitemud Creek
111TH AV
142ND ST
95TH AV
149TH ST
To h
107TH AV
E
156TH ST
87TH AV
76TH AV
W
STONY PLAIN RD
100TH AV
WHITEMUD DR
MAYFIELD RD
170TH ST
G
178TH ST
O R S
U
69TH AV
To Z a f d

SCALE
0
KILOMETERS 2
MILES 2
ROAD
----- PARK BOUNDARY

Food

- Ⓐ Between Friends/Sierras Cafe
- Ⓑ Bistro Praha
- Ⓒ Bones
- Ⓓ Buffet World
- Ⓔ Chef's Table
- Ⓕ Claude's on the River
- Ⓖ Hard Rock Cafe
- Ⓗ Harvest Room
- Ⓘ La Ronde
- Ⓖ Modern Art Cafe
- Ⓙ Olive Garden
- Ⓖ Planet Hollywood
- Ⓚ Pradera
- Ⓛ The Sawmill
- Ⓜ Top of the Inn
- Ⓝ Von's Steak and Fish House
- Ⓞ Xian Szechuan Restaurant

Lodging

- Ⓟ Best Western Cedar Park Inn
- Ⓠ Best Western City Centre
- Ⓡ Best Western Westwood

Lodging (continued)

- Ⓢ Comfort Inn
- Ⓣ Edmonton Inn
- Ⓤ Fantasyland Hotel
- Ⓗ Hotel MacDonald
- Ⓥ International Youth Hostel
- Ⓦ Mayfield Inn
- Ⓧ Sands Motor Hotel
- Ⓨ Travelodge Edmonton South
- Ⓩ Travelodge Edmonton West

Camping

- ⓐ Devon Lions Campground
- ⓑ Half Moon Lake Resort
- ⓢ Kawtikh Retreat
- ⓓ Kinsmen RV Park
- ⓔ Klondike Valley Campground
- ⓕ Oster Lake
- ⓖ Sandy Beach Campground
- ⓗ Whitemud Creek Golf and RV Park

Note: Items with the same letter are located in the same area.

and a popular Sunday brunch. In the same class are **Pradera** in the Westin Hotel, 10135 100th Street, (403) 426-3636; and the **Top of the Inn,** at the Convention Inn, 44404 Calgary Trail, (403) 434-6415.

For moderately priced meals in a lively atmosphere, try the rib dishes at **Bones,** 10220 103rd Street, (403) 421-4747; **The Sawmill's** memorable salad bar, at 4745 Calgary Trail North, (403) 436-1950; the **Olive Garden**, 41st Avenue, 4110 Calgary Trail N.W., (403) 437-3434; and the **Modern Art Cafe** on Bourbon Street in the West Edmonton Mall, (403) 444-2233.

New to Edmonton are the popular **Planet Hollywood** and **Hard Rock Cafe** restaurants, in the West Edmonton Mall.

LODGING

The **Fantasyland Hotel** is perhaps the jewel of the West Edmonton Mall. Luxury personified, it has 354 guest rooms, including 127 decorated according to different themes: Roman, Hollywood Nightclub, Polynesian, Truck, Victorian Coach, Arabian, Canadian Rail, Igloo, and African—each with a full-size Jacuzzi. Kids will like sleeping in the front seat of the Truck suite, which comes complete with working traffic signals and antique gas pumps. In the 600-square-foot Igloo suite, you sleep in a snowhouse on the tundra and can bathe in an iceberg.

Muttart Conservatory

Edmonton Tourism

It's at the west end of the mall, 17700 87th Avenue, (403) 444-3000 or (800) 661-6454, fax (403) 444-3294. Rates are $138–$238 single or double.

A deluxe hotel in the traditional manner, **Hotel MacDonald,** 10065 100th Street, (403) 424-5181 or (800) 441-1414, fax (403) 424-8071, is set picturesquely on top of a hill with a wonderful view of the river. This château-style Canadian Pacific Railway hotel, originally opened in 1915, has been completely restored. Rates run $109–$199 single; $129–$219 double; $20 per extra person.

The **Mayfield Inn,** 16615 109th Avenue, (403) 484-0821 or (800) 661-9804, fax (403) 486-1634, is popular. It has a variety of rooms on ten nonsmoking floors, a dinner theater, full-service salon, exercise and steam rooms, squash and racquetball courts, and a bank. Rates are $78–$88 single or double; $10 per extra person.

Small pets are permitted in the **Edmonton Inn,** 11830 Kingsway Avenue, (403) 454-9521, fax (403) 453-7360, whose entrance is enhanced by a large rock garden and an encircling stream. There's also a sports bar with billiards. Room rates are $65–$105 single; $65–$115 double; $10 per extra person.

Edmonton has three Best Western Hotels. The **Cedar Park Inn** (south Edmonton), 5116 Calgary Trail N., (403) 434-7411, fax (403) 437-4836, has rates of $63–$75 single; $68–$92 double; $10 per extra person. The **Westwood** (west Edmonton), 18035 Stony Plain Road, (403) 483-7770, fax (403) 486-1769, offers $65–$75 singles; $75–$85 doubles; $10 extra. The **City Centre,** 11310 109th Street, (403) 479-2042, fax (403) 474-2204, charges $62–$75 single and $65–$90 double; $5 extra. All three offer indoor pools, exercise rooms, dining, and entertainment. The **Comfort Inn,** 17610 100th Avenue, (403) 484-4415, fax (403) 481-4034, is economical and very comfortable. Pets are permitted, and a restaurant is nearby. Rates are $61–$70 single; $69–$78 double; $8 for an extra person in the room.

The **Travelodge Edmonton South,** 10320 45th Avenue, (403) 436-9770 or (800) 578-7878, fax (403) 436-3529, has 222 rooms with rates of $56–$64 single; $64–$80 double; $8 for an extra person in the room. **Travelodge Edmonton West**'s 226 rooms, at 18320 Stony Plain Road, (403) 483-6031 or (800) 578-7878, fax (403) 484-2358, charges $57–$63 single; $69–$85 double; $8 extra. Corporate, group, sports, and seniors' rates are available at both, along with indoor pools and dining rooms.

A good economy spot is the **Sands Motor Hotel,** 12340 Fort

Road, (403) 474-5476, fax (403) 477-2714, with cocktails, dining, and assistance for the handicapped. Rates run $40–$42 single; $46–$48 double.

The excellent **International Youth Hostel** in Edmonton offers friendship among (usually) a well-traveled mixture of nationalities. It has self-cooking facilities, showers, laundry facilities, and both dormitories and family accommodations. It's at 10422 91st Street, (403) 429-0140, fax (403) 421-0131.

CAMPING

Klondike Valley, on Highway 2 south and Ellerslie Road, (403) 988-5067, advertises itself as Edmonton's most scenic campground. It is nestled in a quiet, natural setting along Blackmud Creek yet is within minutes of the city center and the Edmonton Mall. Rates range $12.50–$19.50; open May 1 through September 30.

Clover Court RV Park, 2104 Yellowhead Trail N.E. (Highway 16 east of the city), (403) 472-6645, has 17 shady sites, city water, laundry facilities, new showers, all services, and $15 rates, and is open year-round. If you don't want to camp, it also has a motel.

The **Devon Lions Campground,** is right on the North Saskatchewan River, next to the Devon Golf and Country Club, (403) 987-4777. It offers hiking, gold-panning, fishing, and canoeing, and it's only 15 minutes from the city center. All services are available.

Half Moon Lake Resort, 21524 Township Road, 520 Sherwood Park, (403) 922-3045, fax (403) 922-3646, has 195 sites, tap water, laundry facilities, a fish pond, beach, minigolf, riding stables, weekend hayrides, paddle-boat rentals, and all services. It's open May through October. Rates are $14–$20. **Kawtikh Retreat,** 51380 Range Road, 205 Sherwood Park, (403) 922-5168, open May through October, has 160 sites, full hookups, hot showers and flush toilets, groceries, and a Laundromat, and is in a quiet spot. Rates are $16–$18.

The **Kinsmen RV Park,** 15 minutes from the West Edmonton Mall, at Riel Drive, 5 kilometers (3 miles) north on 184th Street, off Highway 16X in St. Albert, (403) 419-3434, has washrooms and hot showers, some pull-throughs, water, and power, and is open May through September for RVs only.

Whitemud Creek Golf and RV Park, 16520 41st Street S.W., (403) 988-6800, fax (403) 437-2429, has 60 sites and a trout pond. It's adjacent to a nine-hole golf course and close to the West Edmonton

Mall, Fort Edmonton, and the Valley Zoo. It has all services and is open May through September. Rates are $10–$20.

Sandy Beach Campground, in Elk Island National Park, has 80 sites, but swimming is not recommended. There's a golf course, clubhouse, showers, sewage disposal, play area, canoeing, hiking trails, boat launch, and handicapped facilities. Back-country camping is permitted at nearby **Oster Lake** with a permit. Winter camping facilities do exist, but only at the boat-launch parking lot. Find it 14 km (9 mi) north of Highway 16 (which runs through Elk Island Park), at RR1 Site 4, Fort Saskatchewan, (403) 922-5790, fax (403) 922-2951. Open mid-May through mid-October.

NIGHTLIFE

If you can tear yourself away from the always frenetic Edmonton Mall, the city has a myriad of other nightspots to entertain you—nightclubs, sports bars, comedy clubs, dinner theaters, pubs, casinos, and well-frequented live performances. Look in *Billy's Guide, See Magazine, Where,* and newspapers for up-to-date arts and entertainment info.

Good spots to start are **Club Malibu,** featuring Top 40 hits in a former armory, at 10310 85th Avenue, (403) 432-7300. Try **Yuk Yuk's** in the West Edmonton Mall for nonstop comedy, (403) 481-9857; and **Cook County Saloon,** 8010 103rd Street, (403) 432-2665, for country and western music and free dance lessons.

Edmonton has live theater for all ages. The **Citadel Theater** complex, downtown at 99th Street and 101A Avenue, (403) 425-1820, consists of four individual theaters, an amphitheater, and a beautiful indoor atrium. For an entertaining evening in which the audience is part of the show, try the **Mayfield Dinner Theater,** in the Mayfield Inn on 166th Street and 109 Avenue, (403) 448-9339. The **Stage Polaris** offers family entertainment, (403) 462-1130.

You can't go wrong with nightlife in Edmonton. As Canada's "Festival City," it is noted for more live theater per capita than any other Canadian city.

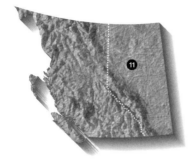

11
NORTHERN ALBERTA

U nlike Alberta's southern half, which is neatly squared off into
sections, its northern half appears on the map as empty green
space; unlike Northern British Columbia, Alberta's north is mostly
lowland. Only three main roads pierce this emptiness: Mackenzie
Highway, north from Grand Prairie and Grimshaw; Bicentennial
Highway, north from Slave Lake; and Highway 63, north from Lac La
Biche. The Peace and the Athabasca Rivers and their tributaries are the
roads that first brought travelers into this wilderness, and are still
important routes. The forest splashes with so many lakes that people
call Northern Alberta "Lakeland." Superlatives are commonplace.
North of Edmonton, Alberta is so vast that it could contain several
European countries. Wood Buffalo National Park is the world's
second-largest national park.

This is adventure country, attracting outdoors lovers all following
the first traders who paddled and portaged westward, then northward,
seeking routes to the Pacific and new fur sources. Follow them. Drive
Mackenzie Highway to the Northwest Territories' Hay River, then to
Wood Buffalo National Park via Fort Smith; or visit Wood Buffalo on
the winter road from Fort Chipewyan. Boat from Fort Chipewyan
through the Peace-Athabasca Delta, a birders' mecca. Drive Highway
63 to Fort McMurray and the world's largest oil sands. Canoe or jet-
boat the Peace River. Fly to a remote fishing lodge. Ride a snowmobile
to a trapline. Be sure to participate in this frontier life (best done with
a local guide/outfitter). ◼

NORTHERN ALBERTA

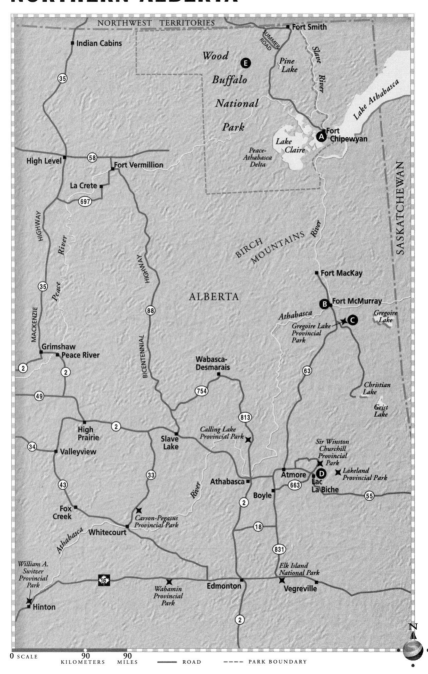

NORTHWEST TERRITORIES

Fort Smith

Indian Cabins

SUMMER ROAD

Wood

E

Pine Lake

Slave River

Buffalo

35

National

Lake Athabasca

Park

Fort Chipewyan

A

Lake Claire

High Level

58

Fort Vermillion

Peace-Athabasca Delta

La Crete

697

HIGHWAY

Peace River

BIRCH MOUNTAINS

River

SASKATCHEWAN

Fort MacKay

35

HIGHWAY

ALBERTA

Fort McMurray

B

MACKENZIE

88

Athabasca

Gregoire Lake

Gregoire Lake Provincial Park

C

Grimshaw

Peace River

BICENTENNIAL

Wabasca-Desmarais

63

Christian Lake

2

2

49

754

Grist Lake

High Prairie

2

813

Calling Lake Provincial Park

Sir Winston Churchill Provincial Park

34

Valleyview

Slave Lake

Lakeland Provincial Park

43

33

River

Athabasca

Atmore

D

Lac La Biche

663

55

Fox Creek

Carson-Pegasus Provincial Park

Boyle

2

Whitecourt

Athabasca

18

William A. Switzer Provincial Park

831

Elk Island National Park

16

Wabamin Provincial Park

Edmonton

Vegreville

Hinton

2

N

Sights

Ⓐ Fort Chipewyan

Ⓑ Fort McMurray

Ⓒ Gregoire Lake Provincial Park

Ⓓ Lac La Biche

Ⓔ Wood Buffalo National Park

A PERFECT DAY IN NORTHERN ALBERTA

I'd wrest myself away from a low-budget day in the West Edmonton Mall and spend a high-budget day getting to Wood Buffalo National Park. Although you can drive north to the Northwest Territories and access the northern end of Wood Buffalo from Fort Smith, the cheaper (though longer) method I prefer is flying to Fort Chipewyan on the Alberta side of the park and taking a boat ride with one of the native guide/outfitters through the Peace-Athabasca Delta for some bird-watching. I would then follow a park naturalist on a "buffalo creep," hoping to see some buffalo wallowing in the sand, then spend a couple of hours photographing white pelicans as they feed and rest on ledges near the Slave River's Rapids of the Drowned by Fort Smith.

SIGHTSEEING HIGHLIGHTS

☆☆☆ **Fort Chipewyan**—On Lake Athabasca, Fort Chipewyan (population 967) is the oldest permanently inhabited settlement in Alberta. It was designated a national historic site in 1939. Called Fort Chip (or just Chip) by the locals, this was the Northwest Company's most important northern fur trading post, built in 1798 to collect furs from the Mackenzie River basin and the Peace River country. The aboriginal people who live in Fort Chip today are still trappers, hunters, and fishers who live a semitraditional lifestyle.

The **Fort Chipewyan Nature Trail and Viewing Platform** is located along the banks of Lake Athabasca. The walk has 77 information signs describing the plant and animal life that may be seen along it.

The **Fort Chipewyan Bicentennial Museum** is modeled after the Hudson's Bay Company store of 1872. It presents the history of the Chipewyan, Cree, Metis, and European settlers and the key role Fort Chip played in Canada's early exploration and fur trade. Details (museum): On Mackenzie Avenue; (403) 697-3844; open year-round Monday through Friday 9 a.m. to 5:30 p.m., Saturday and Sunday 1 p.m. to 5 p.m. Admission: Free but donations are accepted. (½ hour)

★★★ **Fort McMurray**—At the confluence of the Clearwater and Athabasca Rivers, this was a major depot for both the Northwest Trading Company (1790) and the Hudson's Bay Company (1870) on the supply route from northern Saskatchewan to Lake Athabasca. From here, people and goods traveled north by riverboat and paddle-wheeler to the Arctic via Slave River, Great Slave Lake, and the Mackenzie River.

Today Fort McMurray is the service center for the giant **Oil Sands Plants**, one of the world's largest oil deposits, which produce more than 200,000 barrels of oil a day. It's believed that these deposits represent roughly one-third of the planet's known petroleum reserves. Suncor, Inc., and Syncrude Canada, Ltd., have announced plans to expand existing facilities and construct a new mine. Visit the multimillion-dollar **Fort McMurray Oil Sands Interpretive Centre**, (403) 743-7167, at the junction of Highway 63 and Mackenzie Boulevard, to learn how oil is extracted from the sands. The center is open daily May 15 through Labor Day 10 a.m. to 6 p.m., the rest of the year 10 a.m. to 4 p.m. Admission: Adults $2.25, ages 7–12 $1.25; families $5.50.

The **Oil Sands Viewpoint** is 45 km (30 mi) north of the center, and from this vantage point you can see vast production facilities and miles of conveyor belts covering the area of a football field.

Bus tours of the Oil Sands Plants are available daily July through August and may be reserved through the Fort McMurray Visitors' Bureau, (403) 791-4336 or (800) 565-3947. Tours last 3½ hours and cost $10 per person. Children under 12 are not permitted.

Twenty minutes north of Fort McMurray on Highway 63 is the **Bison Gateway**, four massive sandstone sculptures of wood bison marking the beginning of Syncrude Canada's mining area and the **Wood Bison Trail**—that portion of the highway that cuts through the Syncrude Canada site. Park your vehicle near these statues and walk some of the trails, which show what the landscape will look like when Syncrude has completed mining and reclaimed the land. (1 hour)

The **Forestry Interpretive Trail**, across from the Visitors' Bureau, off Highway 63 south, is self-explanatory and has some of Fort McMurray's best scenery. (1 day)

★★★ **Wood Buffalo National Park**—This World Heritage Site was established in 1922 to protect the world's largest free-roaming herd of wood bison; the park is now home to 3,500 or more of these animals. Later, plains bison received refuge in the park, and the two species interbred to form the current hybrid herd. Join a park naturalist on a regularly scheduled summertime "buffalo creep" to see these large, lumbering animals close-up, perhaps wallowing in a sand bath or grazing in a meadow in the subarctic boreal forest.

The park also contains the world's last nesting grounds of the endangered whooping crane and the northernmost nesting grounds of the white pelican. The **Peace-Athabasca Delta**, a massive maze of channels, islands, and marshes, is the staging ground for North America's four major waterfowl flyways, so birds are abundant. Over half a million waterfowl pass through the delta in spring and fall on their annual migration, and many remain to nest.

Wood Buffalo also has noteworthy landforms: extensive gypsum karst formations such as caves, sinkholes, and underground rivers; and salt plains, the remnants of an ancient seabed that once covered North America's inland prairies. If you enter the park from the Northwest Territories side, drive **Parson's Lake Road**, which leads to the **Salt Plains Overlook**. These glistening plains are reminiscent of the Sahara. Take the bends carefully on this narrow, winding road—buffalo may be lurking around each corner.

Details: Park admission is free, and park naturalists in the Fort Smith headquarters conduct excellent guided nature hikes, slide and lecture presentations, and bird-watching and canoeing programs during July and August. The park's gravel roads are open May 1 through November 1, with more convenient access at the northern end. Fort Chipewyan's winter road, which opens December 15 through March 15 (weather permitting), is 400 km (250 mi) long and runs from **Fort McMurray** to **Fort Smith**. Boating, picnicking, and camping are permitted at **Pine Lake**. The park is open in winter for snowshoeing, cross-country skiing, and ice fishing.

For further information, contact the Superintendent, Box 750, Fort Smith, Northwest Territory X0E 0P0; (403) 872-2349. If you're approaching the park from the southern end, at Fort Chipewyan, contact the park office at (403) 697-3662. (2–3 hours)

★★ **Lac La Biche**—This was originally a Hudson's Bay Company trading post, built in 1798. Father Lacombe added a mission in 1853.

Today Lac La Biche is a major jumping-off point for exploring the local area. **Lakeland Provincial Park** showcases some of Alberta's best wilderness lakes and Alberta's first circle-tour canoe route. **Shaw Lake Nordic Ski Area** offers 20 km (12 mi) of groomed scenic trails, and the adjacent recreation area contains four provincial campgrounds, numerous sandy beaches, and a designated trophy-fishing lake. Details: 215 km (134 mi) northeast of Edmonton on Alberta Highway 55; (403) 623-5235, reservations (403) 623-7961. **Sir Winston Churchill Provincial Park**, (403) 623-4144, is on an island in Lac La Biche, joined to the mainland by a causeway. Birders may view more than 200 different bird species here. (minimum 1½ hours)

✵ **Gregoire Lake Provincial Park**—Located 40 km (25 mi) southeast of Fort McMurray, this park provides sportfishing for northern pike and yellow perch and is well-endowed with camping areas, walking trails, and boat-launch facilities. (minimum 1 day)

CONTACTS FOR GUIDED TRIPS

The northern wilderness can be a daunting place when you're going it alone. If you'd prefer to "leave the driving to others," the following guide/outfitters can help. For Northern Alberta information, phone (800) 756-4351.

In Fort McMurray, try **Majic Country Wilderness Adventures**, (403) 743-0766; **Points North Adventures**, (403) 743-9350; or **Weber's Tour and Charter Service**, (403) 790-1777.

In Fort Chipewyan, see **Jumbo's**, (403) 697-3739; **Mr. Fit It**, (403) 687-3830; **Peace Athabasca Delta Tours**, (403) 697-3914; and **Fort Chipewyan Lodge**, (403) 697-3679. **Mikisew Tourism Corporation**, (403) 697-3740, runs a seven-day Wood Buffalo Delta Safari into the national park from Fort Chipewyan. Guided by local First Nations people, this trip includes a boat tour of the delta and a hike across the prairie to view buffalo, eagles, waterfowl, and wolves. Things have a penchant for change in the north, so it's always advisable to make sure a business is still in operation when it's time to make your travel arrangements.

The many guide/outfitters in the Peace River area of northwestern Alberta will take you fishing, hunting, river cruising, wildlife-viewing, horseback-riding, and canoeing. Try **Doig River Outfitters**, (403) 835-5152; **Peace Island Tours**, (403) 624-4295;

Smoky River Adventure Tours, (403) 624-9416; **Outdoors Magnified**, (403) 324-3602; **Wilderness Adventures International**, (403)351-3980 or (403)551-2097. Or if you want to experience a working farm of sheep, cattle, and alpacas, try **R&R Alpacas**, (403) 568-2536.

The following guides specialize in Wood Buffalo National Park but can lead you to other destinations as well. In Fort Chipewyan, try **Scott Flett**, (403) 697-3914; **Vince Vermilion**, (403) 697-3661; **John Rigney**, (403) 697-3740; or **Jumbo Fraser**, (403) 697-3739. **John Rigney** and **Alice Marten-Marcel** run eight-hour boat tours into the Peace-Athabasca Delta for $112; and three- and five-day package tours for $870 and $1,170, respectively. Contact them at Box 178, Fort Chipewyan, T0P 1B0, (403) 697-3929. Guide/outfitters tailor trips to the individual interests of their clients, whether angling, wildlife-viewing, or cultural skills. Most people plan to fish, hike, and camp.

FITNESS AND RECREATION

Camping is popular in Northern Alberta, and the sky's the limit for choice. **Fort McMurray** may be the province's northernmost and most isolated town, but it has every sport and sporting facility you can think of, including sled-dog races, winter bicycle rides, winter golfing, marathons, and triathlon events. It's also a center for fly-in fishing.

The **Clearwater River** originates at Lloyd Lake in Saskatchewan and meets the Athabasca River at Fort McMurray. As the only major river within the western prairie region to flow west, it was an integral part of the river and lake system that brought explorers and fur traders westward during the eighteenth and nineteenth centuries. The Clearwater was declared a Heritage River in 1986 for its contributions to Canadian history. The 118-km (71-mi) canoe route on the Clearwater takes intermediate paddlers four to six days to paddle and portage. File a trip plan with the Alberta Forest Service in Fort McMurray. If you want company while you paddle the Clearwater, take a trip with **Points North Adventures** out of Fort McMurray, (403) 743-9350.

Buffalo creeping is a unique recreational pursuit in **Wood Buffalo National Park**, along with birding and hiking in summer and ice fishing in winter. Jet-boating is a popular pastime on the **Peace River**, but fly-in fishing is the major drawing card for this northern region.

Among the lodges in the Wood Buffalo and Fort McMurray regions that cater to in-house anglers and hunters, or outfitters who fly anglers to their fish and hunters to their game animals, are **Andrew Lake Lodge**, (403) 464-7537; **Christina Lake Enterprises**, (403) 559-2224; **Grist Haven Lodge**, (403) 594-1254; **Island Lake Lodge**, (403) 743-0214; **Kimowin Lake Lodge**, (403) 743-9640; **Magic Country Wilderness Adventures**, (403) 743-0766; **Namur Lake Lodge**, (403) 791-9299; **Northern Sport Fishing**, (403) 791-3412; **Poplar Ridge Outfitters**, (403) 799-9324; and **Steep Bank Wilderness Lodge**, (403) 623-0636.

Among the lodges that cater to fishers in the Peace River country are **Tapawingo Lodge**, on Bistcho Lake, (403) 836-3345; and **Margaret Lake Lodge**, near Fort Vermilion, (403) 926-2278.

FOOD

Your meals in Northern Alberta should be fresh fish fried over an open fire—trout, Arctic grayling, walleye, perch, and whitefish—or maybe moose and caribou stew.

In town cafes, be prepared for plain, homey food and good old-fashioned hospitality with friendly, unabashed service. In Fort Chipewyan, there's the **Athabasca Cafe**, (403) 697-3737; **Chadi's Motel and Coffee Shop**, (403) 697-3777; and the **Fort Chipewyan Lodge**, (403) 697-3679. Two other eateries popular with the locals are **Mah's** and **Alice's Place.**

Dining establishments in Fort McMurray are not much different than those you'd find in a prairie town in the south. This community of 34,000 has nine Chinese restaurants, ten pizza places, 23 general restaurants, and 15 fast-food outlets. It has five restaurants that advertise fine dining: **Cedar's Steak House**, (403) 743-1717; **Earl's Restaurant**, (403) 791-3275; **Frontier Steak House**, (403) 791-2000; **Oliver's**, (403) 743-3301; and **Walters Dining Room**, (403) 791-7900. The Earl's chain is always a good bet, whatever the town.

In La Crete, Alberta's most northerly agricultural town and a largely Mennonite community east of High Level, try some traditional Mennonite food cooked in big outdoor ovens—perhaps roast goose in hunting season? La Crete is well known as a prime goose-hunting spot. In town, try **Country Corner Restaurant**, (403) 928-3161. It has a noon buffet on weekdays and a Sunday brunch. **Dunvegan Tea Room**, (403) 835-4459, near Fairview west of Peace River, is in an actual greenhouse converted to a dining room. You can pick tomatoes right from your table. In Fort Vermilion, try **K-5 Family Restaurant**, (403) 927-4550, for affordable home-style cooking in a relaxed setting.

LODGING

A lodge in the Northern Alberta outback may be a log cabin, a shack, even a tent camp. It's surprising, therefore, to find comparative luxury in some of the northernmost hotels. The best place to stay in Fort Chipewyan is the **Fort Chipewyan Adventure Lodge**, (403) 697-3679. It has every modern amenity, satellite color TV, displays of local crafts, and a full-service restaurant. Experienced guides will take you on various adventure tours. Prices range $85–$95 a room.

Fort McMurray may be isolated, but it has half a dozen good hotels in keeping with its young and aggressive image. **Sawridge Hotel**, 530 Mackenzie Boulevard, (403) 791-7900 or (800) 661-6567, is a classy, full-service hotel where kids under 12 sharing their parents' room stay free. Prices range $66–$145 a night. **Mackenzie Park Inn Convention Centre and Casino**, 424 Gregoire Drive, (403) 791-7200 or (800) 582-3273, has a full-service casino as well as everything else you'd expect in the south, even computer facilities and video lottery terminals. Prices range $68–$125. The most reasonable places to stay in Fort McMurray are **Rusty's Best Canadian Motor Inn**, 385 Gregoire Drive, (403) 791-4646, ($42–$55), and **Twin Pine Motor Inn**, 10024 Biggs Avenue, (403) 743-3391, ($47–$51).

I'd stay at one of the adventure-travel or fly-in fishing lodges even if I weren't going to fish, since they have the resources to let you take advantage of the region's wilderness experiences. Seek out **Grist Haven Lodge** and **Winefred Lake Tent Camps**, 147 km (92 mi) southeast of Fort McMurray, Box 1350, Grand Centre, T0A 1T0, (403) 594-1254. They have private log cabins with kitchen facilities and are located on a sandy beach. Fishing is good on both lakes. The guest cabins at **Gypsy Lake Lodge**, 80 km (50 mi) east of Fort McMurray, (403) 743-3176, are available year-round. The lodge offers a summer flyout to fish Clearwater River for walleye and Arctic grayling.

CAMPING

Northern Alberta is blessed with an abundance of campgrounds and recreational day-use areas provided by the Alberta Parks Service, the Land and Forestry Service, municipalities, and private industry. All are listed in the government's excellent camping guide, *The Alberta Campground Guide*, which is available from Travel Alberta, Box 2500,

NORTHERN ALBERTA

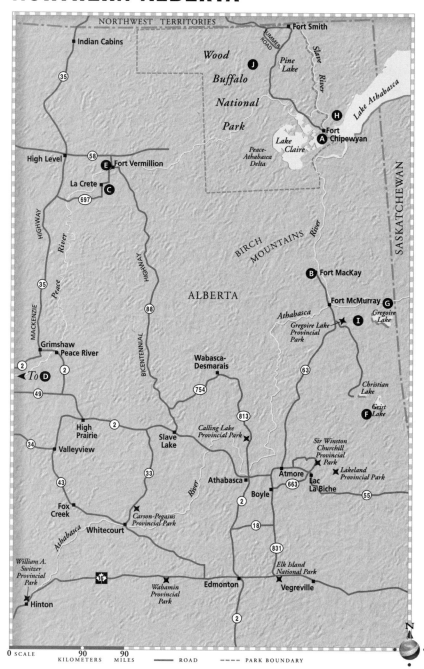

NORTHWEST TERRITORIES

Indian Cabins

Fort Smith

SUMMER ROAD

Wood
Buffalo

Pine
Lake

Slave River

National

Park

Lake Athabasca

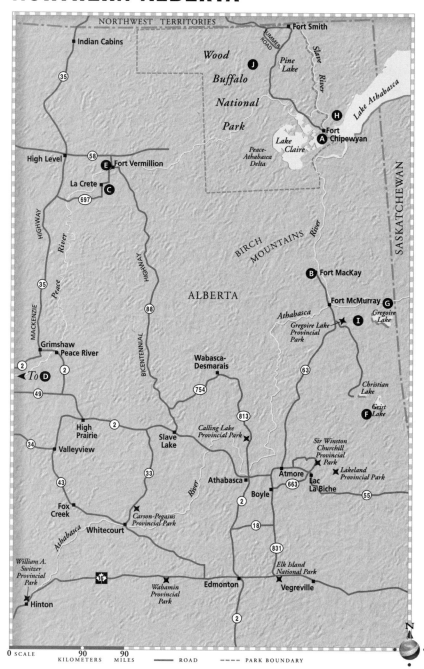

Lake
Claire

Fort
Chipewyan

Peace-
Athabasca
Delta

High Level

Fort Vermillion

La Crete

Peace River

MACKENZIE HIGHWAY

BIRCH MOUNTAINS

River

ALBERTA

Fort MacKay

Fort McMurray

Athabasca

Gregoire Lake
Provincial
Park

Gregoire
Lake

BICENTENNIAL HIGHWAY

Grimshaw
Peace River

To

Wabasca-
Desmarais

Christian
Lake

Grist
Lake

High
Prairie

Valleyview

Slave
Lake

Calling Lake
Provincial Park

Sir Winston
Churchill
Provincial
Park

Lakeland
Provincial Park

Fox
Creek

Carson-Pegasus
Provincial Park

Whitecourt

River

Athabasca

Atmore

Boyle

Lac
La Biche

William A.
Switzer
Provincial
Park

Hinton

Wabamin
Provincial
Park

Edmonton

Elk Island
National Park

Vegreville

SASKATCHEWAN

N

0 SCALE   90
KILOMETERS

90
MILES

ROAD   - - - - PARK BOUNDARY

Food

- Ⓐ Alice's Place
- Ⓐ Athabasca Cafe
- Ⓑ Cedar's Steak House
- Ⓐ Chadi's Motel and Coffee Shop
- Ⓒ Country Corner Restaurant
- Ⓓ Dunvegan Tea Room
- Ⓑ Earl's Restaurant
- Ⓐ Fort Chipewyan Lodge
- Ⓑ Frontier Steak House
- Ⓔ K-5 Family Restaurant
- Ⓐ Mah's
- Ⓑ Oliver's
- Ⓑ Walter's Dining Room

Lodging

- Ⓐ Fort Chipewyan Adventure Lodge
- Ⓕ Grist Haven Lodge on Grist Lake
- Ⓖ Gypsy Lake Lodge
- Ⓑ Mackenzie Park Inn Convention Centre and Casino
- Ⓑ Rusty's Best Canadian Motor Inn
- Ⓑ Sawridge Hotel
- Ⓑ Twin Pine Motor Inn
- Ⓕ Winefred Lake Tent Camps

Camping

- Ⓗ Dore Lake
- Ⓘ Gregoire Lake
- Ⓙ Wood Buffalo National Park

Note: Items with the same letter are located in the same town or area.

Edmonton, T5J 2Z4. The Internet Campground Guide is found at www.AlbertaHotels.ab.ca/campgrounds.

There's organized camping at Pine Lake in **Wood Buffalo National Park**, (403) 872-2349, for $10 a night. It has 36 sites with picnic tables and some wheelchair-accessible sites. **Gregoire Lake**, south of Fort McMurray, (403) 334-2222, is a popular provincial park. Sixty of its 140 campsites have electrical hookups. The park offers a sandy beach and grass, boat- and canoe-rental facilities, and a convenient boat launch. Power sites cost $13; nonpower sites, $11. Firewood is available for sale. There are another dozen parks in the Fort McMurray area as well as many more urban parks and developed trails in the town itself. **Dore Lake** park, 10 miles northeast of Fort Chipewyan, has a floating boat dock, but powerboats are prohibited. There are several Forest Service camps on the Clearwater River and other rivers in Northern Alberta.

Scenic Route: The Deh Cho Connection

The **Deh Cho (Mackenzie River) Connection** is a circular drive which starts at **Grimshaw,** Mile 0 of the Mackenzie Highway, and follows Alberta Highway 35 straight north to the Northwest Territories border and Hay River. It veers west through the Northwest Territories to Fort Simpson on the Mackenzie River; turns south along the **Liard Highway** to meet the Alaska Highway in British Columbia; continues through Fort Nelson and Fort St. John; and finishes at **Dawson Creek,** its other Mile 0. Total distance is about 1,800 km (1,125 mi).

Some highlights near the Northern Alberta section are **La Crete,** a mostly Mennonite community; **Fort Vermilion,** the oldest settlement in Alberta; **Rainbow Lake,** a new community developed by the oil and gas industry; **Zama,** another oil and gas community; and Indian Cabins, the last gas/restaurant service in Alberta before the Northwest Territory border. Of special interest in **Indian Cabins** is a historic log church, a "grave" in a box set high on the branch of a tree, and a cemetery with graves covered by spirit houses.

Compared to the Rockies, this route is not particularly scenic, but it is wild and uncrowded, and you feel like you are taking a step back in time. Take time to ferret around behind the scenes. ◼

THE DEH CHO (MACKENZIE RIVER) CONNECTION

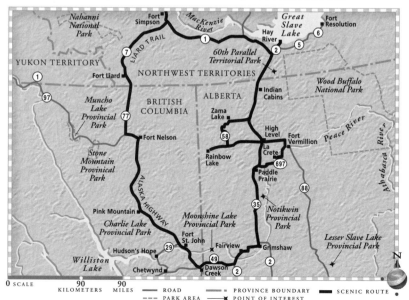

12
CALGARY

Set between rolling foothills to the west and the prairie plains to the east, Calgary offers two worlds: big-city stimulation and accessible wilderness serenity. Images of cowhands, chuck wagons, oil wells, and ski slopes identify Calgary as friendly, energetic, and progressive.

Calgary appeals to both sophisticated and unsophisticated tastes with fashionable shops; a variety of theaters for drama, ballet, symphony, and opera; ultramodern works of art; and restaurants offering every cuisine imaginable—Old World to indigenous Indian to Asian to sizzling, lean Alberta steaks. For those who prefer outdoor pursuits, Calgary has a zoo, a prehistoric park, a pioneer village, botanical gardens, walks along two sparkling rivers, and awesome, hot-air-balloon views of the city and countryside.

Calgary also has other extraordinary assets: the enviable reputation of being the least-expensive city of its size on the entire North American continent and more hours of sunshine each year than anywhere else in Canada. That's a major reason why Calgarians are so outdoorsy—indeed, tiny communities with populations as small as Cherhill (61), Dixonville (90), and Enchant (94) offer camping facilities, often at no charge. ◧

CALGARY

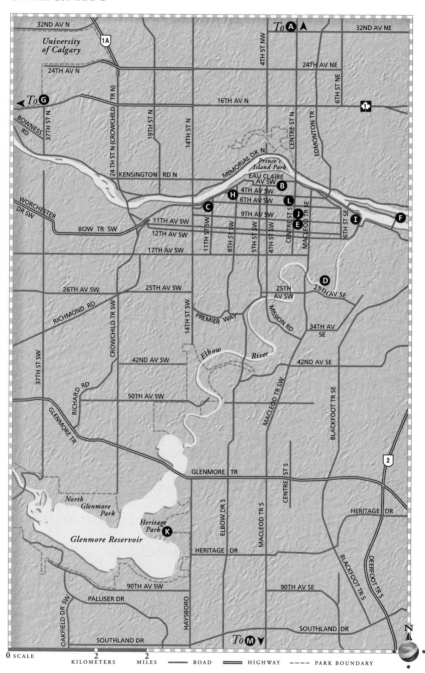

32ND AV N
University of Calgary
1A
24TH AV N
To G
37TH ST N
24TH ST N (CROWCHILD TR N)
19TH ST N
14TH ST N
16TH AV N
4TH ST NW
CENTRE ST N
EDMONTON TR
6TH ST NE
32ND AV NE
24TH AV NE
BOWNESS RD
KENSINGTON RD N
MEMORIAL DR N
Prince's Island Park
EAU CLAIRE AV SW
4TH AV SW
6TH AV SW
9TH AV SW
B
WORCHESTER DR SW
BOW TR SW
11TH AV SW
12TH AV SW
17TH AV SW
H
C
L
J
E
CENTRE ST S
MACLEOD TR SE
6TH ST SE
I
F
11TH ST SW
8TH ST SW
5TH ST SW
4TH ST SW
26TH AV SW
25TH AV SW
25TH AV SW
25TH AV SE
D
37TH ST SW
RICHMOND RD
CROWCHILD TR SW
RICHARD RD
14TH ST SW
PREMIER WAY
MISSION RD
34TH AV SE
42ND AV SW
Elbow River
42ND AV SE
50TH AV SW
MACLEOD TR SW
BLACKFOOT TR SE
GLENMORE TR
GLENMORE TR
2
North Glenmore Park
Heritage Park
K
Glenmore Reservoir
ELBOW DR S
MACLEOD TR S
CENTRE ST S
HERITAGE DR
HERITAGE DR
90TH AV SW
PALLISER DR
OAKFIELD DR SW
HAYSBORO
90TH AV SE
BLACKFOOT TR S
DEERFOOT TR S
SOUTHLAND DR
To M
SOUTHLAND DR
N

0 SCALE
2 KILOMETERS
2 MILES
ROAD
HIGHWAY
PARK BOUNDARY

Sights

A Aerospace Museum

B Calgary Chinese Cultural Centre

C Calgary Science Centre and Centennial Planetarium

D Calgary Stampede

E Calgary Tower

F Calgary Zoo, Botanical Gardens, and Prehistoric Park

G Canada Olympic Park

H Devonian Gardens

I Fort Calgary Historic Park

J Glenbow Museum

K Heritage Park Historical Village

L Lunchbox Theatre

M Spruce Meadows

A PERFECT DAY IN CALGARY

For its size, Calgary has the best variety of activities, parks, golf courses, and restaurants of any city in Canada. But be cautious about a perfect Calgary day on a Sunday—most restaurants are closed. I'd begin with breakfast at the Panorama Restaurant in the Calgary Tower, where I could watch the city revolve around me as I enjoyed my meal. I'd drive the short distance to Fort Calgary, to let my imagination return to the days of Sam Livingston, Calgary's first settler, who confronted the Northwest Mounted Police when they decided to build a fort on his chosen land. I'd then go south, as Sam did, down the Elbow River to where Glenmore Reservoir has now flooded "his" valley, and visit Heritage Park—the Livingston house is part of the pioneer village, and effigies of Sam and his wife are on display.

Once I'd time-machined my return to the present, I'd head downtown to the Silver Dragon Restaurant to indulge myself with a late dim-sum lunch, then head for Olympic Park to get the feel of bobsleigh-racing and ski-jumping with the simulators. Then I'd stand in line for a luge run to test my digestive stamina. Back in town, I'd let my imagination run wild again as I meandered through Prehistoric Park to the Botanical Gardens, to absorb the sights, scents, and beauty of plants from around the world.

In the evening, Hy's would be my choice for a relaxing cocktail before enjoying one of its famed charbroiled steaks. I'd take in an intriguing show in the Planetarium (Science Centre), then let my hair down in one or more of Calgary's nightclubs, dancing to western music and really becoming part (if only temporarily) of "cattle country."

SIGHTSEEING HIGHLIGHTS

★★★ **Calgary Science Centre and Centennial Planetarium—** This was the first multimedia theater in North America. Computer graphics, films, a 12-speaker sound system, and slide visuals that fill the entire dome treat you to an educational and entertaining experience, as do the hands-on exhibits. The Planetarium Star Theatre and the Pleiades Mystery Theatre bring science to scintillating life. Guided tours are available. Details: 701 11th Street S.W.; (403) 221-3700 for show times. Admission: One show and exhibits, or a double-feature dome show is adults $8; seniors and children under 12 $6; families $30. (minimum 2 hours)

★★★ **Calgary Stampede—**This world-renowned international rodeo occurs only in the first two weeks of July and must be booked months ahead to obtain better seats for events you really wish to see. The entire city becomes a ten-day Wild West show—flapjacks, chuck wagons, casinos, a midway, and street dancing create a festival atmosphere that's unparalleled anywhere. The rodeo events cover the entire spectrum. The park also hosts a year-round variety of thoroughbred and harness racing. The Stampede is an unforgettable experience. Details: 14th Avenue and Olympic Way S.E.; (403) 261-0101 or (800) 661-1260. Admission varies according to events and seating. (5 days)

★★★ **Calgary Zoo, Botanical Gardens, and Prehistoric Park—** This complex is world renowned, famous for conservation, scientific studies, education, and recreation. The zoo has more than 1,200 animals, many of which are rare and endangered. Enjoy Breakfast with the Gorillas every second Saturday from 7 to 9 a.m., and the Prehistoric Park, which has 23 life-size dinosaur replicas. Only a few minutes from downtown, fully wheelchair-accessible, and largely built on islands within the Bow River, this complex is a must! Details: 1300 Street and Zoo Road; (403) 232-9300, fax (403) 237-7582; open year-round from 9 a.m. to seasonal closing times. Guided tours available. Admission: Adults $8, seniors $5.50, children ages 2–15 $4, under 2 free. All prices include GST. (4 hours)

☆☆☆ **Heritage Park Historical Village**—Set on a 25-hectare (60-acre) site near the Glenmore Reservoir on Heritage Drive, this park is a re-creation of pre-1915 prairie life and Canada's largest living historical village. Most of its buildings are originals that have been moved to the park—a general store; a blacksmith shop; a Hudson's Bay Company trading post; the Wainwright Hotel; and the Big House, once the home of Calgary's first settlers, Sam and Jane Livingston, and their 14 children. You can see Sam and Jane in wax effigy in the living room of the Big House. For a history of Calgary from the Livingston viewpoint, see my *Tell Me, Grandmother* (McClelland and Stewart Ltd., 1985). As a former teacher, I have taught some of the descendants of Sam and Jane Livingston.

Costumed interpreters bring the village to life. You can ride in a horse-drawn wagon, ride the rails behind a steam locomotive of the period, cruise an active stern-wheeler, and thrill to an antique midway. Guided tours are available. Details: 1900 Heritage Drive S.W.; (403) 259-1900, fax (403) 268-5280; open daily May 18 through September 2, 9 a.m. to 5 p.m., and Saturday, Sunday, holidays, and September 3 through October 14, 10 a.m. to 5 p.m. Admission: Adults $7.50, seniors $6.50, ages 3–16 $4.50. All include a free Stampede-style breakfast if you get there between 9 and 10 a.m. (3 hours)

☆☆ **Calgary Tower**—This 191-meter (627-ft) tower will give you a spectacular view of Calgary and the Rocky Mountains from the Observation Terrace or the revolving restaurant, which serves dishes as superb as the views. Details: 101 9th Avenue S.W.; (403) 266-7171, fax (403) 266-7230; open daily May 16 through September 14 7:30 a.m. to midnight, September 15 through May 15 8 a.m. to 11 p.m. Admission: Adults $3.75; seniors $2.95; ages 13–17 $2.50; ages 6–12 $1.75. (1 hour)

☆☆ **Canada Olympic Park**—This venue for 1988's XV Olympic Winter Games is now a year-round premier sport and tourist attraction. Guided bus tours are available daily for a close-up look at the facilities and the breathtaking view from the top of the 90-meter (295-ft) ski-jump tower. The ski hill offers alpine and cross-country skiing and snowboard programs in winter. The Olympic Hall of Fame and Museum pay homage to Canada's athletes; and you can hurtle down the luge/bobsleigh track for $13 (summer), $39 (winter). In the Olympic Hall of Fame, one simulator re-creates the thrills, twists, turns, and high speeds of bobsleigh racing; another, the 70-meter

(230-ft) "flight" of a ski-jumper. Details: 88 Canada Olympic Road
S.W.; (403) 286-5452, fax (403) 286-7231. Olympic Hall of Fame,
(403) 247-5452. Open daily May through September 10 a.m. to 7 p.m.,
and the rest of the year 10 a.m. to 4 p.m. Admission: Adults $6, ages
6–12, students, and seniors $3. Combination of park and Hall of Fame
is adults $8, seniors, ages 6–12, and students with I.D. $4. Bobsleigh
costs $40 and luge, $12. (2 hours)

✩✩ **Devonian Gardens**—This 1-hectare (2.5-acre), all-indoor site
holds more than 20,000 plants as well as reflecting pools, bridges,
waterfalls, an art gallery, and a play area for the youngsters. Special
stage performances enhance your visit. Details: Downtown Calgary;
(403) 268-3888 for events schedule; open daily year-round from 9 a.m.
to 9 p.m. Admission: Free. (2 hours)

✩✩ **Fort Calgary Historic Park**—Many Calgarians go right by this
spot and do not realize their city began as a fort here in 1875. The spot
was marked by gateways, log stumps, and plaques, and the story told by
audiovisual presentations. Presently the fort is being rebuilt with 1875
tools and will include hands-on interactive displays. On Fridays
between May and October, at the Deane House Historic Site and
Restaurant, visitors enjoy an evening of mirth and mayhem at the
Friday Night Mystery from History Dinner Theater. Details: 750 9th
Avenue, near the confluence of the Bow and Elbow Rivers. (minimum
1 hour)

✩✩ **Glenbow Museum**—This is Western Canada's largest museum
and naturally focuses on the settlement and development of the West,
with rare manuscripts, books, photo collections, artifacts, art, special
international collections, and guided tours. Details: 130 9th Avenue
S.E.; (403) 268-4100, fax (403) 262-4045; open year-round May
through August 9 a.m. to 5 p.m., but not on Monday September
through April. Admission: Adults $5, seniors and students over 7 $3.50;
children under 7 free; families $13. (2 hours)

✩✩ **Spruce Meadows**—This site of world-renowned international
horse jumping and show events is situated amid the rolling foothills just
south of Calgary city limits. Spruce Meadows hosts three major com-
petitions: the National in June, when the best in Canada compete for
honors; the North American in July, between Canada, the United

States, and Mexico; and in September, the top 15 nations in the world in show-jumping compete in an equestrian extravaganza. Each event provides entertainment, exhibits, and excellent food service. The facilities are open year-round, and guided tours are available. Details: Spruce Meadows, RR9, Calgary, T2J 5G5; (403) 974-4200. Admission: Adults $5, seniors and children under 12 free. (1 hour)

☆ **Aerospace Museum**—This wheelchair-accessible museum houses Western Canada's aviation history, with vintage aircraft from 1913 to her latest sleek jets, various engines, artifacts, and art. Guided tours are offered by appointment only. Details: Hangar #10, 64 McTavish Place N.E.; (403) 250-3752, fax (403) 250-8399; open daily all year 10 a.m. to 5 p.m. Admission: Adults $5, seniors $3; 6–18 $2; children under 6 free. (1 hour)

☆ **Calgary Chinese Cultural Centre**—Set in Calgary's Chinatown is this unique museum—the only one in Canada to present Chinese culture exclusively. Exhibitions, an arts and crafts store, and an authentic Chinese restaurant are found in a delightful architecturally correct setting that is wheelchair accessible, with guided tours available. Details: 197 1st Street S.W.; (403) 262-5071, fax (403) 232-6387. Open daily 11 a.m. to 5 p.m. Admission: Adults $2; seniors, students, and children 6–12 $1. (1 hour)

☆ **The Lunchbox Theatre**—Professional one-act plays, musicals, revues, and comedies are produced Monday through Saturday—special evening shows, too—at Canada's longest-running noontime theater. Details: 205 5th Avenue S.W., 2nd level; (403) 265-4297, fax (403) 265-5461; open September through May Monday through Saturday noon to 1 p.m. Admission: $7 per person. (1 hour)

FITNESS AND RECREATION

There are several "leisure venues" scattered around the city. **Calaway Park,** (403) 240-3822, Western Canada's largest amusement park is 11 km (8 mi) west along the Trans-Canada Highway. It's open daily June 23 through September 5 10 a.m. to 8 p.m.; same times but weekends only September 6 through October 13 and May 17 through June 23. Admission, including all rides, shows, special entertainments, and GST, is $17.50 for ages 7–65, $12 for seniors and ages 3–6, free for ages 2 and under, $50 per family (four members). Daytime admission excluding rides is $8, $7 after 5 p.m.

The **Family Leisure Centre,** 11150 Bonaventure Drive S.E., (403) 278-7542, is more adult-oriented, though children are welcome. It offers a wave pool, skating rink, curling sheets, squash and racquetball courts, weight room, and gym. Also more adult-oriented is **Lindsay Park Sports Centre,** (403) 233-8393. Built for the 1983 Western Canada Summer Games, it offers a swimming pool, diving pool, running track, squash courts, weight-lifting room, and three gyms.

The **Southland Leisure Centre,** 19th Street and Southland Drive SW, (403) 251-3505, includes a wave pool and diving tank, two skating arenas, gyms, racquetball, driving range, squash courts, and hot tub. There's also the **Village Square Leisure Centre,** 2623 56th Street N.E., (403) 280-9714, with a wave pool, two ice arenas, arts and crafts rooms, weight training rooms, racquet courts, gyms with rock-climbing walls, and sports halls.

Finally, you can "go-kart'n" at **Kart Gardens International,** at Barlow Trail N.E., and 5202 1st Street S.W., (403) 250-9555, all the way from Kinder Kart'n to bumper boats and bumper cars, to a tight track with lots of twists and turns. An additional feature is an 18-hole minigolf course. Open April through November.

Added to these fitness and recreation ideas are numerous parks where jogging, skateboarding, skating, cycling, and walking can be enjoyed. Of the many waterways and lakes for boating, **Glenmore Reservoir** is for sailboats only. Calgary also boasts at least 11 golf courses, each with its own special beauty and charm.

FOOD

Calgary is home to big juicy Alberta beefsteaks, BBQ, prime ribs, and stacks of syrup-sloshed flapjacks served from a chuck wagon at the Calgary Stampede. Enjoy the city's Western flavor at its many steakhouses, where you'll get a country atmosphere, a saloon, and even free two-step lessons—especially in 1998, which Calgary has declared the "Year of the Cowboy."

Billy MacIntyre's Cattle Company, in the Brentwood Village Mall, Crowchild Trail N.W., (403) 282-6614, prides itself on being Alberta's most award-winning restaurant. It gets attention with its reasonable prices and drinks such as "Skip and Go Naked." Its Rattlesnake Saloon is specially popular after dinner for country and new music dancing. **Ranchman's Restaurant**, 9615 Macleod Trail S., (403) 253-1100, has an authentic Western saloon, a dance hall, plus a museum of rodeo memorabilia and photographs to enliven its Western menu. Real local cowboys go to this saloon, and Thursday night is Ladies' Night, with free admission for women all night and free admission for everyone before 8 p.m. **Dusty's Saloon**, 1088 Olympic Way S.E., (403) 263-5343, serves excellent homemade sausage and buffalo burgers and offers country and western dancing on the city's largest floating dance floor—as well as free two-step lessons on Tuesday and Wednesday. Entrees are under $10.

Of course, to relish unadulterated Grade A Alberta beef, you can always go to the chain steakhouses. **Hy's Steakhouse**, 316 4th Avenue S.W., (403) 263-2222, serves dinners that range from $21–$30, although earlybird specials are offered regularly. There are at least four Keg Restaurants in Calgary, and their steaks and salad bars are predictably good and well-priced. Try the Billy Miner Mud Pie at **Keg Restaurant Glenmore**, corner of 11th Ave. and 5th St. S.W., (403) 226-1036.

For traditions of another kind, sample indigenous native dishes of buffalo, bannock, venison, and rabbit at the **Chief Chiniki Restaurant and Handicraft Centre**, on the Trans-Canada Highway at Morley, (403) 881-3748. **Dante's Cafe and Wine Bar** at 210, 513 8th Avenue S.W., (403) 237-5787, specializes in wild game such as wild boar, reindeer, pheasant, and buffalo. The host is author of a wild game cookbook.

Like Edmonton and Vancouver, Calgary's melting pot population is reflected in its various ethnic restaurants. You'll find them in such neighbourhoods as Eau Claire, Chinatown, Kensington, 4th Street, and Uptown 17th Avenue. Cuisine varies among Japanese, Chinese, Korean, Moroccan, Cajun, Caribbean, Spanish, Italian, French, Dutch, Greek, German, Indian, Pakistani, Indonesian, Irish, Latin American, Mexican, Middle Eastern, Mongolian, Moravian, Peruvian, and, of course, English.

For fat-free vegetarian and Tandoori dishes, try the award-winning **Rajdoot Restaurant**, 2424 4th Street SW, (403) 245-0181. Lunch buffet is a reasonable $7.95; vegetarian dinner buffet Tuesday evenings and Sunday brunch are both $9.95. There are many Italian restaurants in Calgary. **La Dolce Vita Ristorante Italiano** in Calgary's "Little Italy," at 916 1st Avenue N.E., (403) 263-3445, offers fresh seafood, pasta, quail, and veal cooked to perfection. Dinners range $21–$30. I don't know what I like best, the location or the food, at

CALGARY

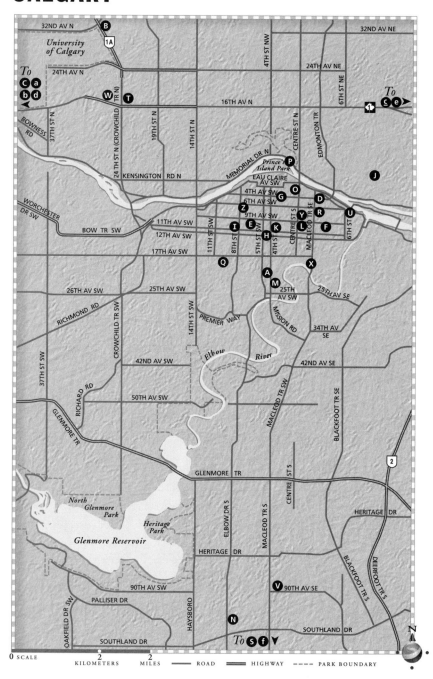

32ND AV N   B   32ND AV NE

University of Calgary   1A

To   c a b d ◀   24TH AV N   24TH AV NE

W T   16TH AV N   To c e ▶   1

BOWNESS RD

KENSINGTON RD N   Prince's Island Park   P   EDMONTON TR   J

MEMORIAL DR N   EAU CLAIRE AV SW

WORCHESTER DR SW   4TH AV SW   G   O   D

6TH AV SW   Z   R   U

BOW TR SW   9TH AV SW   Y

11TH AV SW   I   E   K   L   M   F

12TH AV SW   H

17TH AV SW   Q   X

26TH AV SW   25TH AV SW   A   M   25TH AV SW   25TH AV SE

RICHMOND RD   CROWCHILD TR SW   PREMIER WAY   MISSION RD   34TH AV SE

42ND AV SW   Elbow   River   42ND AV SE

RICHARD RD   50TH AV SW   MACLEOD TR SW   BLACKFOOT TR SE

GLENMORE TR   GLENMORE TR   CENTRE ST S   2

North Glenmore Park   Heritage Park   HERITAGE DR

Glenmore Reservoir   HERITAGE DR

90TH AV SW   V   90TH AV SE

PALLISER DR   N   SOUTHLAND DR

SOUTHLAND DR   To S f ▼   N

0 SCALE   2 KILOMETERS   2 MILES   ■ ROAD   ≡ HIGHWAY   - - - PARK BOUNDARY

Food

A 4th Street Rose Restaurant

B Billy MacIntyre's Cattle Company

C Chief Chiniki Restaurant and Handicraft Center

D The Conservatory

E Dante's Cafe and Wine Bar

F Dusty's Saloon

G Hy's Steakhouse

H Keg Restaurant Glenmore

I The King and I

J La Dolce Vita Ristorante Italiano

K Mother Tucker's

L Owl's Nest Dining Room

L Panorama Dining Room

M Rajdoot Restaurant

N Ranchman's Restaurant

O Regency Palace

P River Cafe

Q Sultan's Tent

R Teatro

K Thai Sa-on

Lodging

S Babbling Brook Bed and Breakfast

T Best Western Village Park Inn

U Calgary International Hostel

V Carriage House Inn

D Delta Bow Valley

W EconoLodge

X Elbow River Inn

Y Palliser

Z Ramada Hotel Downtown

Camping

a Bowridge RV Park

b Calaway Park

c Camp 'n' Water Park

d KOA Calgary West

e Mountain View Farm Campground

f Pine Creek RV Campground

Note: Items with the same letter are located in the same area.

Teatro, 200 8th Avenue S.E. The chef uses a wood-burning oven to prepare inventive renditions of Italian traditions that he calls "Italian Market cuisine." The restaurant is in the historic Dominion Bank building, across from the Centre for Performing Arts.

As everywhere in Western Canada, Thai food is a recent favorite. Some like the **Thai Sa-on**, 351 10th Avenue S.W., (403) 264-3526, for consistent quality. Others prefer **The King and I** at 822 11th Avenue S.W., (403) 264-7241, for such exotics as marinated chicken wrapped in *pandulus* banana leaves. Even more exotic is the **Sultan's Tent**, 909 17 Avenue S.W., (403) 244-2333, Calgary's first Moroccan restaurant, which is made to look like the inside of a Berber tent. Try the six-course, 2½-hour "Sultan's Feast."

Chinese restaurants have been around a long time in Calgary. One of the favorites is **Regency Palace**, a large seafood restaurant on top of Dragon City Plaza, (403) 777-2288, where buffets give good value and daily dim sum is popular.

Although eating out can be fairly cheap in Calgary, here are some choices that give the most for your money. **Mother Tucker's**, 345 10th Avenue S.W., (403) 262-5541, has a children's menu and an extensive salad bar. Dinners run $11–$20. You get a fresh and healthy multi-ethnic menu and low prices (under $10 entrees) at the **4th Street Rose Restaurant**, 2116 4th Street S.W., (403) 228-5377. Your best value is the ever-changing gourmet menu at SAIT (Highwood Dining Room Hospitality Careers), a world-class, student-operated training facility at 1301 16th Avenue N.W., (403) 284-8612. Don't count on it at weekends, despite the lavish five-course meals served weekdays.

At the other end of the price scale is the **Panorama Dining Room**, atop the Calgary Tower in Palliser Square at 101 9th Avenue S.W., (403) 266-7171. The restaurant revolves slowly to give fabulous views of the city and the surrounding countryside, the foothills, and the Rockies. Dinners start at $31, and you have to pay $5.50 extra to ride the elevator whether dining or not, but it's worth the splurge. If you can afford a few other splurges, try **The Conservatory**, 209 4th Avenue, (403) 263-1980, situated in the lovely Delta Bow Valley; or the **Owl's Nest Dining Room** in the Westin Hotel Calgary, 320 4th Avenue, (403) 266-1611. These offer fine dining in a tastefully formal atmosphere.

You know there's got to be something good about a restaurant when all it needs in a magazine ad is its name. This is the **River Cafe**, located across the bridge from Eau Claire Market in Prince's Island

Park, (403) 261-7670. Its setting is romantic and its menu poetically written, even though it serves Northwest Canadian.

LODGING

Calgary doesn't have a Fantasyland Hotel like the West Edmonton Mall, but it does have 10,000 hotel rooms, which range from the deluxe to the quaint. And Calgarians are known worldwide for their genuine friendliness and hospitality. How to choose one place over another? You might want to consider distance from downtown, the airport, or the light rail transit system (LRT); fitness facilities; or proximity to parks and riverbank trails. You'll have difficulty getting specific room rates unless you know specific dates.

Probably the oldest (1914) and best known is the **Palliser**, a typically regal Canadian Pacific (CP) Hotel that the locals sometimes call Calgary's Castle by the Tracks or the Top Bunk. The Palliser is a large, renovated, turn-of-the-century hotel that is likely to attract visiting dignitaries. Located at 133 9th Avenue S.W., it is conveniently connected via skywalk to the convention center, the performance

Calgary night skyline

John Sharpe

center, and the Glenbow Museum. Phone (403) 262-1234 or (800)
441-1414. Rates generally range from $250–$350 a night, but there's a
discount for seniors, and rates can change according to demand.
Chocoholics may be interested in the hotel's ritual of "Death by
Chocolate"; others will enjoy its ritual of afternoon tea ($14.95).
    Another first-class downtown hotel is the **Delta Bow Valley**, at
209 4th Avenue S.E., (403) 266-1980, (800) 268-1133 (Canada), or
(800) 877-1133 (U.S.). It has fully equipped fitness facilities and an
award-winning dining room called The Conservatory. Children are
welcome. The hotel has a Kids Creative Centre, and those under 6 eat
free. Rates range $125–$225. The **Ramada Hotel Downtown**, 708
8th Avenue S.W., (403) 263-7600 or (800) 661-8684, is only 2 blocks
from the Eaton Centre and half a block from the LRT. It has an
outdoor heated pool, poolside rooms, and the usual fitness facilities.
Rates range from $109–$155.
    There are four Best Western hotels but in terms of ambiance, my
choice would be the **Best Western Village Park Inn**, 1804 Crowchild
Trail N.W., (403) 289-0241 or (800) 528-1234. It is the smallest of the
four but has a lovely atrium, and the rates are slightly lower, too. A
double room is $110. If you prefer your foliage outside, try the **Elbow
River Inn and Casino**, across from Lindsay Park Sports Centre and
Stampede Park, on the banks of the Elbow River. It is a few minutes'
walk from the city center. Phone (403) 269-6771 or (800) 661-1463.
    In the medium price range, try the **Carriage House Inn**, a luxury
hotel in the suburbs, at 9030 Macleod Trail S., (403) 253-1101 or (800)
661-9566. It has a pub, a sports bar, a nightclub, and a Sunday brunch
buffet. Rates are in the $100–$165 range.
    There are many options for the budget-conscious. The **Econo-
Lodge** at 2440 16th Avenue N.W., (800) 553-2666, has attractive
rooms with complimentary coffee. Rooms range from $58–$149. A
B&B with a memorable name is the **Babbling Brook Bed and
Breakfast**, at 939 124 Avenue S.W., (403) 251-0340. Its yard overlooks
a brook and walking trails and is close to Fish Creek Park. For names
of numerous other B&Bs, contact the B&B Association of Calgary, Box
1462, Station 'M', Calgary, Alberta T2E 1P3, (403) 531-0065.
    Another alternative for budget travellers between May and August
is SAIT (Southern Alberta Institute of Technology), at 1301 16th Avenue N.W., (403) 284-8013. Rates start at $15.50 per night. Then there
are hostels. **Calgary International Hostel**, at 520 7th Avenue S.E.,
(403) 269-8239, offers basic accommodations within walking distance

to many of the city's attractions. For information on other hostels, contact Southern Alberta Region, 203-1414 Kensington Road N.W., Calgary T2N 3P9, (403) 283-5551, or e-mail NAB&HostellingIntl.ca

CAMPING

With the sunniest skies in Canada and friendly people, Calgary is attractive to campers. **Camp 'n' Water Park**, RR7, Site 2, Box 504, Calgary, (403) 273-5122, fax (403) 248-5590, has 180 sites, 100 of which are open year-round. Off the highway, with pull-throughs, pay phone, coin laundry, firepits and firewood, a sanistation, waterslide and bumper board, power, water, and sewage—and only 20 minutes from the Stampede grounds or the airport (shuttle service available)—this campground east of Calgary (at the junction of Highways 1 and 1A) is a comfortable, quiet place. Rates range $13–$22.

KOA Calgary West is at the western city limits on Highway 1, at Box 10, Site 12, RR1, Calgary, T2M 4N3, (403) 288-0411, reservations (800) 562-0842, fax (403) 286-1612. Like most KOAs, it offers full hookups, tent and trailer space, RV supplies, LP gas, laundry facilities, a recreation room, heated pool, minigolf, nature walks and trails, plus shuttle services to the Stampede, downtown, the zoo, and Heritage Park. Rates are $19–$22.

Mountain View Farm Campground has 189 sites, is open year-round, and is just 3 km (2 mi) east of Calgary, at Site 8, Box 6, RR6, T2M 4N3, (403) 293-6640, fax (403) 293-4798. It has a coin phone, laundry, firewood, propane, videos, minigolf, a petting zoo, and a BBQ and dance in the evenings. It offers tours, and German is spoken. Rates run $14–$20.

Bowridge RV Park, immediately across from Canada Olympic Park at 8220 Bowridge Crescent N.W., (403) 288-4441, fax (403) 288-4441, has 50 fully serviced sites for tents or RVs, and is open year-round. Only 12 minutes from downtown; near McDonald's, Robin's Donuts, and Wendy's; and offering a shuttle service to the Stampede; it's an ideal spot. City water, showers, coin laundry, and an outdoor pool complete the picture. Rate per night is $23.50.

Calaway Park has 109 regular and 150 overflow sites, with all services available for most. It's in a country setting at RR2, Site 25, Comp 20, (403) 249-7372, yet only 10 km (6 mi) from the city, and offers a coin laundry, showers, a grocery, and shuttle service to the Stampede. Within walking distance are a driving range and Canada's largest amusement park. Rates are $15–$21.

Pine Creek RV Campground, just 1.6 km (1 mi) south of the city on Highway 2, is fully fenced, with a security gate. In a country setting near Spruce Meadows Equestrian Centre, golf courses, shopping centers, restaurants, and churches, it also offers pull-throughs, hookups, TV lounge, billiard room, horseshoe pits, pitch 'n' putt golf, and immaculate washrooms, showers, and laundry facilities. Wheelchair accessible. Box 174, De Winton, T0L 0X0, (403) 256-3002, fax (403) 254-9280. Reservations suggested. Rates quoted on inquiry.

Other campgrounds are farther out in the general area. Net surfers should check the **Internet Campground Guide**: www.AlbertaHotels.ab.ca/campgrounds

For hostels, contact Southern Alberta Region #203, 1414 Kensington Road N.W., T2N 3P9, (403) 283-5551, fax (403) 283-6503, e-mail NAB@HostellingIntl.ca

NIGHTLIFE

Calgary offers nightclubs with music (and meals) to suit just about every taste—from blues and jazz at **Mad Jack's Saloon**, 438 9th Avenue S.E., to **Electric Avenue**, on 11th Avenue. Country dancing is very popular and can be enjoyed at **Bronco Billy's**, 10440 7th Avenue S.W.; or the **Rockin' Horse Saloon**, 24-7400 Macleod Trail S., (403) 255-4646. Calgary boasts a full range of the performing arts, too. Phone (403) 270-6700 or (403) 297-8000 for detailed information about what's happening.

13
DRUMHELLER VALLEY

Drumheller, a town of some 7,000 people on the Red Deer River, is a convenient location from which to explore Alberta's Badlands. The rolling farmland east of Calgary suddenly drops from the prairie to the river through a skeleton of steep, dry canyons that Albertans call "coulees." These are the Badlands, where stark layers of multicolored rock, bared by the eroding forces of wind, water, and ice over 70 million years, tell the story of time through the fossilized remains of gargantuan creatures that once roamed this river valley.

This is Dinosaur Country, where in 1884 Joseph Tyrrell discovered the skull of a dinosaur, and where the town of Drumheller now houses the world-famous Royal Tyrrell Museum. As you look down into the arid coulees or up at the rock-capped hoodoos, it is hard to believe that this semidesert was once a forested swamp.

More than 500,000 people visit the Drumheller Valley annually. Over 50 intriguing attractions located within a 100-square-km (60-square-mi) area await them. You can return to the Badlands time and time again and still be as intrigued as the first time you visited. Drive the figure-eight Dinosaur Trail, hike, or perhaps golf in the middle of these weird rock formations. You might also watch a dig in progress (or participate yourself), or let your children enjoy the thrill of an afternoon's actual excavation at an advertised day camp. ◼

DRUMHELLER VALLEY

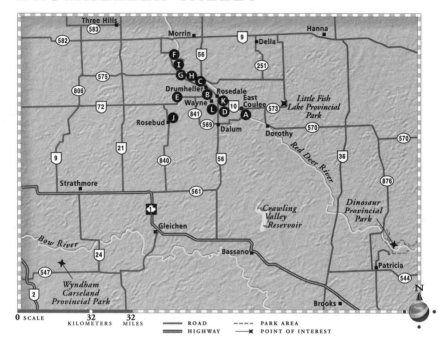

Sights

- **A** Atlas Coal Mine Museum
- **B** Canadian Badlands Passion Play
- **B** Drumheller Dinosaur and Fossil Museum
- **A** East Coulee
- **C** Homestead Antique Museum
- **D** Hoodoos
- **E** Horseshoe Canyon
- **F** Horsethief Canyon
- **G** Little Church

- **H** McMullen Island in Midland Provincial Park
- **I** North Dinosaur Trail
- **B** Reptile World
- **J** Rosebud Theatre
- **K** Rosedale and the Swinging Suspension Bridge
- **H** Royal Tyrrell Museum
- **L** Wayne

Note: Items with the same letter are located in the same town or area.

A PERFECT DAY IN THE DRUMHELLER VALLEY

My perfect day in Dinosaur Country begins in the morning at the Royal Tyrrell Museum and the afternoon on either or both of the loop drives. On my way to the museum, I let my imagination run wild. How did this barren, moon-like world look when clothed in forests and swamps? How did it sound with the bellows of huge, rampaging beasts? Once inside the museum, I gaze enraptured at the immense creatures towering over me and realize how insignificant any of us really are. Every time I visit I have to pull myself away from each exhibit, hurrying to the next visual, the next simulation, the next explanation, or the next development in the passage of time—there's so much else to be seen.

Out on the first loop drive, there's the luxuriance of Prehistoric Park; on the second loop are famous hoodoo sandstone columns and abandoned creations of Rosebud Man. As I cook my evening steak on the Rosedeer Hotel's barbecue, I wonder, how long before we are the subjects of discovery, excavation, and conjecture?

SIGHTSEEING HIGHLIGHTS

★★★ **Canadian Badlands Passion Play**—Portraying the life and passion of Jesus Christ, the Passion Play is set in an outdoor amphitheater just south of Drumheller, where you'll be seated quite comfortably on wooden-backed benches. Including intermission, the performance takes all of three hours and has been described as a "life-changing and moving experience."

Cold drinks are provided in the amphitheater before the play and during intermission, and there are ample washroom facilities, indoors and out. The main building is wheelchair accessible; if you have any handicapped or special needs, inform the office at the time of booking. Tickets go on sale at the beginning of November at the Passion Play office and may be purchased by cash, check, Visa, or MasterCard. Seating is assigned, and tickets are mailed to you after payment. A free ticket is given to each group purchasing 15 or more. Details: Tickets: Adults $15, children under 13 $7.50, no GST. For tickets and location of amphitheater, contact the Canadian Badlands Passion Play Society, Box 457, Drumheller, T0J 0Y0; (403) 823-7750, fax (403) 823-8170. (3 hours)

★★★ **Horseshoe Canyon**—This is most visitors' first experience of the area as they drive north on Highway 9 from the Trans-Canada, where a typically straight and seemingly never-ending prairie road takes a sudden, sharp right turn at a rough-grassed parking lot overlooking the site. For others, it may be their last look as they leave, since this is the only road in and out of the area. Although the canyon can be viewed almost from your vehicle, it's best to walk down to its floor to really appreciate the sedimentary strata and alternating layers of volcanic ash that form the steeply banked cliffs. Hiking, walking, and scrambling up and down are very popular in this area, but take special care! In wet weather these badland slopes become treacherous. The soil is actually bentonitic clay, used in lubricating oil drills and (hold your breath!) in manufacturing toothpaste and cosmetics. When wet, this clay can swell to ten times its volume, becoming soggy glue. In such weather it's unwise (to say the least) to park or drive off the road—your car may well remain "glued" there until conditions are much drier.

If you walk for any distance or time, always take a canteen of water—temperatures are often considerably hotter "down there" in the canyon or coulee. But do walk. It's an experience well worth the time, effort, and perspiration. (1 hour)

★★★ **Little Church on Loop #2**—Situated near the Royal Tyrrell Museum is the Little Church, also called the Chapel of Contemplation. On the rare occasion I was alone there, I experienced a most peaceful aura. This tiny church is visited by tens of thousands of people a year— just six at a time. (15 minutes)

★★★ **Loop Drives**—Two scenic loops can actually form a figure-eight drive, though they are distinct. One, 60 km (37 mi) long, follows the north bank of the Red Deer River Valley; the other returns along the south bank. The road passes McMullen Island, the Little Church, a canoe rental site, and a go-kart track. It changes direction suddenly as it reaches **Horsethief Canyon**. Here are the best views of the multilayered cliffs so typical of these Badlands. Another two sharp turns later and the road drops almost into the Red Deer River. The little cable-operated **Bleriot Ferry** (free) will take you across to a sharp climb up to the flats and **Orkney Viewpoint**, where marvelous photographic views of the Red Deer River Valley may be captured; then on to Drumheller Prehistoric Park's short but intriguing walks and its many lookouts.

Take Highway 10 between Drumheller and Rosedale for the start of the second loop, then turn onto Highway 10X. The road winds and weaves along and across the Rosebud River (a tributary of the Red Deer River), using 11 uniquely narrow bridges in a very short distance (sufficiently unique that this stretch of road and bridges is featured in *Ripley's Believe it or Not*). At the small community of **Wayne**—where the films *Running Brave*, *Draw*, and *2001: A Space Odyssey* were filmed—the whole family can safely enjoy the "pleasures" of the Wild Horse Saloon. Highway 569 then takes you from Dalum to the **Atlas Coal Mine Museum**, a provincially designated historic site with guided tours available. This is close to **East Coulee**, a coal-mining town with a museum and cultural center in the old school, where you can muse on the mining equipment used years ago and see what a 1930s "high style school" was like.

When you begin the return run on Highway 10, you'll soon see the **Hoodoos** off to your right. These spectacular rock formations result from the erosive force of thousands of years of wind and weather, and are "capped" by harder rock. Picnic facilities are available here for rest and contemplation. Continue on to Rosedale to see the unique **Swinging Suspension Bridge** (originally built without "sides") that miners crossed to work in the now-buried Star Coal Mine, and imagine yourself walking across *that!* A cable-trolley system was installed later so coal cars could also be transported across more easily—not, one gathers, for the miners' safety. If you have time, turn north from Rosedale, then west for a short distance on Highway 576, where a buffalo herd grazes. (1 hour)

★★★ McMullen Island in Midland Provincial Park on Loop #1— McMullen Island is a rare and delightful surprise after the area's barren drylands. This cool, natural, and lushly vegetated microcosm of another world lies to the right as you drive from Drumheller to the Royal Tyrrell Museum. Details: Within Midland Provincial Park, beside the highway. Free. (1 hour)

★★★ Rosebud and the Rosebud Theatre—Open year-round, the Rosebud Theatre is a popular place for dinner and entertainment. Country-style meals are served accompanied by live music, then guests enjoy either family theater or a variety show in the Rosebud Opera House. Other local attractions are Akoiniskway Gallery, Rosebud Craft Shop, and the Centennial Museum. A visit to Rosebud makes a very pleasant break from a vacation's often-all-too-hectic pace. Because of the great popularity of these dinner shows, purchase your tickets early; contact the box office (open Monday through Saturday 9 a.m. to 5 p.m.) by phone at (800) 267-7553 from Alberta, (403) 677-2350 from elsewhere, or fax (403) 677-2390.

Show dates: March 17 through June 3, June 9 through June 24, July 14 through September 30, and November 10 through December 23. Admission includes dinner: Adults $27 for the matinee, $30 for the evening show, with special rates for children. (3–4 hours)

★★★ **Royal Tyrrell Museum**—This world-famous complex always fascinates me. It displays life-size models, full skeletons, fossils, hands-on exhibits, computer simulations, films, a preparation laboratory, and an indoor science garden that illustrate millions of years of geological and biological progressions, all of which are updated as soon as new information becomes available. Good free parking, a cafeteria, and a picnic area are available; an excellent souvenir/bookstore keeps browsers browsing. It is possible—advisable for a first visit—to have a guided tour by appointment (phone ahead for reservation), but audio guides are available, too. Details: On Highway 838, 6 km (4 mi) north-west of Drumheller; (403) 823-7707, fax (403) 823-7131; open daily Victoria Day weekend (usually the third weekend in May) through Labor Day (first Monday in September) 9 a.m. to 9 p.m.; the rest of the year Tuesday through Sunday 10 a.m. to 5 p.m.; closed December 25. Admission: Adults $6.50, seniors $5.50, ages 7–17 $3, families $15. (minimum 3 hours)

★★ **Drumheller Dinosaur and Fossil Museum**—What was the original Dinosaur Museum has particularly interesting exhibits: a duck-billed dinosaur *(Edmontosaurus)*, an ice age bison *(Occidentalis)* skull in which a rounded stone is embedded (was there a *David* living in North America in those days?), and the first intact *Pachyrhinosaurus* skull ever found. Many Indian artifacts are also displayed among the other attention-piqueing facets of the "time that was." Details: 335 1st Street E.; (403) 823-2593; open July through August 10 a.m. to 6 p.m. and May, June, September, and October 10 a.m. to 5 p.m. Admission: Adults $2, seniors $1, ages 6–18 75 cents. (1 hour)

★★ **Homestead Antique Museum**—If you've ever wondered about how Grandpa or Grandma *really* lived, this museum contains more than 4,000 catalogued items of their time. Details: 901 N. Dinosaur

Trail on Highway 9; (403) 823-2600; open daily mid-June through Labor Day 9 a.m. to 8 p.m., and mid-May through mid-June and September 5 through October 9 9 a.m. to 6 p.m. Admission: Adults $3, seniors and students $2. (1 hour)

★★ **Reptile World**—Here are more than 150 reptiles and amphibians, some of which are the rarest in the world. Have a hands-on experience if you dare. Allow an hour minimum, much more if you have children. Details: 1222 Highway 9 S.; (403) 823-8623; open daily June 1 through October 31 10 a.m. to 10 p.m.; the rest of the year 10 a.m. to 6 p.m. Admission: Adults $3.95, seniors and ages 4–16 $2.75. (1–2 hours)

FITNESS AND RECREATION

Drumheller has good hiking, swimming, fishing, and golfing; and some campsites and parks have fitness trails.

Back to Nature Trail Rides, (403) 823-8760, offers hourly guided tours through scenic spruce coulees where deer, birds, and beaver are likely to be found. Rustic camping is also available. The outfit is 28 km (18 mi) from Drumheller and open daily May through fall.

Badlands Adventure Tours (contact them through the Wild Horse Saloon in Wayne, 403-823-4555) offers mountain bike and canoe rentals; horseback and raft tours down the Red Deer River; ranch barbecues; and serviced and nonserviced camping.

ESPECIALLY FOR KIDS

Badlands Go-Kart Park, (403) 823-7352, with over 1,700 feet of track, gives a fast, fun ride. It's on the North Dinosaur Trail, 4 km (2.4 mi) west of the Royal Tyrrell Museum, and is open all week from the May long weekend through September 10 a.m. to 9 p.m. Youngsters can let off steam at **Funland Amusements**, between Drumheller and the museum. Nearby **Drumheller Aquaplex** will then let them cool off before bedtime while Mom and Dad relax in a hot tub. Both are open daily.

FOOD

Despite its small size, Drumheller has a good variety of restaurants, ranging from Greek to Chinese to Western, with the usual fast-food outlets for the famished. Smorgasbord lunches are reasonably priced.

DRUMHELLER VALLEY

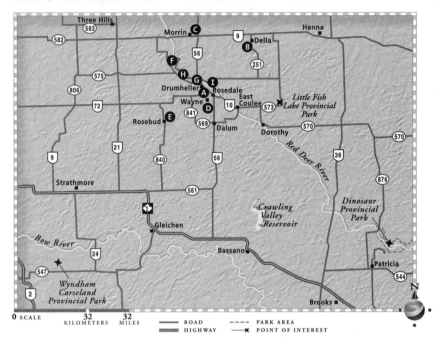

Food

- **A** Diana Restaurant
- **A** Drumheller Elks Clubrooms
- **A** Drumheller Inn
- **A** Fred and Barney's Family Restaurant
- **A** Jack's Bistro
- **B** Mother's Mountain Tea House and Country Store
- **C** Prairie Inn
- **D** Rosedeer Hotel and Last Chance Saloon
- **A** Stavros Family Restaurant
- **A** Yavis Family Restaurant

Lodging

- **A** Alexandra International Hostel
- **A** Badlands Motel

Lodging *(continued)*

- **A** Drumheller Inn
- **A** Inn at Heartwood Manor
- **A** Newcastle Country Inn
- **E** Rosebud Country Inn and Tea Room B&B
- **A** Taste the Past B&B
- **A** Victorian House B&B

Camping

- **F** Bleriot Ferry Provincial Recreation Area
- **G** Dinosaur Trailer Park
- **H** Dinosaur Trail RV Resort
- **A** River Grove Campground and Cabins
- **I** Wild Horse Saloon Campground

Note: Items with the same letter are located in the same town or area.

At **Diana Restaurant**, 388 Centre Street, (403) 823-3030, you'll find mostly Chinese dishes, but there are Western dishes, too. All are good portions and served in a comfortable setting. At 54 Centre Street are the **Drumheller Elks Clubrooms**, (403) 823-2494, where you can enjoy a smorgasbord or a good hot meal for $6 and up. **Fred and Barney's Family Restaurant**, 1222 Highway 9 South, (403) 823-3803, is another excellent smorgasbord spot, offering a selection of 45 items including soup, salad bar, and a wide variety of Chinese and Western foods for $7.95 lunch or $9.95 dinner. **Jack's Bistro**, 70 Railway Avenue East, (403) 823-8422, is a small cafe serving excellent pasta and really good meals starting at $5.

The **Drumheller Inn**, 100 South Railway Avenue S.E., (403) 823-8400, has a delightfully elegant Skylight Dining Room with a bar. Meals here are excellent and run $8–$25. For Greek and Western dishes, the **Stavros Family Restaurant**, 190 Railway Avenue W., (403) 823-6362, is tops, with meals at $8–$15. The **Yavis Family Restaurant**, in the Valley Plaza Shopping Centre, (403) 823-8317, has a family area rather like a European roadside cafe, along with the Prop Room, a lounge, sports bar, and pool room decorated with an aircraft propeller. Awesome burgers are served here, according to enthusiastic locals. Entrees run $6.65–$15.45, with special dishes for seniors and children.

Mother's Mountain Tea House and Country Store, just northeast of Drumheller, 102 First Avenue West, Delia, (403) 364-2057, spent two years restoring an old Crown Lumber building to its former glory, now complete with antique furniture and gleaming maple floors. Breads, soups, sandwiches, salads, and light meals are freshly homemade, whether for family orders, groups, or whole busloads. Entrees range $7–$10. The Tea House is wheelchair accessible. The store is filled with craft items from around Alberta and prides itself on old-fashioned country atmosphere. The owners speak English, German, and French.

Rosedeer Hotel and Last Chance Saloon, 1 Jewel Street, Wayne, (403) 823-9189, wants your steak to be done the way you like it, so you have the option of doing it yourself! Decor includes such memorabilia as a boar's head, stuffed rattlesnakes, traps, and music boxes.

The **Prairie Inn** in Morrin, where you can also see a prairie sod house, is reputed to serve the best hamburgers in the world—huge, yet priced at only $6.75.

LODGING

The **Inn at Heartwood Manor**, 320 N. Railway Avenue, (403) 823-6495, is an outstanding place to stay in Drumheller. It looks a bit garish from the outside but is warm and comfortable inside. All ten of its rooms have private baths, nine have whirlpool tubs, five have fireplaces, and two have wheelchair access. Rates run $79–$120 and include a large pancake breakfast. The Inn also offers a full spa, with emphasis on Asian healing arts; packages include a full-body massage, makeovers, pedicures, glamour photography, and manicures.

The **Drumheller Inn**, 100 S. Railway Avenue (Highway 9), (403) 823-8400, fax (403) 823-5020, is a large complex with 100 rooms. **Newcastle Country Inn**, 1130 Newcastle Trail, (403) 823-8356, fax (403) 823-2458, has 11 air-conditioned rooms and offers a complimentary breakfast with rates of $49–$89.

Apart from its comfortable rooms, the **Badlands Motel**, in a country setting at 801 Dinosaur Trail, (403) 823-5155, fax (403) 823-7653, is so well known for its WHIFS (Waffles, Hamburgers, Ice cream, Flapjacks, and Salads) that there are big lines on Sundays. A train set hangs from the ceiling to delight the many youngsters eating here.

Drumheller also has interesting and historic B&Bs. **Taste the Past B&B**, 281 2nd Street W., (403) 823-5889, was built by a Drumheller coal baron in the early 1900s. It's an original mansion, with each room decorated in period antiques. Rates range from $55 single to $65 double. **Victorian House B&B**, 541 Riverside Drive W., (403) 823-3535, overlooks the Red Deer River and the Badlands. Rates are reasonable, ranging from $40 single to $65 double. **Rosebud Country Inn and Tea Room B&B**, on Highway 840 in the village of Rosebud near the popular Rosebud Theatre, (403) 677-2211, is a beautiful place in which each of the ten bedrooms has a queen sleigh bed, antique furnishings, private bath, and balcony with scenic view. Rates are $79–$99. For information about other B&Bs in the area, write Drumheller B&B Association, Box 865, Drumheller, Alberta T0J 0Y0.

The **Alexandra International Hostel**, 30 Railway Avenue North, (403) 823-1749, is a lively place that fits the budget and provides the conviviality for which such international accommodations are known.

CAMPING

These are all pleasantly quiet and offer scenic walks particularly suited for late afternoons or evenings. Both **Dinosaur Trailer Park**, (403) 823-9333, and **Dinosaur Trail RV Resort**, (403) 823-3291, are along Dinosaur Trail North; **River Grove Campground and Cabins**, (403) 823-6655, is on Poplar Street, just north of the bridge in town. Each sits alongside a river, which adds to the walks' scenery.

The **Wild Horse Saloon Campground** in Rosealee, south of Drumheller, is also on a river, as is the **Bleriot Ferry Provincial Recreation Area**, northwest of Drumheller.

SIDE TRIP: DINOSAUR PROVINCIAL PARK

Dinosaur Provincial Park is a natural preserve that is designated a UNESCO World Heritage Site because of the richness and diversity of the 35 dinosaur species (75 million years old) already found there, as well as those still embedded in its deeply eroded Badlands. Indeed, the fossilized remains of nearly 300 species of Cretaceous-period animals and plants have been discovered here. Many of the specimens displayed in the Royal Tyrrell Museum came from here, and the museum conducts major digs every summer in this area.

The park covers over 7,300 hectares (more than 18,000 acres) with self-guiding trails to reveal its natural and cultural history. Lying alongside the Red Deer River, the park is approximately 150 km (95 mi) southwest of the Royal Tyrrell, but it's well worth the additional driving distance or taking one of the special interpretive tours, some of which are wheelchair accessible.

The **Badlands Bus Tour** takes you on a two-hour ride (led by a park staff member) into the very heart of Dinosaur Provincial Park to see and hear what's so unique about it—and why it's a World Heritage Site. Because not all of the buses can accommodate wheelchairs, phone ahead, (403) 387-4342, to make necessary arrangements.

The **Centrosaurus Bone Bed Hike** takes some two-plus hours and goes to a weirdly shaped area about the size of a football field, where you see firsthand one of the world's most exciting excavation sites. The **Fossil Safari Hunt** is also a two-plus-hour hike to a micro-vertebrate fossil site in the Natural Preserve to see fossils and discover exciting new facts about the creatures that lived in this river delta 75 million years ago. Guides lead both of these hikes. Remember to wear proper walking shoes and a hat, and bring sunscreen, binoculars, a camera, and water.

Tickets for these three tours are sold at the Field Station (located in Dinosaur Provincial Park) at 8:30 a.m. for the morning tour and 12:30 p.m. for the afternoon tour. Tours are limited to 17 to 24 participants, so in July and August especially, plan to arrive 30 minutes early. Tickets cost $4.50 adults and $2.25 ages 6–17; youths under 6 are free but require a ticket stub.

Further information is available from the Bookings Officer, Royal Tyrrell Museum, P.O. Box 7500, Drumheller, T0J 0Y0, (403) 823-7707, fax (403) 823-7131, e-mail rtmp@dns.magtech.ab.ca

14
KANANASKIS COUNTRY

Albertans consider Kananaskis to be "God's own country," 4,250 square km (1,540 square mi) of wilderness and a prime four-season recreational area that is easily accessible from Calgary. But most people drive right by it as they hurtle along the Trans-Canada to Banff and Lake Louise. Until the Winter Olympics were held in 1988 in Calgary and Canmore, the region was little known except by Calgarians. Now, as Banff and Jasper National Parks become increasingly overcrowded, Kananaskis continues to attract attention.

Kananaskis begins just south of Highway 1, and extends south on Highway 40 to the intersection of Highways 532 and 940. It encompasses three provincial parks—Bow Valley, Peter Lougheed, and Bragg Creek. On its outskirts are the artists' colony of Bragg Creek and the service center of Canmore. Parts of Highway 40, the park's main thoroughfare, are closed December 1 through June 15.

"Kananaskis" means "a meeting of the waters." The Bow and Kananaskis Rivers and their tributaries provided the corridor that led Captain John Palliser through the Rockies between 1857 and 1860, just as they had the aboriginal peoples over 10,000 years before. Except for Kananaskis Village, there are no townsites, no thousands of international tourists looking for shops and quick scenery fixes. Rather, the area has abundant and unparalled opportunities to appreciate the outdoors. Once, after a painful slog up a mountain in Sheep Valley behind a pack of barking hounds, I looked up a tree and saw three wild cougars—a thrilling experience. ◼

KANANASKIS COUNTRY

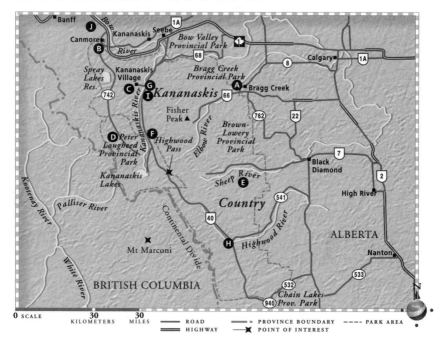

Sights

- **A** Bragg Creek
- **B** Canmore
- **C** Kananaskis Village
- **D** Peter Lougheed Provincial Park
- **E** Sheep River Valley

Food

- **F** Boulton Creek Trading Post
- **G** Boundary Ranch
- **B** Drake Hotel
- **B** Fireside Inn

Food (continued)

- **B** Gasthaus Restaurant
- **H** Highwood House
- **I** Kananaskis Golf Course
- **J** Lady Macdonald Teahouse
- **C** Lodge at Kananaskis
- **D** Mt. Engadine Lodge
- **B** Rose and Crown
- **B** Sinclair's

Note: Items with the same letter are located in the same town or area.

A PERFECT DAY IN KANANASKIS COUNTRY

Choose a day in mid-September, when crowds have thinned, the skies are deep sapphire blue, and the fall leaves are most intense. And prepare to move like a whirlwind. You could drive through Kananaskis Country from Canmore to Canmore via Highway 40 in three hours—but don't. Start at the northern end where Highway 1 meets Highway 40 and head south along the Kananaskis River, a route called the Kananaskis Trail.

Take time to notice how the palette of color changes, from the lime gold poplars of the valley to the blood red of willows to the burnt gold of the alpine larches. In Peter Lougheed Provincial Park, turn right at the Kananaskis Lake Trail on a 40-minute detour to the parking lot between Upper and Lower Kananaskis Lakes for one of the day's many "Kodak Moments"—the view to the southwest of mountain-framed Mangen Glacier. Back down Highway 40, take the gravel road to the left over Elpoca Creek for another short detour. Stop near the bridge and look up at the cliff face for mountain goats. Another rewarding stop is further south along Highway 40 through the Highwood Pass, which, at 2,206 meters (7,280 ft), is the highest drivable pass in Canada. Take the 5.6-km (3.5-mi), 1½-hour Ptarmigan Cirque Trail on the left side of the road. Beside the stepped waterfalls, you're likely to see hoary marmots and lots of fossils. Back at your car, stop for pie or muffins and coffee at nearby Highwood House. Complete the loop back to Canmore or Calgary through the cattle and cowboy country of the foothills.

GETTING AROUND KANANASKIS COUNTRY

The following contacts will help you get around the area: Barrier Lake Information Centre, (403) 673-3985; Kananaskis Village Information Centre, (403) 591-7555; Peter Lougheed Provincial Park Information Centre, (403) 591-6344; Kananaskis Country Headquarters, (403) 297-3362. Ron Chamney, Visitor Information Coordinator and member of an organization called the Friends of Kananaskis, is a particularly useful contact. You can reach him at (403) 678-5508 or www/world-web.com/ kananaskis

SIGHTSEEING HIGHLIGHTS

★★★ **Kananaskis Village**—This is less a village than a central square surrounded by three ritzy hotels and impeccably landscaped grounds with ponds, waterfalls, and gardens: the **Lodge at Kananaskis** and **Hotel Kananaskis**, both part of the Canadian Pacific (CP) Hotels and Resorts chain, (800) 441-1414, and the **Kananaskis Inn Best Western**, (800) 528-1234. Kids from the Calgary Children's Hospital visit before ice-up each year to fish out the rainbow trout that are stocked in the hotel ponds in the spring. The only mail address you need to know is Kanaskis Village, Alberta T0L 2H0.

Adjacent to the hotels is the Village Centre, which consists of a convenience store, a leisure center, a sports equipment rental shop, the start of interconnected hiking and skating trails, and a 36-hole championship golf course. **Kananaskis Country Golf Course** was designed by Robert Trent Jones, who planned every tee shot to line up with a different mountain peak. Every drive is a painting, making it difficult to keep your eyes on the ball. Locals advise players at the fourth hole on the Mount Lorette side of the course to watch out for grizzly bears. They've been seen on the slopes above the course and could be another reason why it's difficult to keep your eyes on that ball. Rates for 18 holes range from $31 for a senior Canadian resident to $45 for a nonresident adult. For tee times, call (403) 591-7272.

About five minutes from the Village Centre off Highway 40 is the **Nakiska Ski Area**, on Mount Allan, (403) 591-7777, which was one of the venues for the 1988 Calgary Winter Olympics. Winter activities include downhill and cross-country skiing, skating, sleighriding, and dogsledding. In summer, use the trails for hiking and biking. Details: Address: Box 100, Kananaskis Village, Alberta T0L 2H0; (403) 591-7495; open year-round. (½ day; 2 days if golfing)

★★★ **Peter Lougheed Provincial Park**—At more than 500 square km, this was the largest provincial park in Alberta until the recent declaration of the Elbow-Sheep Wildlife Provincial Park, also in Kananaskis Country and now a globally recognized Special Place. Glacial streams, evergreen valleys, clear sparkling lakes, and towering mountains leave an indelible impression. Go to the Park Visitor Centre for orientation, maps, and detailed information on trails and campsites. The hiking trails vary from barrier-free trails for persons limited in mobility to high alpine back-country adventures. There are 85 km (53 mi) of groomed cross-country ski trails, 12 km (7.5 mi) of paved biking trails, and one equestrian trail. Campgrounds vary from rustic walk-in tent-type to pull-through trailer sites. See "A Perfect Day" for suggested activities. For a bite to eat, stop in at the Boulton Creek Trading Post and Highwood House. Details: Phone (403) 591-7226 for campground reservations or (403) 591-6345 for the Visitor Centre.

One of the most special places in Peter Lougheed (and perhaps the world) is **William Watson Lodge**, a special needs facility that provides accommodations in a mountain setting for people with physical, mental, or sensory limitations. The lodge has eight cabins that house two to four apartments, all of which are self-contained and wheelchair accessible at a cost of $25–$35 a night for up to eight people. It has two campgrounds, one with plug-ins that have oxygen units to recharge wheelchair batteries. Reservations are essential. Details: Box 130, Kananskis Village, Alberta T0L 2H0; (403) 591-7227. (minimum 1 day)

✹✹ **Sheep River Valley**—It's known for its abundance of bighorn sheep, which you can easily see grazing in the valley or scrambling up the rocks on either side of the river. Bighorn Lookout in the Sheep River Wildlife Sanctuary has a meadow observation blind overlooking a popular bighorn gathering site. Because of its varied wildlife—sheep, cougars, ground squirrels, dippers, grouse—the University of Calgary established a Biological Field Station here. Details: Information Centre, Bag 1, Bragg Creek, Alberta T0L 0K0; (403) 933-7172. Or contact Fish and Wildlife in Calgary at (403) 297-6423. (½ day)

✹ **Bragg Creek**—The rural hamlet Bragg Creek lies just 40 km (25 mi) southwest of Calgary on Highway 22, and it's been a year-round recreation mecca for Calgarians since the 1920s. It is still a favorite weekend drive for city dwellers, but it has now developed into a shopping and cultural center as well. Its main street, known as Heritage Mile, is lined with craftshops, antique emporiums, and restaurants. It has several bed and breakfasts and a popular restaurant, Barbecue Steak Pit, 43 White Avenue, (403) 949-3633. In mid-November, Bragg Creek puts on an Artisans' Arts and Crafts Show and Sale. (½ day)

✹ **Canmore**—In 1883 Canmore was a coal-mining region. Today it is a fast-growing service center or jumping-off point for attractions in Kananaskis Country and Banff National Park. It is just off Highway 1, or the Trans-Canada, the major artery into the Rockies. Leave the business strip and browse around the shops, eateries, ponds, and pathways of the **Towne Center**. Park at the IGA grocery store and walk the **Boardwalk Trail** along Policeman's Creek to look for birds and watch ducks. In fall, you'll see monster 3-foot brown trout in this skinny waterway. Also in fall, watch for migrating golden eagles; 7,500 a year have been counted in Canmore. The **Canmore Nordic Centre**, with its 56 km (35 mi) of groomed woodland skiing, biking, hiking, and orienteering trails, was built for the 1988 Winter Olympics. The Nordic Centre is on the Smith Dorrien/Spray Trail. Phone (403) 678-2400. Details: Canmore is in the Kananaskis' northwest corner, near Banff and alongside the Trans-Canada Highway. (½ day)

FITNESS AND RECREATIION

There's lots to keep you fit in Kananaskis Country; the whole region is geared toward physical activity, both indoors and outdoors in all seasons. Major activities are skiing and hiking but there's probably nothing you can't do here—either independently or as part of an organized group. Facilities such as **Nakiska**, at Mount Allan, adjacent to Kananaskis Village, (403) 591-7777, **Canmore Nordic Centre**, (403) 678-2400, and **Fortress Mountain**, near Peter Lougheed Provincial Park, (403) 591-7108 or 264-5825, are modern, all-encompassing, and well-organized. To get the flavor of Kananaskis Country, make sure to walk a trail, ski a slope, ride a horse, and kayak a lake; if you can, climb a peak, too. I would try trekking with llamas and **Bragg Creek Tours and Travels**, (403) 949-3400. Others won't want to miss golfing at **Kananaskis Country Golf Course**, adjacent to the Lodge at Kananaskis, (403) 591-7071.

FOOD

You'll dine well in luxurious surroundings amid spectacular mountain scenery at any of the restaurants in either of the two CP Hotels in Kananaskis Village. Sunday brunch for $19.95 at The Peaks in the **Lodge at Kananaskis**, (403) 591-7171, is especially recommended. At other times, watch for specials if price is important. Meals at the

Kananaskis Golf Course, (403) 591-7070, are quite reasonable considering its country club atmosphere. A large bowl of seafood chowder is good value for around $5, and a bonus is the possibility of seeing grizzly bears from the clubhouse windows. You can have pheasant under glass inside and grizzlies through glass outside!

You won't find the following restaurants advertised in the glossy magazines, but they are places locals swear by. They say the food, service, and scenery at the **Boulton Creek Trading Post**, the Kananskis Lakes Trail in Peter Lougheed Provincial Park, (403) 591-7678, is as good as anywhere. The menu is standard burgers, lasagne, pizza, and roast chicken, but you can get a lunch for $6–$11, and the servers take the trouble to recognize clients and make them feel welcome. Try the rhubarb strawberry muffins and chocolate cake served regularly at **Highwood House**, at the junction of Highwood with Highway 40, also in Peter Lougheed Park, (403) 558-2144. Also highly praised are the barbecued steaks and cowboy fare of beans, buns, and spuds at the **Boundary Ranch**, on the east side of Highway 40 near Kananaskis Village, (403) 591-7171. And locals like dining on the deck of **Mt. Engadine Lodge**, on the Spray Lake Road, (403) 678-2880, because the setting in this wildest part of Kananaskis Country is so incredible.

Canmore is said to have more restaurants per capita than anywhere else in North America and, compared to Banff and Calgary, prices are very reasonable. The best deal in town is lunch at the **Drake Hotel**, 909 Railway Avenue, (403) 678-5131. Lunch specials, including homemade soup, salads or fries, and entrees such as *nasi goreng* and calamari, average $5.95, and the portions are large. Those who like plates heaped with bacon and eggs with their coffee for $3–$4 go to the **Fireside Inn**, at 718 8th Street, (403) 678-9570 or (403) 678-6677. For a friendly English pub atmosphere, though not necessarily English food (which to this writer is a plus), try the **Rose and Crown**, at 749 Railway Avenue, Canmore, (403)678-5168.

My favorite dining experience in Kananaskis Country is to take a helicopter ride with Mountain Wings Helicopters, (403) 678-4848 or (403) 678-486, from Canmore up a nearby mountain to the **Lady Macdonald Teahouse** for afternoon tea or a sunset supper.

The **Gasthaus Restaurant**, 1723 Mountain Avenue, Canmore, (403) 678-5000, serves authentic European cuisine in a cozy atmosphere. Try Bavarian liver dumpling soup, grilled bratwurst or schnitzel, followed by hot apple strudel. Enjoy mountain views, casual

KANANASKIS COUNTRY

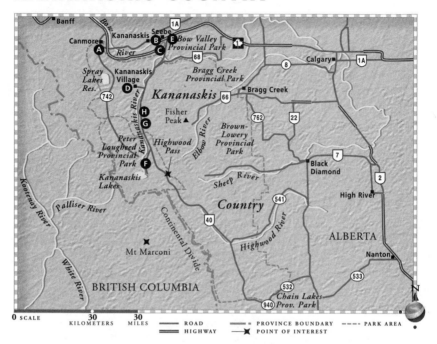

Lodging

- Ⓐ A-1 Motel
- Ⓑ Bow Valley Motel
- Ⓒ Brewster's Kananaskis Guest Ranch
- Ⓒ High Country B&B
- Ⓓ Hotel Kananaskis
- Ⓓ Kananaskis Inn Best Western
- Ⓐ Kiska Inn B&B
- Ⓓ Lodge at Kananaskis
- Ⓔ Rafter Six Ranch Resort
- Ⓓ Ribbon Creek Hostel
- Ⓐ Stockade Log Cabins

Camping

- Ⓕ Boulton Creek Campground
- Ⓕ Canyon Campground
- Ⓕ Cataract Campground
- Ⓕ Elkwood Campground
- Ⓕ Interlakes Campground
- Ⓕ Lower Lake Campground
- Ⓖ Mt. Kidd RV Park
- Ⓕ Mount Sarrail Campground
- Ⓗ Sundance Lodges and RV Park

Note: Items with the same letter are located in the same town or area.

elegance, and innovative cuisine at **Sinclair's,** 637 8th Street, Canmore, (403) 678-5370. Here you can select from a varied menu made from fresh ingredients. Lunch and dinner are served from 11 a.m., and entrees are $6–$16. Reservations are advised.

LODGING

If you can't camp, pick a place with an intimate view of mountains close to outdoor activities. New accommodations and restaurants are being developed all the time that cater to visitors as well as such new residents as Arnold Schwarzenegger. The three big all-season hotels are in Kananaskis Village: The **Lodge at Kananaskis,** (403) 591-7171, **Hotel Kananaskis,** (403)591-7711, and the **Kananaskis Inn Best Western** (403) 591-7500. Rates vary from $220-$550 in the CP Hotels and $85-$295 at the Best Western.

A more authentic Western feel is found at **Brewster's Kananaskis Guest Ranch,** 2 km (1.3 mi) from the Trans-Canada Highway in Seebe, (403) 673-3737 or (800) 691-5085. It's an oldie but a goodie. It belongs to the famous Brewster family, some of whom took the tourist route from carriages to buses, and others of whom stayed in horses. From your renovated turn-of-the-century cabin or chalet, you can go horse-back-riding, rafting, jet-boating, heli-hiking, and fly-fishing in addition to the usual hotel amenities of swimming in the pool or soaking in the hot tub. The Brewsters can handle group barbecues of up to 1,200 people—fancy events that include rodeos, gunfighters, cowboy poets, and native dancers. Ten-day packages are available, but daily rates range $70–$170.

The **Rafter Six Ranch Resort,** 2 km (1.3 mi) south of the Trans-Canada at the Seebe exit, (403) 673-3622, also has a heritage atmo-sphere and Western feel. In fact, its motto is "Where the West Stays Alive." It consists of a log lodge and cabins and offers trail and pack trips, hay and carriage rides, an antique photo parlor, and a dance hall. Another attraction is their Passing of the Legends Museum, which houses native and pioneer relics.

For economy and some character, try **Stockade Log Cabins,** Box 575, in the Canmore–Harvie Heights part of town, (403) 678-5212. Cabins cost between $68–$98 a night. For plain economy, try the **A-1 Motel,** Box 339, Canmore, (403) 678-5200, where rates go from $35-$65. The **Bow Valley Motel** in Canmore has similar rates, (800) 665-8189.

There are many B&Bs in Canmore. Reserve through a registry such as **High Country B&B**, Box 772, Turner Valley, (888) 509-1965. The themed rooms in **Kiska Inn B&B**, at Deadman's Flats in Canmore, are intriguing. So is Kiska's decadent hot gourmet breakfasts such as stuffed fruit crepes drizzled with a special chocolate sauce. Contact Kiska at (888) 533-7188 or www.info&kiska.ab.ca on the Internet. Rates range from $85–$110. A useful hostel located on the access road to Kananaskis Village is **Ribbon Creek Hostel**, (403) 762-4122. Rates are $12 for members, $16 for nonmembers.

CAMPING

As expected, there are lots of campgrounds in Kananaskis Country. Most are not fancy, but you go to this region for the outdoor experience, not for the sophistication of the campsite. There are six campgrounds in Peter Lougheed Provincial Park, (403) 591-7226. Families prefer the two largest ones—**Boulton Creek** and **Elkwood**—which have tap water and amphitheaters that put on award-winning interpretations. The others—**Canyon, Cataract, Interlakes, Lower Lake,** and **Mount Sarrail**—are smaller, pump water, and sell firewood.

Mt. Kidd RV Park, on Highway 40, 28 km (17.5 mi) south of the Trans-Canada near Kananaskis Village, is more of a resort than a campground. This is high-end camping. It offers facilities for every possible type of recreational vehicle, or tenter, many designed for winter use. The park features saunas, showers, whirlpool, game room, lounge, and fast-food counter inside—and tennis courts, bicycle and walking paths, children's play areas, wading pool, and outdoor amphitheatre. Mt. Kidd even has a gift shop, an arcade, and banking. Box 1000, Kananaskis Village, Alberta T0L 2H0, (403) 591-7700, open year-round.

Sundance Lodges (Tipis) and RV Park, (403) 591-7122, on Highway 40, 21 km (13 mi) south of the Trans-Canada near Kananaskis Village, offers camping with a difference. Apart from regular campsites, it features hand-painted tipis with wood floors, beds, and mattresses (rent bedding and cook kits), lanterns, hot showers, groceries, and the opportunity for horse-riding, rafting, golfing, hiking, and fishing for $14.95 a night.

15

BANFF/LAKE LOUISE

The transcontinental railway tracks were edging their way toward the forbidding Rocky Mountains in 1883 when three workers discovered hot water simmering in the ground. Tourism was born— and so was Banff! Two years later, the area was protected as a tourist mecca to help pay for the new Canadian Pacific Railway. Banff is the oldest and most visited of Canada's national parks. Along with three other national parks straddling the Continental Divide and some neighboring provincial parks in British Columbia, Banff is a World Heritage Site in recognition of its outstanding scenery.

At 1,372 meters (4,530 ft), Banff is the highest town in the country. It sits beside the Bow River, cradled by mile-high mountain peaks: to the north, the Cascade Mountains and Mount Norquay; to the south, the Sulphur Mountains; to the east, Mount Rundle. Chateau Lake Louise and the Victoria Glacier are 58 km (36 mi) to the northwest. Add a red canoe and a Mountie in his red serge on horseback, and you have the world's view of Canada. It is a picture perfect scene that attracts more than 4 million visitors a year, many of them Japanese. ◪

BANFF/LAKE LOUISE

N

Strathmore

21

Red Deer

2

Olds

27

Airdrie

Cochrane

Calgary

27

1A

Bow River

Kananaskis Country

Rocky Mountain House

752

584

40

Forest Reserve

Lake Minnewanka

Mountains

E

B

A

Banff

Canmore

Kananaskis Village

11

DAVID THOMPSON HIGHWAY

Rocky

734

1A

C

Banff National Park

93

Siffleur Wilderness

Lake Louise

Louise

Lake

Louise

Kootenay National Park

93

D

F

BOW VALLEY PARKWAY

Peyton Lake

Yoho National Park

95

Bighorn Wildland

White Goat Wilderness

Recreation Area

93

ALBERTA

BRITISH COLUMBIA

Golden

ICEFIELDS PARKWAY

Athabasca Glacier

Jasper National Park

Glacier National Park

PARK AREA

PROVINCE BOUNDARY

PLACE OF INTEREST

HIGHWAY

ROAD

0 SCALE 33 MILES

33 KILOMETERS

Sights

- **Ⓐ** Banff Centre
- **Ⓐ** Banff Park Museum
- **Ⓐ** Banff Springs Hotel
- **Ⓑ** Bankhead Mine
- **Ⓒ** Bow Valley Parkway
- **Ⓐ** Cascade Gardens
- **Ⓐ** Cave and Basin National Historic Site
- **Ⓓ** Lake Louise
- **Ⓔ** Lake Minnewanka
- **Ⓐ** Luxton Museum
- **Ⓕ** Moraine Lake
- **Ⓐ** Natural History Museum
- **Ⓐ** Sulphur Mountain Gondola
- **Ⓐ** Upper Hot Springs Pool
- **Ⓐ** Whyte Museum of the Canadian Rockies

Note: Items with the same letter are located in the same town or area.

A PERFECT DAY IN BANFF/LAKE LOUISE

One day here is like offering only one selection from a newly opened box of mixed chocolates! I recommend catching the 7:30 a.m. eight-minute gondola ride up Sulphur Mountain and hiking one of the trails to build a good appetite for breakfast at The Summit, Canada's highest restaurant.

Back down in the valley, I'd drive Highway 1A, the Bow Valley Parkway, to the Great Divide to watch a single small creek dividing in midflow and beginning two long journeys, one to each side of the continent. Then I'd take a 1-km (.6-mi) walk through Johnston Canyon to Lower Falls on a boardwalk anchored to the canyon walls; or a 6-km (3.75-mi) hike to the Ink Pots, seven cold-water springs bubbling into clear pools in an open meadow.

At Lake Louise I'd take yet another obligatory picture of the famous turquoise-colored lake, then probably rent a red canoe and paddle Louise's waters to enjoy a closer look at Victoria Glacier. Later in the afternoon, I'd drive up a 12-km (7.5-mi) road to Moraine Lake, set below the Valley of Ten Peaks, a lake that rivals Lake Louise in both beauty and fame.

It would be a tossup whether to stay at Chateau Lake Louise that night to wait for its special early bird breakfast and see the Victoria Glacier at dawn, or return to the Banff Springs Hotel for a soak in its mineral springs. I probably wouldn't be spending the night in the Presidential Suite for $3,000. But then again, if it was my perfect day, perhaps I would.

SIGHTSEEING HIGHLIGHTS

★★★ **Banff Springs Hotel**—This imposing castle in the clouds is a blend of Scottish baronial and French chateau charm. Its past clientele was the rich and famous—Winston Churchill, Marilyn Monroe, and the King of Siam. Current guests are more likely to be early-rising tourbus passengers. Back in 1885, the first visitors went to Banff to "test the waters," that is, the natural mineral waters springing out of a cave at the base of Sulphur Mountain. The hotel recently added a spa, The Solace, which covers 3,270 square meters (35,000 sq ft), cost $12 million to build, and is open daily to the public from 6 a.m. to 10 p.m. Details: Admission is $40 a day for unlimited use. Services range from simple massages to aroma- or hydrotherapy to facials, which begin at $60. You can't miss the hotel in Banff, but the mailing address is Box 960, Banff, Alberta T0L 0C0; (800) 441-1414. (1½ hours)

★★★ **Bow Valley Parkway**—Also called Highway 1A, this parkway is a more leisurely route between Banff and Lake Louise than the Trans-Canada Highway 1. It is only 58 km (34 mi) long, but drive it slowly to savor its viewpoints and wildlife. Animals are best viewed at dawn or dusk. Watch for elk, deer, bighorn sheep, and coyotes. The Hole-in-the-Wall, a cavern cut into the rock face by meltwaters from the glacier that once completely filled the Bow River Valley, sits near the Mule-shoe Picnic area, 11 km (6.8 mi) from Banff. The road's flat terrain makes it popular with cyclists. At Lake Louise, take the gondola up Whitehorn Mountain for a closer look at the glaciers. (3 hours)

★★★ **Lake Louise**—First discovered by Tom Wilson in 1882, this lake is a rare jewel, 4.5 km (2.8 mi) west of the highway near its junction with Highway 93. The nearby chateau and landscaped grounds, designed to blend in with their natural surroundings, are a great place to view the spectacular lake. Wilson, a CPR scout, originally named it

Emerald Lake, for its emerald green and aquamarine color. The name
was later changed to Louise, to honor Queen Victoria's daughter, and
the glacier that rises behind it was renamed to honor the Queen
herself. One of the most popular trails goes 3 km (2 mi) around the
lake to the foot of the glacier. Two other trails lead to teahouses, an
appropriate reward for your walk. Both the village of Lake Louise and
Chateau Lake Louise have recently been expanded (within national
park guidelines) to cope with increased visitation. (minimum 1 day)

★★★ **Moraine Lake**—In the Valley of Ten Peaks, this must-see lake is
an emerald set beneath ten glaciated peaks, the northern of which is
the third highest in Banff National Park. (At one time Lake Moraine
appeared on the Canadian $20 bill.) Details: Located on the north side
of the Trans-Canada Highway, just off the Lake Louise Ski Area access
road. (minimum 1 hour)

★★ **Banff Park Museum**—Western Canada's oldest natural history
museum is a rustic 1903 building housing wildlife specimens from the
1860s. It's now a National Historic Site displaying the birds and
mammals found in Banff National Park. There's also a reading room
and a new Discover Room. Details: 93 Banff Avenue; (403) 762-6100,
box office (403) 762-6300, (800) 413-8368 (North America); open daily
in summer 10 a.m. to 6 p.m. (free tours 11 a.m. and 3 p.m.), off-season
10 a.m. to 3 p.m. Admission: Adults $2, seniors and children $1,
families $5. (1 hour)

★★ **Lake Minnewanka**—The lake and especially the two-hour boat
tour present you with what is probably the most spectacular scenery in
the entire Canadian Rockies. You can also rent a boat or charter fishing
services here. Facilities are all wheelchair accessible. Details: Follow
the Minnewanka Loop Road; (403) 762-3473; cruises leave at 10:30
a.m. and 12:30, 3, and 5 p.m., with a 7 p.m. sunset cruise in July and
August. Cost: Adults $22, ages 5 to 11 $11, under 5 free. (2 hours)

★★ **Sulphur Mountain Gondola**—The Sulphur Mountain Gondola
is an eight-minute ride up Sulphur Mountain to 2,285 meters (7,500
feet). At the summit, enjoy the view of surrounding mountains and
valleys or the miniaturized village beneath. You can walk an alpine trail
or dine at the Summit Restaurant. Details: On Mountain Avenue, 3.2
km (2 mi) from downtown Banff; (403) 762-2523, fax (403) 762-7493;

open June 8–21 8 a.m. to 8 p.m., June 22 through August 18 7:30 a.m. to 9 p.m., August 19 through September 9 7:30 a.m. to 8 p.m., the rest of the year 8:30 a.m. to 6 p.m. Admission: Adults $10, children $5. (½ hour–2 hours)

🟊🟊 **Upper Hot Springs Pool**—This site has been renovated, with changing rooms and a large outdoor pool in which the water temperature averages 38°C (108°F). There are bathing suit and towel rentals, lockers and therapeutic massage (book ahead), and it's all wheelchair accessible. Details: Located to the right along Mountain Avenue, 4.5 km (2.8 mi) from Banff townsite; (403) 762-1515, for massage (403) 762-2966; open daily June 21 through September 15 9 a.m. to 11 p.m., September 16 through June 20 10 a.m. to 10 p.m. (Friday and Saturday to 11 p.m.). Admission: Adults $7, seniors and ages 3–16 $6; children under 3 free. (1 hour)

🟊🟊 **Whyte Museum of the Canadian Rockies**—This wheelchair-accessible museum presents the rich changes in the cultural history and fine arts of the Rocky Mountain area, and features a heritage collection, archives, and an art gallery. Special programs, photographs, gallery tours, and lectures depict the variety of lifestyles in these mountains. Details: 111 Bear Street; (403) 762-2291; open daily May 19 through June 30 9 a.m. to 11 p.m., July and August weekdays 10 a.m. to 9 p.m. and weekends 10 a.m. to 6 p.m. Admission: Adults $3, seniors and students $2; under 12 with adults free. (1 hour)

🟊 **Banff Centre**— A prestigious School of Fine Arts presents an Arts Festival each summer from early June through September (the largest such festival in North America). Talented artists from Canada and around the world who attend the school are showcased. Details: St. Julien Road; (403) 762-6300 or (800) 413-8368. (1 hour)

🟊 **Bankhead Mine**—Take an easy walk through the ruins of the site of a 1900s coal mine, colliery, and town in which interpretive plaques explain the mine workings. Details: 7.4 km (4.5 mi) from Banff on the Lake Minnewanka Loop Road; always open for viewing. (1 hour)

🟊 **Cascade Gardens**—This is one of the finest historic landscapes in Western Canada, with flower gardens, gazebos, and pools. Gardens are open whenever the building is, but you can see parts over the top even when closed. Details: In the Park Administration grounds at the end of Banff Avenue; (403) 762-1550. Admission: Free. (½ hour)

✸ **Cave and Basin National Historic Site** (also called the **Centennial Centre**)—This is the spot where hot springs were first discovered in 1883; it soon became a mecca, particularly for the wealthy who sought its curative waters, and led to the establishment of Banff. The pool here is now closed, but interactive exhibits, films, a boardwalk, and history and nature tours recount the effects on the surrounding marshes, flora, and fauna. Details: 311 Cave Avenue; (403) 762-1557; open daily September through May 9:30 a.m. to 5 p.m., June through August 9 a.m. to 6 p.m. Admission: Adults $2.25, seniors $1.75, ages 6–18 $1.25, families $5. (1 hour)

✸ **Luxton Museum**—The history of Native Indians of the Canadian Rockies and Northern Plains is told through life-size scenes depicting tipis, travois, and ornamental costumes. Museum is wheelchair accessible. Details: 1 Birch Avenue; (403) 762-2388; open daily May 15 to October 15 9 a.m. to 9 p.m., October 15 to May 14 Wednesday through Sunday 1 to 5 p.m. Admission: Adults $5, seniors and students $3.75, children $2, under 6 free, families $11.50. (1 hour)

✸ **Natural History Museum**—The geological evolution of the Rocky Mountains is portrayed with dioramas and a display featuring Castlegar Cave (which is under the Columbia Icefield) diagrams, models and audiovisuals, rocks and minerals, fossils, and dinosaur bones. There's also a life-sized Bigfoot, the legendary creature that is rumored to live in remote regions such as this. The museum is wheelchair accessible. Details: 112 Banff Avenue; phone/fax (403) 762-2388; open daily in May 11 a.m. to 6 p.m., in June 10 a.m. to 6 p.m., July through August 10 a.m. to 8 p.m., September through October 10 a.m. to 6 p.m. Admission: Freé. (1 hour)

FITNESS AND RECREATION

Fitness and recreation possibilities are endless in the Banff–Lake Louise area. Summer visitors will enjoy walking, hiking, cycling, can-oeing, golfing, kayaking, white-water rafting, horseback-riding, jet-boating, rock-climbing, ATV tours, fishing, caving, climbing, heli-copter tours, and wildlife-viewing. In winter, downhill and cross-country skiing, tobogganing, dog-sledding, and ice-climbing attract thousands of visitors.

There are tours or outfits offering just about everything. **Mountain Coasters** is one of several guides who provide guide-accompanied and van-supported cycle tours of the area for $80 full day or $50 half-day, (403) 678-6670.

Lake Minnewanka Boat Tours takes visitors the 27-km (17-mi) length of the lake in glass-enclosed launches, with guides giving geological details, local history, and tall stories. (For times, prices, and phone numbers, see Sightseeing Highlights.)

Banff Fishing Unlimited provides for fly-fishing, spin-casting, trolling, or jigging, at (403) 762-4936. A world-famous golf course is at the **Banff Springs Hotel**, (403) 762-6801; other courses are **Kananaskis Country Club**, (403) 591-7272, and **Canmore Golf Course**, (403) 678-4784.

Interpretive hikes are offered in the Banff–Lake Louise areas by **Parks Canada** staff June 15 through September 15. Phone (403) 762-1550 (Banff) or (403) 522-3833 (Lake Louise).

Alpine Helicopters, (403) 678-4802, based in Canmore, offers flightseeing tours from 20 minutes ($85) to one hour ($185).

Boundary Stables, (403) 591-7171, has one-hour ($19.50), two-hour ($30.50), and full-day horseback tours ($85, including lunch). **Holiday on Horseback**, (403) 762-4551, offers hourly to multiday pack trips (from $21), breakfast rides, evening steak fries, and overnights. The Explorer is a full-day trip, lunch included. Accommodation in back-country lodges is provided on longer trips. **Banff Springs Hotel** corral offers hourly rides ($25) and a three-hour trip ($52) (see Sightseeing Highlights for phone and fax numbers).

FOOD

Eating in Banff and Lake Louise, mecca for busloads of wealthy overseas tourists, can be expensive, so strive to get a little value for your money.

For an authentic Western meal in the Rockies, try a horseback or covered-wagon ride to a wilderness cookout at the end of the trail. Between June 15 and September 15, **Brewster Cowboy's BBQ Barn** offers a ride around Lake Louise followed by a BBQ steak dinner for $54; (403) 522-3511, ext. 1210, or (403) 762-5454. **Warner Guiding and Outfitting Ltd.**, of the Trail Rider Store in Banff, (403) 762-4551, takes guests on rides to Sundance Canyon for a Mountain Breakfast Ride and Evening Steak Fry ($49) and a covered-wagon luncheon cookout ($39). Steaks are accompanied by cowboy beans, spuds, and Caesar salad.

Banff Springs Hotel, on Spray Avenue in Banff, (403) 762-6860, offers sophisticated dining and dancing in the Rob Roy Room; Japanese dishes such as *shabu*, sushi, and sukiyaki at the Samura; Italian food at the Pavilion; and traditional German food, fondues, and entertainment at Waldhaus. These restaurants are open 6 to 10 p.m. Family-type meals and prices are available at the Koffie Huis for breakfast, lunch, and dinner.

The **Tom Wilson Rooftop Restaurant** in the Chateau Lake Louise, (403) 522-3511, offers superb views, piano music, and continental cuisine. The Victoria Room serves a buffet breakfast, lunch, and table d'hôte dinner, with a fireplace, live music, and good views. The elegant Edelweiss serves innovative European food while offering spectacular lake and glacier views, and the Poppy Room has family fare. You get light meals while you dance at the Glacier Saloon and finger foods while you drink at the Alpine Lounge. My favorites are the early bird special breakfast to get me up to watch dawn on Victoria Glacier, and lunch in the garden on the Lakeside Terrace. If you just want ice cream, go for a Glacier Scoop.

On one of my visits to Banff Springs Hotel and Chateau Lake Louise, I cooked my own steaks in the campground but splurged on desserts and chocolate in the heady atmosphere of Canada's two famous fairy-tale castles. Once, at Banff Springs, my sister spent hours gussying herself up to appear for a formal dinner but found herself alone at 9 p.m. with just the piano player for company. Tourists, especially bus tourists, dine early, go to bed early, and get up early.

Banff has two award-winning restaurants: **Le Beaujolais**, on the corner of Buffalo Street and Banff Avenue, (403) 762-2712, and its more economical affiliate, the **Bistro Restaurant**, on the corner of Wolf and Bear Streets, (403) 762-8900. Most individual entrees at Le Beaujolais run in the $30 range, three-course table d'hôte meals cost about $40–$46, and the six-course chef's surprise, a few dollars more. Personally, I find that the French dishes look artistic but lack substance, and add-ons are expensive. I'd rather join other Banff residents at The Bistro for hearty bouillabaisse, seafood crepes, or Alberta steaks—items that run between $10–$20.

Highly recommended by the locals is **Ticino**, a Swiss-Italian

BANFF/LAKE LOUISE

Food

- Ⓐ Baker Creek Bistro
- Ⓑ Banff Springs Hotel
- Ⓑ Bistro Restaurant
- Ⓒ Brewster Cowboy's BBQ Barn
- Ⓑ Bumper's, The Beef House
- Ⓑ Coyote's Grill
- Ⓑ Craig's Way Station
- Ⓑ Earl's
- Ⓑ Edo of Japan
- Ⓓ Emerald Lake Lodge
- Ⓒ Lake Louise Station
- Ⓑ Le Beaujolais
- Ⓔ Moraine Lake Lodge
- Ⓑ Sukiyaki House
- Ⓑ Summit Restaurant
- Ⓑ Ticino
- Ⓒ Tom Wilson Rooftop Restaurant
- Ⓑ Warner Guiding and Outfitting Ltd.

Lodging

- Ⓐ Baker Creek Chalet and Guest Lodges
- Ⓑ Banff International Hostel
- Ⓑ Banff Springs Hotel
- Ⓑ Castle Mountain Hostel
- Ⓒ Chateau Lake Louise

Lodging (continued)

- Ⓑ Douglas Fir Resort and Chalets
- Ⓑ Eleanor's House
- Ⓕ Johnston Canyon Resort
- Ⓒ Lake Louise International Hostel
- Ⓔ Moraine Lake Lodge and Cabins
- Ⓒ Skoki Lodge
- Ⓑ Y Mountain Lodge

Camping

- Ⓖ Castle Mountain
- Ⓕ Johnston Canyon
- Ⓒ Lake Louise 1
- Ⓒ Lake Louise 2
- Ⓗ Mosquito Creek
- Ⓘ Protection Mountain
- Ⓙ Rampart Creek
- Ⓐ Tunnel Mountain Trailer Court
- Ⓐ Tunnel Mountain Village 1
- Ⓐ Tunnel Mountain Village 2
- Ⓚ Two Jack Lake Main
- Ⓚ Two Jack Lakeside
- Ⓛ Waterfowl Lake

Note: Items with the same letter are located in the same town or area.

restaurant at 415 Banff Avenue in Banff, (403) 762-3848. It's noted for its Swiss decor, Swiss-dressed waitstaff, and well-prepared food.

Probably the first restaurant that comes to everybody's lips in Banff is **Bumper's, The Beef House**, at 603 Banff Avenue. Bumper's is a family restaurant that offers top service and good value, with Alberta beef specials (prime ribs, steaks, and baby back ribs), B.C. salmon, an all-you-can-eat salad bar, and a children's menu. Entrees are about $8–$18. Another economical choice is **Craig's Way Station**, a popular diner known for its legendary all-day breakfasts costing less than $10 and its menu of over 50 selections, including homemade burgers and 14 varieties of chicken. Craig's has a seniors' menu and menus for Little Pardners that begin at $2.49. It's located at 461 Banff Avenue, beside Esso, (403) 762-4660.

The highest restaurant in Canada, with absolutely the best view around, is the **Summit Restaurant**, on top of Sulphur Mountain, Mountain Avenue, Banff, (403) 762-5438. You can get there by gondola if you don't want to climb. But make it by 8 p.m., when the gondola closes, or you'll miss out on casual deli-type dining such as burgers, chicken fingers, fish and chips, and homemade soups.

Coyote's Grill, at 206 Caribou Street in Banff, (403) 762-3963, is known for its open kitchen, Southwestern decor, and menu selections such as char-grilled meats, fish, vegetables, vegetarian burritos, black bean salads, Southwestern sushi rolls, and eight innovative pastas. Dinner entrees range from $10–$15, and breakfast and lunch start at $5. **Earl's**, upstairs at Banff Avenue and Wolf Street in Banff, (403) 762-4414, is always a good overall choice for tourists and locals alike. Food is fresh, prices are reasonable, and the staff is popular.

Japanese restaurants abound in Banff—from the elegant and traditional **Sukiyaki House**, on the 2nd floor of Park Avenue Mall, 211 Banff Avenue, (403) 762-2002; to the fast-food kiosk **Edo of Japan**, in the Food Court of Cascade Plaza, 317 Banff Avenue, (403) 762-9251. Favorites at Sukiyaki are sushi, *shabu shabu*, and hot-pot sukiyaki.

You get a lot of value-added atmosphere when you dine in the Lake Louise area. At lovely **Moraine Lake Lodge**, on Moraine Lake Road, 13 km (8 mi) from the Village of Lake Louise, (403) 522-3733, you can sit in a casually elegant atrium dining room (or cafe or outdoor patio) overlooking the famous view of the lake set below the Valley of Ten Peaks. The lodge's breakfast buffet consists of Muesli, fruit, croissants, and muffins for less than $10. Dinner is a choice of game paté, tenderloin beef, caribou, salmon Wellington, lemon chicken, or grilled sea bass. Open daily May 28 to October 2.

Emerald Lake Lodge, 40 km (25 mi) west of Lake Louise, (250) 343-6321, has a similar outstanding location. Hearty soups, homemade bread, free-range chicken, and a game platter are specialties. You have a choice at **Lake Louise Station**, 200 Sentinel Road on the Bow River, (403) 522-2600: roadside dining in a 1920s log railway station or elegant eating in a vintage dining car with wood panelling, immaculate linen, silverware, and perhaps the sound of a transcontinental train passing by. The menu reflects the difference: from pizzas, burgers, and homemade soups to fresh salmon, red spring trout, and honey-mustard curry organic chicken. Open daily 11:30 a.m.–11 p.m. (dining car 6 p.m.–9 p.m.). Lunch $4–$12 and entrees $8–$24.

Partway between Banff and Lake Louise, closer to Lake Louise, is the **Baker Creek Bistro**, an intimate log cabin restaurant so popular that you must reserve even if you are staying in the nearby Baker Creek Chalets, Box 57, Lake Louise, Alberta T0L 1E0, (403) 522-2182.

LODGING

Without doubt, **Banff Springs Hotel**, Banff's picture-postcard perfect castle in the clouds since 1888, is the biggest and the best. Its Presidential Suite with a private glass elevator rents for $3,000 a night, Canada's most expensive accommodation, but you can also get a room for as "little" as $215 in the off-season. In winter, the hotel offers an all-inclusive "winter wonderland experience" starting at $215 per person per day for deluxe accommodation, daily use of Solace Spa and Fitness Centre, three meals a day in your choice of hotel restaurant, plus activities such as skiing, skating, snowshoeing, dogsledding, and sleighriding. Not a bad deal for a day, except that the days may not be long enough to fit everything in.

All rooms have minibars; the hotel has outdoor and indoor pools, a golf course, tennis courts, riding stables, exercise rooms, and a new and comprehensive spa. Located at 405 Spray Avenue across a bridge only 500 meters from downtown, the opulent Banff Springs can scarcely be missed. Phone (403) 762-2211 or (800) 441-1414.

The Rockies' other castle is newly renovated **Chateau Lake Louise**, on the shores of Lake Louise looking across to Victoria Glacier. It has nearly the same amenities as Banff Springs but not quite the same opulent ambiance. For me, Chateau Lake Louise has the edge over Banff because of its stunning scenery, its many trails close by, and its distance from downtown. Prices are comparable, from about $250–$450. Address: Box 178, Lake Louise, Alberta T0L IE0, (403) 522-3511 or (800) 441-1414.

Another "view property" is **Moraine Lake Lodge and Cabins**, on Moraine Lake, Box 70, Lake Louise, Alberta T0L IE0, (403) 522-3733. It was designed by Arthur Erickson, famous architect of the new Canadian Embassy in Washington, D.C. Rates vary from $175–$290.

Fun for the family is the **Douglas Fir Resort and Chalets**, on Tunnel Mountain Road, Box 1228, Banff, Alberta T0L 0C0, (403) 762-5591 or (800) 661-9267. A unique feature is its two giant indoor waterslides to keep the kids busy. The resort has a variety of rooms, from studios to A-frame chalets, to suit many tastes, all with kitchens and fireplaces. Rates are $188–$238 in high season, $108 and up in low season. A little easier on the budget and often chosen for weddings for its romantic atmosphere is **Baker Creek Chalets and Guest Lodge**, on the Bow Valley Parkway between Banff and Lake Louise, Box 66, Lake Louise, (403) 522-3761. Chalets have red roofs, red shutters with hand-painted flowers, decks and flowerboxes, fireplaces, and kitchens. Rates range $75–$225.

Johnston Canyon Resort, also between Banff and Lake Louise on the Bow Valley Parkway, has 41 old-fashioned but comfortable cabins that offer reasonable rates ($65–$158). It also has a tennis court, hot tub, dining facilities, gas station, and groceries. It is adjacent to one waterfall and is on a renowned trail to seven others.

There are several bed and breakfasts in the Banff area for you to consider. Try **Eleanor's House**, at 125 Kootenay Avenue between the centre of Banff and Banff Springs Hotel, (403) 760-2457. Eleanor House (yes, really!) calls her home "Alberta's finest." Rates for her two units are $85–$125. Check her home page at www.banff.cyberstream. net/eleanor.

For the budget-conscious, there are several hostel-type accommodations: **Lake Louise International Hostel and Alpine Centre**, in the townsite, (403) 522-2200; **Banff International Hostel**, on Tunnel Mountain Road, (403) 762-4122; and **Castle Mountain Hostel**, in Banff, (403) 762-4122. A little more expensive but with a variety of room types is the **Y Mountain Lodge**, at 102 Spray Avenue in downtown Banff, (403) 762-3560. It used to be a hotel. Basic dormitory accommodations start at $19; a double room with private bath is $79; and family rooms with three double beds (but shared hostel bathroom and shower facilities) cost $79. **Skoki Lodge**, 14.5 km

(9 mi) from the Lake Louise ski area, (403/522-3555), is a beautiful 1930 log lodge and cabins, open Christmas to April and June to September. However, you can't drive to Skoki—you'll have to hike or ski.

CAMPING

The many public campgrounds in Banff National Park are available on a first-come, first-served basis. No reservations are accepted, so it's wise to settle into a site early in the day and stay awhile. If you want to stay overnight in the back country, you must get a free park use permit obtainable at information centers in the Banff and Lake Louise townsites. You need a $3 permit for a campfire. Rates per night vary from $9–$20, according to the location and the services available. All Banff area campsites listed can be reached at (403) 762-1550 (or by fax 403/762-3380). For the Lake Louise campgrounds: (403) 522-3980.

Castle Mountain has 43 sites, tap water, and flush toilets but no services. Hiking trails are nearby. It's 2 km (1 mi) north of Castle Junction on Highway 1A, open June 23 through Labor Day. **Johnston Canyon** has 132 sites, tap water, sewage disposal, flush toilets, and showers. It's wheelchair accessible, with phone facilities and hiking trails, 26 km (16 mi) west of Banff on the Trans-Canada Highway.

Mosquito Creek has 32 sites, tap water, and hiking trails, 23 km (14.5 mi) north of Highway 1 on Highway 93. It's open mid-June through mid-September and for winter camping (20 sites) with self-registration. **Protection Mountain** has 89 sites, tap water, flush toilets, and good hiking trails. It's 11 km (8 mi) west of Castle Junction on Highway 1A, open June 23 through Labor Day.

Tunnel Mountain Trailer Court has 321 RV-only sites, tap water, flush toilets, sewage disposal, all services, and is wheelchair accessible. It's 2.5 km (1 mile) northeast of Banff on Tunnel Mountain Road, open mid-May through late September.

Tunnel Mountain Village 1 has 618 RV-only sites, tap water, showers, flush toilets, sewage disposal, and phone, and is wheelchair accessible. With good hiking trails and an interpretive amphitheater, it's 4 km (2.5 mi) northeast of Banff on Tunnel Mountain Road, open mid-May through late September. **Tunnel Mountain Village 2** has 222 designated and walk-in sites, tap water, power only, phone, wheelchair accessibility, and an interpretive amphitheater. It's 2.5 km (1.6 mi) northeast of Banff on Tunnel Mountain Road and open year-round; winter camping is permitted.

Two Jack Lake Main has 379 sites, tap water, flush toilets, sewage disposal, hiking trails, and phone facilities. Located 13 km (8 mi) northeast of Banff on Lake Minnewanka Road, it's open mid-June through Labor Day.

Two Jack Lakeside has 74 sites, tap water, showers, flush toilets, sewage disposal, canoeing, hiking trails, and phone. Located 12 km (7 mi) northeast of Banff on Lake Minnewanka Road.

Rampart Creek has 50 sites, tap water, and hiking trails. Located 88 km off Highway 1 and north on Highway 93. Waterfowl Lake has 116 sites, tap water, flush toilets, and sewage disposal. You can canoe or hike, and there are interpretive talks in the amphitheater. Located 57 km (35 mi) off the Trans-Canada Highway and along Highway 93, it's open mid-June through mid-September.

Lake Louise 1, in Lake Louise on Highway 1, has 189 sites, tap water, phone, sewage disposal, hiking, fishing, and winter camping in the RV area. Open mid-May through early October. Lake Louise 2 has 220 tent-only sites, tap water, and flush toilets. Open mid-May through early October.

THE ARTS

The Banff Festival of the Arts presents a variety of performances, including jazz, dance, chamber music, musical theater, and drama, with solo and ensemble performances, between early June and the end of August. For details, phone (403) 762-6300 or (800) 413-8368.

For two to three days each early November, the Banff Film Festival of Mountain Films is held in Banff. Phone (403) 762-6157 for more information. In the second week of June, the Banff TV Festival showcases the world's best TV productions. The Rocky Mountain Shakespeare Theatre Company, (403) 522-3555, presents two Shakespeare plays between mid-July and the end of August.

16

KOOTENAY COUNTRY

The dramatic but unhurried Kootenay country in southeastern British Columbia is reminiscent of Vancouver Island as it was years ago. The Kootenays (west and east) are still pristine despite a late 1800s influx of miners seeking gold, silver, lead, zinc, and copper; there was another influx in the early 1900s of Doukhobors—Russian immigrants escaping religious persecution—and now the encroachment of loggers and dam builders. Its dramatic scenery—parallel ranges of massive, glacier-clad mountains, rugged peaks, long rivers, elongated lakes, and copious hot springs—stand out in a province famous for its scenery. Though all roads lead to the Kootenays, the region is still a quiet and unspoiled backwater that attracts artists and lovers of the outdoors. Locals call it Shangri-la.

As well as the fabulous scenery, the Kootenays are rich in history. Ghost towns, abandoned mines and smelters, restored paddle-wheelers, heritage buildings, and living museums attest to the area's mining-related boom-and-bust economy. Trail and Kimberley celebrated their centennials in 1996; Grand Forks, Greenwood, and Nelson, in 1997.

There are no freeways but plenty of good two-lane highways, logging roads, hiking trails, cross-country ski trails, and free ferries. Circular driving routes ranging 70 to 450 km (42 to 315 mi) allow convenient access to the region's on- and off-road attractions. ◼

KOOTENAY COUNTRY

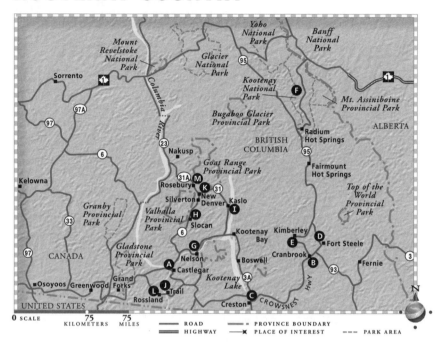

Sights

- **Ⓐ** Castlegar
- **Ⓑ** Cranbrook Railway Museum
- **Ⓒ** Creston Valley Wildlife Management Area
- **Ⓓ** Fort Steele Provincial Heritage Park
- **Ⓔ** Kimberley
- **Ⓕ** Kootenay National Park
- **Ⓖ** Nelson
- **Ⓗ** Slocan Valley
- **Ⓘ** S.S. *Moyie*
- **Ⓙ** Trail

Food

- **Ⓖ** All Seasons Restaurant

Food (continued)

- **Ⓚ** Apple Tree
- **Ⓒ** Blondie's Bistro
- **Ⓖ** Book Garden
- **Ⓙ** Colander Restaurant
- **Ⓐ** Gabriel's
- **Ⓐ** Gardeli's
- **Ⓐ** Gold Rush Books and Expresso
- **Ⓖ** Max and Irma's
- **Ⓛ** Olive Oyl's
- **Ⓖ** Rice Bowl
- **Ⓐ** Spinning Wheel Vegetarian Eatery
- **Ⓛ** Sunshine Cafe
- **Ⓘ** Treehouse Restaurant
- **Ⓜ** Wild Rose Restaurant

Note: Items with the same letter are located in the same town or area.

A PERFECT DAY IN THE KOOTENAYS

My perfect day would be a 323-km (202-mi) circular drive through a blend of history and unsurpassed beauty. Start early in Nelson, an 1880s mining town, and look at some of its 350 heritage buildings. Travel west and north along the Slocan River Valley, the route taken by thousands of fortune seekers in the 1890s. Visit the ghost town of Sandon and move on to New Denver, where the Nikkei Internment Memorial Centre commemorates the shocking displacement of Japanese-Canadians during World War II.

The road then winds its way along the west shore of Slocan Lake to the unspoiled wilderness of Valhalla Provincial Park. Here, tumultuous creeks and waterfalls, crystal clear lakes, and stands of tall timber offer hours of hiking possibilities. Later, relax in the Ainsworth Hot Springs, watching stalagmites and stalactites growing in the horse-shaped cave before driving the last few miles back to Nelson. After eating a well-earned and filling dinner at the All Seasons Restaurant, sit back, loosen your belt, and reflect on a day well spent.

SIGHTSEEING HIGHLIGHTS

★★★ **Creston Valley Wildlife Management Area**—During spring and fall, more than 250,000 birds—migratory ducks, geese, and swans—fly into this 6,880-hectare (17,000-acre) bird refuge/outdoor education center to feed and rest. This preserve has the highest density of osprey in the world. It offers a variety of nature hikes and canoe trips and operates a campground for people exploring the marshlands and taking part in the nature programs. Details: 10 km (6 mi) northwest of Creston; (250) 428-3259; open May through Thanksgiving. Admission: Adults $3, families $7. (1½ hours)

★★★ **Fort Steele Provincial Heritage Park**—The park represents an 1890–1905 East Kootenay town. Fort Steele began in 1864 as Fisherville when gold was discovered at nearby Wild Horse Creek. More than 60 buildings have survived or been restored or reconstructed. Street dramas, quilting demonstrations, stagecoach rides, steam-train rides, and live theater help re-create that life of a hundred years ago, when Fort Steele was the site of the first Northwest Mounted Police post in British Columbia. The fort was named after Samuel Steele, the Mountie who peacefully settled tensions between Kootenay Indians

(First Nations) and newcomers bent on mining and farming. Details: 3 km (2 mi) southwest of Fort Steele on Highway 93/95; (250) 489-3351; living history programs presented daily 9:30 a.m. to 5:30 p.m., mid-June through Labor Day. Admission: Adults $5.50, over 65 and ages 13–18 $3.25, ages 6–12 $1, families $10.75. (½ day)

★★★ **Kimberley**—Once a mining town, Kimberley is now a winter sports center and tourist hub, calling itself the "Bavarian Town of the Rockies." Many of its buildings have a Bavarian Alpine decor, and the pedestrian-only downtown shopping area known as the Platzl features the world's largest operating cuckoo clock and a wandering minstrel who plays an accordion. Nearby is Cominco's (Consolidated Mining and Smelting of Canada Limited) Sullivan Mine, one of the world's largest underground lead and zinc mines. Kimberley Ski and Summer Resort, at the ski area above town via Gerry Sorenson Way, has a 1,223-meter (4,045-ft) alpine slide that winds down Kimberley ski slope. A chairlift takes you up North Star Mountain to the launch site. Details: (250) 427-4881; alpine slide open daily late June through Labor Day 10:30 a.m. to 7:30 p.m. Cost: Single ride $3.50, book of ten $30, book of 20 $50. Downhill skiing available December through April. (1 day minimum, but the charming atmosphere could entice you to stay even longer)

★★★ **Kootenay National Park**—Named a World Heritage Site because it represents the Rocky Mountain landscape, Kootenay is easily accessible from Highway 93 between the Banff-Jasper Highway and Radium Hot Springs. This was a travel corridor for local First Nations peoples long before it was the first road built by European newcomers through the central Rocky Mountains. Every twist and turn reveals something interesting to explore—gray-white-striped limestone Marble Canyon; towering red sandstone cliffs of the Redwall Fault; ochre-tinted Paint Pots cold springs once used by First Nations people to make body paint, decorate their tipis, and draw their rock paintings; and at the park's southern end, popular Radium Hot Springs, which has both a hot pool (35–47°C/95–117°F) and cool pool. Of the numerous hiking trails, two of the best are Floe Lake Trail and Stanley Glacier Trail.

Details: On the western slopes of the Rocky Mountains adjoining Banff and Yoho National Parks. Although the park is open all year, its three campgrounds are open only mid-May through early September. Fees range $12–$17.50 a night per site. Visitors must obtain a park

motor-vehicle pass at the entrance before driving the park, and back-country campers must obtain a wilderness pass. Admission for private motor vehicles is by daily ($8), three-day ($16), or annual ($50) permit. Radium Hot Springs pools, (250) 347-9485, are open daily 9 a.m. to 10 p.m. Admission: Adults $4, seniors and ages 3–16 $3.50. For further information, contact Superintendent, Kootenay National Park, Box 220, Radium Hot Springs, British Columbia V0A 1M0; (250) 347-9615. (minimum 1 day)

★★★ **Nelson**—Situated on a steep hillside overlooking the west arm of Kootenay Lake, this was once an iron- and silver-mining boom town. Today it has the second-highest concentration of heritage buildings (350) per capita in British Columbia. Francis Rattenbury, the famous architect of Victoria's Parliament buildings and the Empress Hotel, designed Nelson's impressive courthouse and city hall. Most of the town's historic buildings are open to the public, with free guided (early July through Labor Day) and self-guided tours highlighting Nelson's arts, crafts, and antiques. Nelson may have more artists and craftspeople per capita than any other city in Canada, so you'll find lots of live theater, musical events, art galleries, bookstores, and marble sculptures in parks and along boulevards, plus two colleges. Take a ride on restored Streetcar 23 along the shores of Kootenay Lake. Seek out local locations for movies you may have seen, such as Steve Martin's *Roxanne*. Details: For further information, contact Nelson Chamber of Commerce, 225 Hall Street, Nelson, British Columbia V1R 5X4; (250) 352-3433. (1 day)

★★ **Castlegar**—On the west bank of the Columbia River at the junction of Highways 3 and 3A, the "crossroads of the Kootenays," Castlegar is surrounded by Doukhobor "farm communes." In the 1920s British Columbia held about 90 such communes, each occupied by about 60 people who cleared the virgin forest to farm, build sawmills, plant orchards and gardens, operate jam factories, and try to remain as independent as possible from outside influences. Their motto was "Toil and a Peaceful Life," and their communes' Russian names translate as "Blessed," "Meadowland," "The Beautiful," and "The Cross." In Brilliant, at the bottom of Airport Hill in Castlegar, is a Doukhobor suspension bridge across the Kootenay River, built of hand-poured concrete in the early 1900s to connect with the old Doukhobor settlement of Ootischeniye ("Valley of Consolation").

Nowadays, many Doukhobors are dispersed and integrated into the mainstream of provincial life. The **Doukhobor Historical Village** is a replica of a Doukhobor commune. At the village's Doukhobor Museum, descendants of the original Doukhobor settlers (a pacifist group of unorthodox Russian immigrants who lived here from 1908 to the 1930s) guide visitors and explain their customs. The adjacent Doukhobor Restaurant serves traditional vegetarian meals and sells books and handicrafts. Details: Opposite the airport in Castlegar just off Highway 3A; (250) 365-6622; village is open daily May through September 9 a.m. to 5 p.m. Admission: Adults $4, students $3, first senior citizen $3, each additional senior citizen $2, families $4 for first adult, each additional member $2. (½ day)

Zuckerberg Island Heritage Park and Chapel House— Accessible by a pedestrian suspension bridge, this 2.2-hectare (5.5-acre) island shows some of the area's history, from the original Interior Salish First Nations to the Doukhobors. The park is named after a Russian who arrived in 1931 to teach local Doukhobors and who settled on the island. Details: In the vicinity of 7th Avenue and 8th Street, Castlegar, near the confluence of the Columbia and Kootenay Rivers; call Castlegar City Hall, (250) 365-7227, or Zuckerberg Island, (250) 365-5511, for information. Admission by donation. (1 hour)

The **Hugh Keenleyside Dam** has Western Canada's only navigation lock, which lifts river traffic some 15 meters (75 ft) to new lake levels as needed. The dam retains the Arrow Lakes Reservoir (part of the Columbia River system), which extends 232 km (145 mi) north to Revelstoke. This long, narrow waterway is popular with anglers who fish for kokanee salmon, rainbow and Dolly Varden trout, walleye pike, sturgeon, and lingcod. It's also a highway for tugs and log booms heading for downstream sawmills and pulp mills. Details: 8 km (5 mi) upstream from Castlegar's town center via Columbia Avenue. (1 hour)

★★ **Cranbrook Railway Museum**—This museum has restored a set of railway cars from the $1-million Trans-Canada Limited (a luxury train built in 1929), a caboose, and a Canadian Pacific Railroad (CPR) station built in 1900. The dining car has displays of original CPR china, glassware, and silver. Here you can enjoy tea and light refreshments. A business car contains an original dining room, sitting room, and bedrooms. Then there's the combination baggage and sleeping car which contains the interpretation area. A model railway display depicts the 1900s era of rail travel. Details: Downtown Cranbrook, on

Highway 3/95; (250) 489-3918; open daily year-round. Admission: Adults $6, over 65 $4.60; students with ID $3, families $14.95. (1 hour)

★★ **Slocan Valley ("Silvery Slocan")**—Most towns in the Slocan Valley owe their existence to silver. Mines around Slocan, New Denver, Silverton, and Sandon worked until high production costs and low ore prices ended the boom. Logging, milling, and tourism are now the valley's three main industries. Visit Sandon ghost town, once the wealthiest mining community on the whole continent. A 2-km (1.3-mi) trail from Sandon takes you up through alpine meadows to Idaho Peak Lookout for wonderful views.

For a change of pace, explore part of Valhalla Provincial Park, which encompasses most of Slocan Lake's western shore. In Norse mythology Valhalla was "heaven" (a magnificent palace), and reaching Valhalla was the greatest honor a Norse warrior could attain. Wilderness enthusiasts say the same about Valhalla Park's rock palaces. Although Highway 6 along Slocan Lake's eastern shore gives superb views of the rugged Valhalla Range mountains to the west, you need a boat to cross the lake and reach the park's main trailheads. Valhalla's most popular hike is the Evans Creek–Beatrice Lake Trail, reached from the village of Slocan by a connecting trail. Details: For information and a trail guide, contact Valhalla Wilderness Society, Box 224, New Denver, British Columbia V0G 1S0; or B.C. Parks, RR3, Nelson, British Columbia V1L 5P6; (250) 825-4421. (1 day)

★★ **Trail**—Trail was established in the 1890s, when a small smelter was built to serve the rich gold and copper mines in nearby Rossland. Local mines are played out, but Trail is now the home of the world's largest zinc- and lead-smelting complex, operated by Cominco. Silver, lead, and zinc ores from Alberta, the Kootenays, the Northwest Territories, and the United States are smelted here to produce refined metals, chemicals, and fertilizers. Don't miss the guided tours of its metallurgical operations. Details: (250) 368-3144; Cominco tours June through August Monday through Friday 10 a.m.; by appointment the rest of the year; closed some holidays. Admission: Donations. (1 day)

★ **S.S. *Moyie***—This 49-meter (162-ft) ship was the last commercial stern-wheeler to serve in British Columbia. Launched in Nelson in 1898, it served camps and settlements on Kootenay Lake until 1957.

As an official historic site, it now houses Kaslo's travel information center and museum, presenting local history, photographs, and artifacts. Details: Front Street, Kaslo; (604) 353-2525; open daily 9 a.m. to 6 p.m. Admission: Adults $4, over 60 and ages 13–19 $3, ages 6–12 $2. (½ hour)

FITNESS AND RECREATION

Many of the miners who flooded into Kootenay country a century ago—as well as the loggers and railroaders who followed—came from Scandinavia, bringing skiing to this region and building the first lifts. Skiing is the passionate interest of current residents; Canada's most famous skier, Nancy Greene, came from Rossland.

For its area, Rossland's **Red Mountain**, (250) 362-7700 or (800) 663-0105, has more advanced and expert terrain (60 percent) than any other ski resort in British Columbia. Two rounded ancient volcano peaks descend through a labyrinth of powder-filled glades and gullies.

With more than 18 courses nearby, golfing is big in the Kootenays, and few places have better scenery. Courses carved from the forest are surrounded by towering mountains punctuated with shimmering glacier-fed lakes. **Kokanee Springs Golf Resort**, Crawford Bay, (800) 979-7999, sets the standard. Some courses offer RV facilities so golf enthusiasts can stay close to the action.

Abundant lakes, streams, and rivers give Kootenay country an edge for swimming, boating, and fishing. **Christina Lake** is reputed to be the clearest, warmest lake in the province. Houseboating is popular on **Kootenay Lake**, near Kaslo. Some of the largest freshwater sport fish in North America are found in its ice-free waters, including the largest breed of rainbow trout in the world. Other fishing hotspots are the **Columbia** and **Kootenay Rivers**, where you can fly-fish for sturgeon, walleye, and kokanee salmon.

The many parks and trails in this region allow a variety of hiking and climbing opportunities near road access. Try **Valhalla Kokanee Glacier, Top of the World Provincial Parks**, and the **Purcell Wilderness Conservancy**. Further north, in the Rockies, try **Mount Revelstoke National Park, Yoho National Park**, and **Mount Robson Provincial Park** (Robson is the Canadian Rockies' highest peak). The less energetic or those preferring to stay closer to civilization can check out nature trails in the **Castlegar** area and art and heritage walking trails in most Kootenay towns. For a different kind of hiking, go underground in **Cody Caves Provincial Park**, near Ains-worth Hot Springs, for a guided or self-guided spelunking adventure. For information, contact Kokanee Creek Provincial Park, RR3, Nelson, British Columbia V1L 5P6, (250) 825-4421.

After days spent on these activities, the Kootenay has a variety of hot springs for relaxation; **Nakusp, Ainsworth, Fairmont**, and **Radium** are the best-known. Don't miss Ainsworth's horseshoe-shaped cave, once a mine shaft, where you can gaze at stalagmites and stalac-tites while you soak. Phone **Ainsworth Hot Springs Resort**, (250) 229-4212 or (800) 668-1171.

FOOD

A few decades ago, the Kootenays attracted a lot of hippies and alternative lifestyle-lovers, who have left their mark on the region's restaurants. You may not find a lot of high-end fine dining, but reasonably priced good food is served in funky, intriguing places.

Due to its large Doukhobor population, Russian food is easy to find, especially in Grand Forks and Castlegar. Locals rave about the borscht at the **Spinning Wheel Vegetarian Eatery**, on Highway 3A across from the airport, Castlegar, (250) 365-7202.

Nelson has many good eateries. The funky but well-respected **All Seasons Restaurant**, 620 Herridge Street, (250) 352-0101, offers a "inland left coast cuisine" menu. The meals are memorable, the por-tions mountain-sized, and the wine list an award-winner. Dinner costs $15–$20, a bit expensive for the rest of the Kootenays but well worth even a detour to get there. The **Rice Bowl**, 459 Ward Street, (250) 354-4129, also functions as an art gallery and specializes in organic foods and Japanese sushi. It has a nice ambiance, with lots of stained glass and other arts and crafts on display. The **Book Garden**, 556 Josephine Street, (250) 352-1812, is a cafe within a bookstore. Prices range $6–$12. **Max and Irma's**, 515A Kootenay Street, Nelson, (250) 352-2332, is a good midrange restaurant noted for its pizzas and calzone (try smoked salmon and peppercorn pizza).

In Castlegar, you'll find **Gabriel's**, a French restaurant at 1432 Columbia Street, (250) 365-6028. Its comfortable atmosphere makes it popular for fine dining. Families seeking good, plain Italian food at reasonable prices will like **Gardeli's Restaurant and Pub**, 1502 Columbia Street, (250) 365-7006.

In Rossland, locals like **Sunshine Cafe**, 2116 Columbia Street,

KOOTENAY COUNTRY

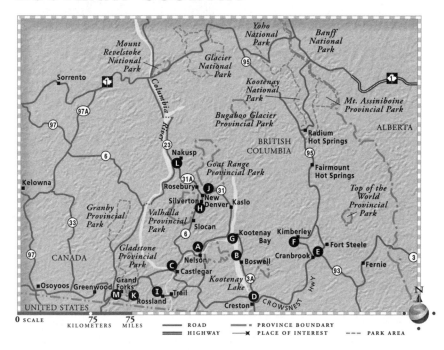

Lodging

Ⓐ Dancing Bear Inn
Ⓑ Destiny Bay Resort
Ⓒ Fireside Inn
Ⓓ Hacienda Inn
Ⓔ Heritage Estate Motel
Ⓐ Heritage Inn
Ⓕ Inn of the Rockies
Ⓔ Inn of the South
Ⓐ Inn the Garden
Ⓖ La Chance Swiss B&B
Ⓗ Mistaya Country Inn
Ⓒ Mountain Retreat Guest House
Ⓘ Ram's Head Inn
Ⓙ Sweet Dreams Guest House
Ⓘ Tara Shanti Retreat

Lodging (continued)

Ⓘ Uplander Hotel
Ⓗ Wedgewood Manor

Camping

Ⓚ Camp Beverly Hills
Ⓒ Castlegar RV Park Campground
Ⓚ Christina Lake RV Park
Ⓚ Christina Pines Tent and Trailer Park
Ⓐ City Tourist Park, Nelson
Ⓔ Cranbrook City Centre Campground
Ⓛ Nakusp Hot Springs Campground
Ⓜ Riviera RV Park

Note: Items with the same letter are located in the same town or area.

(250) 362-7630. **Olive Oyl's**, 2167 Washington Street, (250) 362-5322, is known for "incredibly good food." Have coffee at **Gold Rush Books and Espresso**, 2063 Washington Street, (250) 362-5333.

In New Denver, the **Apple Tree**, 210 6th Avenue, (250) 358-2691, is an excellent choice for coffee, homemade soups, sandwiches, and baked goods.

Eat around an actual tree at the popular **Treehouse Restaurant**, 419 Front Street, Kaslo, (250) 353-2955. Less classy but popular with families is the **Colander Restaurant**, 1475 Cedar Street, Trail, (250) 364-1816, where you eat your spaghetti at banquet tables—and are encouraged to make a mess. Two other eating places frequented by locals are the **Wild Rose Restaurant**, in Roseberry near Nakusp, (250) 358-7744; and **Blondie's Bistro**, in Creston, (250) 428-5858.

LODGING

The Kootenay doesn't have four-star luxury resorts, but there is an abundance of charming chalets, cottages, and inns; plenty of motels; and lots of basic accommodations. Compared to the rest of British Columbia, prices are moderate. Reservations are recommended during July and August for bigger centers, such as Nelson or Cranbrook.

In Nelson, the **Heritage Inn**, centrally situated at 422 Vernon Street, (250) 352-5331, is a big, old-style hotel with period rooms. Its Library Lounge is a popular meeting place for drinks. Prices range $52–$78. Also near downtown in a beautifully restored Victorian heritage home is **Inn the Garden**, 408 Victoria Street, (250) 352-5331. Prices range $60–$120, including a full breakfast.

Hostelers and other budget-conscious travelers get excellent value for their lodging dollar at **Dancing Bear Inn**, 155 Baker Street, (250) 352-7573. It's a warm, friendly place where guests cook in the communal kitchen, swap stories around the fireplace, or join organized activity programs. Single rooms cost $17–$20, doubles and triples, $34–$45.

Typical of Kootenay charm with a European flavor is **Tara Shanti Retreat**, 134 Riondel Road, Kootenay Bay, (800) 811-3888, with a sun deck, sauna, and hot tub providing views of Kootenay Lake and Glacier. Rates range $40–$100. Also in Kootenay Bay is **La Chance Swiss B&B**, (250) 227-9477, near the free Kootenay Bay ferry and Kokanee Springs Golf Course. Rooms are quite luxurious, with fireplaces or Jacuzzis, and there are also fully equipped housekeeping cabins and a cheerful restaurant. Rates are $40–$50.

Wedgewood Manor, in Crawford Bay, (800) 862-0022, is a Victorian-era house on a 20.2-hectare (50-acre) country estate with extensive gardens and hiking and bicycling trails. Prices range $79–$110 and include complimentary breakfast and evening tea.

Destiny Bay Resort, 11935 Highway 3A, (800) 818-6633 or (250) 223-8234, open between April and October, has sod-roofed cottages overlooking Kootenay Lake near Boswell. No TV or phones ensures tranquility. The price range of $160–$200 includes a gourmet four-course dinner and a buffet breakfast for two.

Mistaya Country Inn, (250) 358-7787, a secluded B&B ranch on 36 hectares (90 acres) in the Slocan Valley at Silverton, offers easy hiking access to Valhalla and Kokanee Glacier Provincial Parks and is near Slocan Lake for swimming, canoeing, and fishing. Rates range $40–$65. **Sweet Dreams Guest House**, in New Denver on Slocan Lake, (250) 358-2415, has romantic views of Valhalla Wilderness Park and the New Denver Glacier. Rates range $50–$85.

Mountain Retreat Guest House in Castlegar, (250) 365-6578, is another Victorian-style home with spectacular views, the customary fireplace, plus a piano in the living room. Also in Castlegar is the **Fireside Inn**, (800) 499-6399, with both simple sleeping and house-keeping units, a pub, and a family restaurant. Rates range $55–$68.

In Rossland, try the more modern **Ram's Head Inn**, (800) 661-6335 or (250) 362-9577, set in a forest at the base of Red Mountain. Rates are $45–$152. At the **Uplander Hotel**, Columbia Avenue, (250) 362-7375, rates are $53–$99; rooms with kitchenettes cost an extra $10.

In Cranbrook, the **Inn of the South**, (250) 489-4301 or (800) 663-2708, is a classy place with a nightclub and cocktail lounge. Rates are $55–$84. In beautiful Kimberley (which you must visit), the **Inn of the Rockies**, 300 Wallinger Avenue, (250) 427-2266, is a full-service hotel with rates ranging $42–$67.

Creston's **Hacienda Inn**, overlooking the Creston Valley, (800) 567-2215, has rooms ranging $45–$65; and the **Heritage Estate Motel's** rooms, in Cranbrook, (250) 426-3862, are a reasonable $38–$50.

CAMPING

Two popular camping areas in the Kootenays are **Christina Lake** and along the north shore of Kootenay Lake on **Highway 3A**. For July and

August visits, it's wise to reserve space. Provincial and national parks provide the best campgrounds in that their locations are selected for nearby hiking, swimming, boating, or fishing. Most campsites have road access, but you'll have to boat, ski, or hike in to wilderness backcountry spots. Sites may not have electrical hookups or shower facilities, but most parks have developed hiking trails, and parks officers offer excellent free interpretive programs. To find out if a campsite is full, call West Kootenay Parks and Outdoor Recreation District Office, (250) 825-4421. For other information, contact District Manager, Ministry of Environment and Parks, Kokanee Creek Park, RR3, Nelson, British Columbia V1L 5P6. Remember B.C. Parks' handy Discover Camping phone number, for provincial campground reservations anywhere in the province: (800) 689-9025.

Kootenay is popular camping country, so lots of commercial private campgrounds stay open between spring and fall, plus little-known B.C. Forest Service wilderness campsites. For maps and other information, write to Regional Recreation Officer, Ministry of Forests, 518 Lake Street, Nelson, British Columbia V1L 4C6, or call (250) 354-6200.

Near popular Christina Lake, try **Christina Lake RV Park**, (250) 447-9421; **Christina Pines Tent and Trailer Park**, (250) 447-9587, only 4 blocks from the lake; **Riviera RV Park**, (250) 442-2158, 19 km (11.4 mi) west of the lake in Grand Forks; or **Camp Beverly Hills**, (250) 447-9277. **Castlegar RV Park Campground**, on Highway 3 between Christina Lake and Castlegar, (250) 365-2337, is attractive. **Nakusp Hot Springs Campground**, on the Kuskanax River by a hot-springs pool that's open year-round and near hiking, fishing, and cross-country skiing, is a good choice. Sites are $12–$14 per vehicle, and since no reservations are taken, it's first come, first served. The **City Tourist Park** in Nelson is handily downtown, at 90 High Street. Sites are $13–$16 for two persons. Phone (250) 352-9031 in season, May through September, or (250) 352-5511 off-season. Cranbrook also has a downtown site, **Cranbrook City Centre Campground**, (250) 426-2162. Within walking distance of golf, mall, indoor and outdoor pools, and softball field, it's open March through November. Cost is $14–$20 per vehicle (no credit cards), and kids stay free.

Scenic Route: Kootenays to Alberta

The Crescent Pass Route:

From Cranbrook, go east along Highway 3 to Fernie and Sparwood, then to Coleman and Blairmore, and on to either **Waterton Lakes National Park**, **Calgary**, or the **Drumheller** area. This road winds (and I mean *winds*) through some of the most spectacular mountain scenery there is, going over **Crowsnest Pass** (1,396 meters/4,580 ft). This is one of only three passes that cut through the Canadian Rockies. About 35 km (22 mi) inside the Alberta border is the site of the town of **Frank**, which was virtually obliterated in 1903 by a massive rockslide of some 74 million tons. The slide tore the top off Turtle Mountain and swept 1.6 km (1 mi) across the valley to bury roads, rail lines, homes, and whole farms, leaving the area so unstable that the remaining mountain continues to be monitored.

The Kootenay Lake Route:

Another route is to drive Highway 3A north from Creston along the eastern shore of Kootenay Lake to **Kootenay Bay** and take the free

KOOTENAYS TO ALBERTA

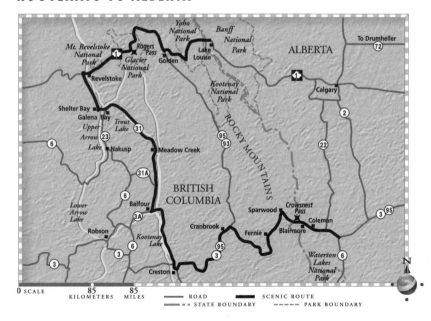

ferry across the lake to **Balfour**. Go north again on Highway 31, which parallels the lake's western shore for some 70 km (44 mi), to the community of **Meadow Creek**. The road becomes gravel (but still good in all weather) and skirts **Trout Lake** to **Galena Bay**, where you take another free ferry ride to **Shelter Bay** (check for ferry times before you begin this trip). Drive north on Highway 23 to **Revelstoke**.

A brief detour will take you to **Mica Dam**, for free guided tours at 11 a.m. and 1:30 p.m. or self-guided tours daily: from 8 a.m. to 8 p.m. mid-June through mid-September; 9 a.m. to 5 p.m. mid-September through October 31 and mid-March through mid-June. Here are lighted displays, topographical maps, and audiovisuals on the design, construction, and function of the dam. (250) 837-6515.

The Rogers Pass Route:
From Revelstoke, follow the Trans-Canada Highway via **Mount Revelstoke National Park** and world-famed **Roger's Pass** to **Glacier National Park** and **Golden**, then through **Yoho National Park** and **Kicking Horse Pass** to **Lake Louise**. A miniside trip in Yoho Park will take you to **Takkakaw Falls**, at 305 meters (1,000 ft) the highest sheer waterfall in Canada. Its total drop is 385 meters (1,265 ft).

17

THE OKANAGAN SIMILKAMEEN

In my early 1960s search for a Western Canada residence, I was told to consider only two areas: Vancouver or the Okanagan; I tried both. Today, more mellow, I'd choose the Okanagan, now rivaling Victoria as a B.C. retirement capital. Unlike rainy Vancouver, the Okanagan's semi-arid climate with warm summer temperatures records more sunshine than most of Canada. Besides 250-plus lakes (boating, fishing, swimming) and sandy beaches (strolling, sunbathing), it has over 40 golf courses; three exceptional ski resorts; over 25 wineries/vineyards; abundant orchards, farms, and ranches; and activities for all ages and interests.

Okanagan Valley, nearly 240 km (150 mi) along a string of lakes from Osoyoos (south) to Enderby (north); and Similkameen Valley, 115 km (72 mi) from Osoyoos (east) to Princeton (west), comprise the Okanagan Similkameen. Take a leisurely drive along Highways 3 and 97, visiting every temptation—a roadside stand; a winery, cheese factory, fruit or game farm; a hot-air balloon ride or waterslide; or perhaps a sunny beach. Stop often for photos—the Okanagan is picture-perfect, with lush orchards, rolling hills, and colorful lakes.

More adventurous? Drive Highway 33's mountain route on the lake's other side, including the famous (now abandoned) Kettle Valley Railway route. Cycle or hike Myra Canyon's 8 km (5 mi) of 18 heart-stoppingly high railway trestles. Better still, drive both sides of the valley in a circle linking eastside mountain roads to popular westside towns. North American tour-bus operators rate the Okanagan among the continent's top 100 destinations. ◼

THE OKANAGAN SIMILKAMEEN

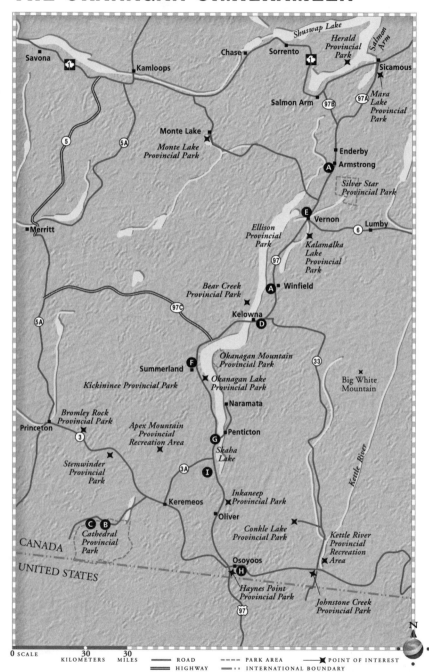

Sights

A Agritours

B Cathedral Lakes Lodge

C Cathedral Provincial Park

D Father Pandosy's Mission

E Historic O'Keefe Ranch

F Kettle Valley Steam Railway

D Okanagan Food and Wine Festival

G Okanagan Game Farm

D Okanagan Orchard Tours

H Pocket Desert

I Vaseux Lake

Note: Items with the same letter are located in the same town or area.

A PERFECT DAY IN THE OKANAGAN

Start in Osoyoos on a pleasant day in May, when cherry, peach, pear, plum, and apple blossoms are turning the lakeside hills into flower gardens, and drive north to Vernon along the west side of the Okanagan Valley. Pick up a calendar of events for the Okanagan Wine Festival and decide on the highlight for that day—a guided tour of several wineries with lunch or dinner included; a horse- or tractor-drawn tour of an orchard; perhaps both. I'd photograph the intriguing Spotted Lake near Oliver, look for birds and bighorn sheep by the bluffs of Vaseaux Lake, wander through the Okanagan Game Farm in Penticton, and watch an alpaca herd in Winfield. For supper, I'd dine and dance aboard the 1948 paddle-wheeler MV *Fintry Queen*, on Lake Okanagan out of Kelowna, between courses, keeping an eye out for the Okanagan's legendary sea monster, Ogopogo. Those in the know describe him as a creature with a snake-like body that may include several humps, a dark green outer skin, and a head the size of a horse's. I'd sleep by the water, perhaps at Kelowna's sumptuous Grand Hotel. In winter a perfect day means skiing at Silver Star Mountain Resort or Big White Ski Resort.

WINE COUNTRY

The Okanagan Similkameen has become one of Canada's premier wine-producing regions. Each vineyard varies with its exposure to sunlight, soil type, drainage, and proximity to lakes and rivers, all of which influence the wine. The region has a wide variety of European varietal grapes, including Riesling (also left on the vine to freeze for ice wine), chardonnay, pinot blanc, and pinot noir. Among the most notable wineries are the **Cedar Creek Estate** near Kelowna, (250) 764-8866; the **Gray Monk Estate** in Winfield, (250) 766-3168 or (800) 663-4205; the **St. Hubertus Estate** near Kelowna, (250) 764-7888 or (800) 989-WINE; and the **Sumac Ridge Estate** near Summerland, (250) 490-0451. The historic **Quails' Gate Estate** near Westbank, (250) 769-4451 or (800) 420-WINE, features an 1873 log-cabin wine shop.

Most of the region's two dozen or so wineries are clearly marked by highway signs on the Okanagan Wine Route. Some wineries offer tastings and tours by appointment only, so it's best to phone ahead. Get your Wine Festival Passport stamped at each winery to earn prizes.

For further information, contact the Okanagan Wine Festival Society, 1030 McCurdy Road, Kelowna, V1X 2P7, (250) 861-6654; or the Okanagan Wine Festival Office, 185 Lakeshore Drive, Penticton, V2A 1B7, (250) 490-8866 or (800) 972-5151.

SIGHTSEEING HIGHLIGHTS

★★★ **Cathedral Provincial Park and Cathedral Lakes Lodge**—You have two choices if you want to explore this beautiful park near Keremeos. You can drive to a base camp along a 21-km(13-mi) gravel road from Highway 3 near the Ashnola River, then rough it by hiking up a 15-km (9-mi) trail to 2,000 meters (7,000 ft) and the private facility of Cathedral Lakes Lodge. Private vehicles are not allowed on the park road, but if you want a one-hour, quicker alternative to hiking, your second choice is to pay to use the lodge's four-wheel-drive vehicle.

Cathedral Provincial Park is a stunningly beautiful wilderness in the Cascade Mountains, which Canada shares with the United States. The park's turquoise lakes and alpine meadows are guarded by jagged peaks that stand majestically against the skyline. It has 85 km (53 mi) of hiking trails that lead to the park's main features—curious rock formations with names such as Smokey the Bear, Devil's Woodpile,

Stone City, and the Giant Cleft. You'll probably see mule deer, mountain goats, and California bighorn sheep. Even if you can't wangle a ride to the alpine and have to hike, the scenery on top is worth the climb. Details: Box 399, Summerland, V0H 1Z0; (250) 494-6500. $2 fee charged June through September; cash only.

Cathedral Lakes Lodge, in the alpine wilderness on Lake Quini-scoe, features 50 km (31 mi) of hiking trails, four trout-stocked lakes, and free canoes. You can choose a cabin, a room in the chalet, or the lodge itself. All have good views and hot water, but showers and toilets are shared. Reservations are recommended. Details: Contact the lodge c/o Site 4, Comp 8, Slocan Park, V0G 2E0; (250) 226-7560 or (250) 492-1606; open June 1 through October 15. Cost: $115–$190 a day. Alternatively, try (250) 499-5848 or cellular phone (250) 492-1606 off-season; or write RR1, Cawston, British Columbia V0X 1C0. No credit cards, but checks accepted. (time depends on hiking preferences)

✫✫✫ Okanagan Food and Wine Festival—Classified as one of the Top 100 events in North America by international bus-tour organizers, this biannual festival (May and October) has become so popular that some events sell out months before they occur. Most of the wineries link up with local restaurants and tourist attractions to provide food, wine, and travel packages. During consumer tastings and wine judgings in the fall, visitors are offered such enticements as pig roasts, winemak-ers' dinners, salmon bakes, chocolate buffets, train rides, and wine bik-ing tours. A popular event is a floatplane ride to the top of the Kettle Valley Railway and a cycle back to town, during which riders learn a bit of history and enjoy wine and cheese in an exotic location. Details: Contact Okanagan Adventure Company, 1330 Water Street, Kelowna; (250) 862-9155 or (800) 862-9155. Cost: $99. (2 days)

✫✫✫ Roadside Produce—Lots of people tour the Okanagan Similkameen in fall to take advantage of fresh fruits and vegetables from roadside stands. Keremeos is known as the Fruit Stand Capital of the World, with more than 25 stands in town. Stop and tour one of the orchards—it's a fun way to get your produce and learn some-thing of the process. Try the Kelowna Land and Orchard Company, 2930 Dunster Road, Kelowna V1Y 7R2, (250) 763-1091, for a wagon ride on a working orchard. You'll learn the Oriental way of growing apples—in paper bags right on the tree—in order to pro-duce flawless fruit. After the tour you get samples. (½ day)

★★ **Agritours**—Many Okanagan Valley ranches and farms welcome visitors. Try a tour and sample some cheese at the **Armstrong Cheese Factory**, 3155 Pleasant Valley Road, Armstrong, (250) 546-3084. Have a honey farm vacation at a working bee-farm B&B, 2910 North Glenmore Road, Kelowna, (250) 762-8156. Feed and milk the dairy goats at **Paradox Farm**, Enderby, (250) 838-7766. Catch some trout and sample some venison at the **Fink Trout, Deer, Elk and Bison Farm**, Mabel Lake Road, Enderby, (250) 838-7621. Watch how raw fiber is spun into wool at the **Okanagan Alpaca Company**, 11014 Bond Road, Winfield, (250) 766-3175. Take a hike with **High Country Llama Adventures**, Meadow Valley, Summerland, (250) 494-8329. Visit the **Okanagan Crockers Ostrich Farm**, 112 Westside Road, Kelowna; call ahead, (250) 769-6693. Take the self-guided walking tour of **Davison Orchards**, RR4, Davison Road, Vernon, V1T 6L7, (250) 549-3266. You have a tremendous choice of farms, orchards, farmers' markets, and apiaries in the Okanagan. (1 hour each)

★★ **Father Pandosy's Mission/Pandosy Mission Provincial Heritage Site**—The first agricultural site and the first European settlement in the Okanagan Valley, the mission was set up in 1859 by three Oblate missionaries as a base to convert the aboriginal inhabitants, traders, and free settlers. Father Pandosy is well known for planting the first apple tree in the valley. Tour four of the original buildings remaining, including the church. Details: 2279 Benvoulin Road, Kelowna; (250) 762-6911 or (250) 860-1384; open April through Thanksgiving, dawn to dusk. Admission by donation. (½ hour)

★★ **Historic O'Keefe Ranch**—Founded in 1867 as the headquarters of a vast cattle empire, the ranch became a historic site in 1977. Visitors can tour original buildings such as the O'Keefe Mansion, St. Anne's Church, the general store, and the blacksmith's shop. It also features a ranching gallery, a popular ranch-house restaurant, and stagecoach rides. Details: 12 km (7 mi) north of Vernon; (250) 542-7868; site is open daily Mother's Day through Thanksgiving 9 a.m. to 5 p.m. Admission: Adults $5, over 65 and ages 13–18 $4, ages 6–12 $3, families $15. (1½ hour)

★★ **Kettle Valley Steam Railway**—Spanning southern British Columbia from Hope to Rock Creek at the entrance of the Kootenay, this railroad was designed in 1916 to open up new mining areas (and to stave off competing American attempts to do likewise). It was known as "McCulloch's Wonder," after the Canadian Pacific Railway engineer who pushed the railway through to completion despite mudslides, avalanches, and the deaths of many construction workers, and was regarded as one of the greatest engineering feats in railway history. By 1959 the railway was abandoned for lack of traffic and the difficulty of maintaining it under adverse conditions. Parts of the line have been restored for hiking and cycling.

To get to Myra Canyon and some picturesque trestles situated high over deep canyons, take the K.L.O. Road out of Kelowna to McCulloch Road. About 2 km (1.2 mi) after the pavement ends on McCulloch Road, power lines cross above the road in a clearing. On the right is the Myra Canyon Forest Service Road, an active logging road that can be messy in bad weather. Follow this road for 8 km (5 mi) and park. Walk for 15 minutes and you will find the trestles. You can travel the railway bed all the way to Penticton, or as far as you like and return to your vehicle. Another entry point to the Kettle River Railway bed is from Naramata.

In Summerland, near Trout Creek Canyon, you can re-live that old-railway-days feeling by taking a ride in a 1924 Shay Locomotive on a portion of preserved track in this area. This one-hour ride departs at 11 a.m. from the Summerland train station, mostly on weekends but daily from July 29 through August 12. Details: For a more detailed schedule, contact Kettle Valley Railway, Summerland; (250) 494-8422. Admission: Adults $7.50, seniors and ages 13–18 $6.50, ages 4–12 $4.50. (1½ hours)

★★ **Okanagan Game Farm**—About 1,000 animals of 130 species from around the world live here, in spacious surroundings that emulate their native habitats. Details: Scenically situated on Highway 97 overlooking Skaha Lake 9 km (5 mi) south of Penticton; (250) 497-5405; open daily 8 a.m. to dusk. Admission: Adults $9; ages 5–17, $7. (2 hours)

★★ **Pocket Desert**—It can get so hot in Osoyoos that visitors actually fry eggs on the sidewalks. The Pocket Desert is Canada's only true desert, the northern extremity of America's Great Basin Desert. This area of unirrigated land extends 48 km (30 mi) north to Skaha Lake and west along the Similkameen River. A Federal Eco-Reserve, it features such rarities as spadefoot toads, Pacific rattlesnakes, and Calliope hummingbirds. Details: Off Road 22 near Osoyoos. (1 hour)

✿✿ **Vaseux Lake**—In this excellent wildlife-viewing area are mountain goats, California bighorn sheep, and a wide variety of birdlife.
Trails access nearby Vaseux Lake Canadian Wildlife Service Sanctuary
and Vaseux Lake Provincial Park. You can swim and fish in the lake for
largemouth bass and rainbow trout. Details: Near Highway 97, 16 km
(10 mi) north of Oliver. (1½ hours)

FITNESS AND RECREATION

Now that you've eaten and imbibed your way around the Okanagan
Similkameen, you'd better concentrate on getting in shape. So forget
sun-baking on the sandy beaches and go for another swim, preferably
in **Kalamalka Lake**, "the lake of many colors," on the outskirts of
Vernon. Stop at the viewpoint on Highway 97, 5 km (3 mi) south of
25th Avenue in Vernon, to take panoramic photos. Look over the lake
to **Kalamalka Lake Provincial Park**, popular with swimmers, boaters,
and cross-country skiers who want to avoid the biggest crowds. There
are dozens of places to stop for a swim along the west side of
Okanagan and **Skaha Lakes**.

Kids will have fun at one of the many Okanagan waterslides:
Wonderful Waterworld, Penticton, (250) 493-8121; **Wild Waters
Waterslide Park**, Kelowna, (250) 765-9453; **Atlantis Waterslides and
Recreations**, 7 km (4 mi) north on Highway 97A at Pleasant Valley
Road, outside of Vernon, (250) 549-4121.

Okanagan Bobsliding, 8 km (5 mi) north of Vernon on Highway
97A, (250) 542-0104, offers a 580-meter (1,903-ft) ride down a stain-
less steel bobslide. A mechanical lift takes riders to the lift site.

Residents and visitors alike make the most of water in the sunny
Okanagan. If they're not swimming, boating, skiing, sliding, and fishing it, they're floating it. The **Penticton River Channel**, a 6-km (3.8-
mi) canal that connects Skaha and Okanagan Lakes, is a drawing card
for anyone with a flotation device. Locals love it. As many as 30,000
people float it on a hot summer weekend. You can rent dinghies and
tire tubes. For the more active, there's climbing **Skaha Bluffs** at
Penticton; golfing at **Predator Ridge** in Vernon; heli-biking, air-
biking, and mountain biking in places like the Kettle Valley Railway;
and trail-riding almost anywhere.

The Okanagan Similkameen is determined to catch up to
Whistler in the current expansion of ski facilities at its three main ski
destinations: **Silver Star Mountain Resort** near Vernon, **Big White**

Ski Resort near Kelowna, and **Apex Resort** near Penticton. Apex is currently suffering from political and financial problems, but the other two are significantly upgrading their summer and winter facilities. For further information, contact Silver Star Mountain Resort, Box 2, Silver Star Mountain, V0E 1G0, (250) 542-0224 or (800) 663-4431; Big White Ski Resort, Box 2039, Station R, Kelowna, V1X 4K5, (250) 765-3101 or (800) 663-2772; or Apex Resort, Box 1060, Penticton, V2A 7N7, (250) 492-2880 or (800) 387-2739.

I like Silver Star for its 1890s Gaslight Era village, which reminds me of the days of the Old Canadian West. If you're planning a ski holiday, remember to ask about packages—they can be very economical, especially for families. The Okanagan is super for the skier: the snow is light, dry, and plentiful; the ski season is long; the air is dry and mild; the sun shines generously; and prices are reasonable.

FOOD

When you're tired of roadside stands but still want to feel you're in the outdoors, settle by the creek that runs through the **Garden Cafe and Courtyard Dining Room** in the Best Western Vernon Lodge and Conference Centre, 3914 32nd Street (Highway 97), Vernon, (250) 545-3385 or (800) 663-4422. Dine in a magnificent three-story indoor courtyard atrium filled with tropical plants, swim in the pool, or sit in the whirlpool. In such a setting the food may be secondary, but here you won't compromise on taste or service. Entrees range $15–$30.

One of the most elegant of Kelowna's restaurants is the **Vintage Dining Room** at the Coast Capri Hotel, 1171 Harvey Avenue, (250) 860-6060, ext. 229. Specialties such as escargots, chateaubriand, and lobster tails may be fairly expensive, but the meal will be memorable. Lunch Monday through Friday, dinner every day, Sunday brunch recommended.

The Aberdeen family, pioneers of the Okanagan's fruit-growing industry, built Guisachan House, now a historic site, in 1891. Designed in the Indian colonial bungalow style, it now houses the **Guisachan House Restaurant**, 1060 Cameron Avenue at Gordon Drive, Guisachan Heritage Park, (250) 862-9368, serving lunch daily and dinner Thursday through Sunday. Entrees range $15–$25. In Keremeos, try fresh baked goods and lunch in the **Tea Room** of another Heritage Trust building, the Grist Mill, on Upper Bench Road, 1 km (.6 mi) off Highway 3A, (250) 499-2888.

THE OKANAGAN SIMILKAMEEN

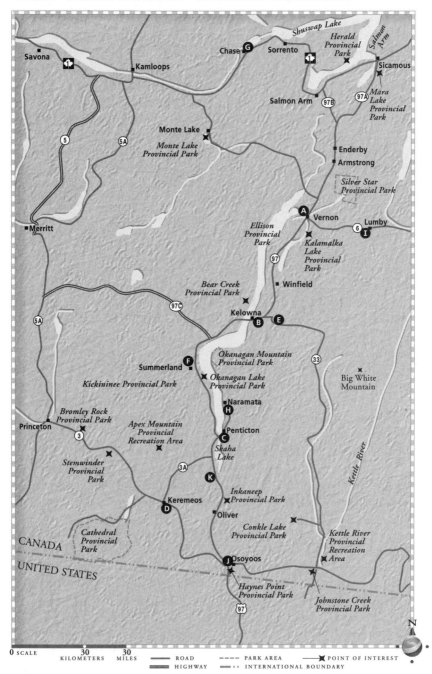

Food

Ⓐ Garden Cafe and Courtyard Dining Room

Ⓑ Earl's

Ⓒ Granny Bognor's

Ⓓ Grist Mill Tea Room

Ⓑ Guisachan House Restaurant

Ⓒ Mickey Finn's Restaurant

Ⓒ Salty's Beach House

Ⓔ Schoolhouse Cafe Pub

Ⓕ Shaughnessy's Cove Waterfront Pub and Restaurant

Ⓒ Theo's Greek Restaurant

Ⓑ Vintage Dining Room

Lodging

Ⓐ Best Western Vernon Lodge

Ⓐ Castle on the Mountain B&B

Ⓒ God's Mountain Crest Chalet

Ⓑ Grand Okanagan Lakefront Resort and Conference Centre

Ⓒ Hostelling International Penticton

Ⓑ Hotel Eldorado

Ⓑ Lake Okanagan Resort

Ⓕ Lakeshore Memories B&B

Ⓐ Melford Creek Country Inn and Spa

Lodging (continued)

Ⓖ Quaaout Lodge

Ⓑ Samesun International Travel Hostel

Ⓗ Sandy Beach Lodge

Ⓑ Stay 'n' Save Motor Inn

Camping

Ⓕ Bear Creek Provincial Park

Ⓘ Echo Lake Fishing Resort

Ⓑ Hiawatha RV Park

Ⓖ Lakeshore Tent and RV Park

Ⓕ Okanagan Lake Provincial Park

Ⓙ Shady Lagoon Campsite

Ⓚ Vaseux Lake Provincial Park

Note: Items with the same letter are located in the same town or area.

In Penticton, **Granny Bognor's**, in a heritage house at 302 Eckhardt Avenue West, (250) 493-2711, is noted for desserts and artistic presentation. Duckling and veal sweetbreads are specialties of its wide menu, where entrees range $21–$30. Dinners Tuesday through Saturday. With its whitewashed walls, red tiled floors, heavy rough-hewn beams, and tree-lined staircase, **Theo's Greek Restaurant**, 687 Main Street, (250) 492-4019, might be an outdoor patio in the Greek Islands. Rabbit and octopus are the specialties of this popular restaurant, and entrees range $11–$20.

A unique feature of **Shaughnessy's Cove Waterfront Pub and Restaurant**, 12817 Lakeshore Drive North, Summerland, (250) 494-1212, is its free shuttle service from homes or hotels. If you like dining over water, Shaughnessy's is as close as you can get. Try their fish 'n' chips or stew served in hollowed bread. Lunch and dinner are served daily, and meals are inexpensive (less than $15). Other casual and fun eateries are **Salty's Beach House**, 1000 Lakeshore Drive West, Penticton, (250) 493-5001; and the **Schoolhouse Cafe Pub**, on Highway 33 near Kelowna, (250) 491-1020, a brewpub favorite with skiers on their way home from Big White. The popular chain **Earl's**, which has restaurants in Vernon and Kelowna, is always a good choice for the variety of its food at $5–$30 prices.

One of the best deals in Penticton is **Mickey Finn's Restaurant**, 57 Padmore Avenue, (250) 493-3883, which has had loyal clientele since 1977. A 7-ounce steak, including vegetables, soup, a salad bar, bread, and choice of potato, rice, or French fries, costs just $7.95.

LODGING

For Okanagan Similkameen reservations and travel information, call (800) 663-1900 or (800) 972-5151. As expected in such a year-round resort area, there's a wide range of accommodations from which to choose. Many offer golf and ski packages in one inclusive price. To rent a vacation home right on a ski mountain, phone or fax Silver Star Ski Accommodation Management at (250) 542-3090.

What could be grander than the **Grand Okanagan Lakefront Resort and Conference Centre** on the shores of Okanagan Lake and within walking distance of downtown Kelowna? Among 10 hectares (25 acres) of beach, parkland, and lagoons, this luxury hotel at 1310 Water Street, (250) 763-4500 or (800) 465-4651, offers a variety of units at $115–$330. **Lake Okanagan Resort**, on a steep hillside at 2751

Westside Road, Kelowna, (250) 769-3511 or (800) 663-3273, has a golf course, tennis courts, marina, summer camp, naturalist programs, horseback-riding, cycle and heli-tour packages, and lodgings that range $130–$180. **Hotel Eldorado**, 500 Cook Road, Kelowna, (250) 763-7500, has an excellent reputation; a waterside boardwalk and cafe; cozy antique-filled rooms; and a lakeside dining room, bar, and grill. Rooms vary from $89 (off-season) to $125 and up. Clean and friendly **Stay 'n' Save Motor Inn**, 1140 Harvey Avenue, Kelowna, (250) 862-8888 or (800) 663-0298, is more affordable for families ($69–$120).

B&Bs are abundant. Try the **Castle on the Mountain B&B**, 8277 Silver Star Mountain Road, S-10, C-12, (250) 542-4593 or (800) 667-2229, close to the ski resort in Vernon. This imposing house includes an outdoor Jacuzzi and the Eskila Gallery, showing artworks by the host and other B.C. artists. Standard double rate is $65 a night, but it has a stargazer's tower suite for $135–$145 a night. **Lakeshore Memories B&B**, 12216 Lakeshore Drive, RR1, Site 14, Comp 9, Summerland, (250) 494-5134, is another heritage home. It overlooks Okanagan Lake and is near golf, wineries, swimming, and an art gallery. Smoking outside only and no children under 10. Rooms range $60–$75. **Melford Creek Country Inn and Spa** is a wood and stone country château at 7810 Melford Road, RR3, S11, C102, Vernon, (250) 558-7910, 1 km (.6 mi) off Silver Star Road. Its luxury spa includes a heated pool, a Roman whirlpool, a sauna, and massage therapy. Cost is a reasonable $75 for a standard double room year-round. Another executive-type retreat is **God's Mountain Crest Chalet**, above Skaha Lake on Lakeside Road, Penticton, (250) 290-4800.

For the budget-conscious, there's **Hostelling International Penticton** at 464 Ellis Street, (250) 492-3992. Prices vary from $13.50 (single) to $37 (three persons). **Samesun International Travel Hostel**, 730 Bernard Avenue, Kelowna, (250) 763-9800, is also centrally situated. Prices range from $15 (single) to $35 (three persons). Families like **Sandy Beach Lodge**, 4275 Mill Road, Box 8, Naramata, (250) 496-5765; reservations may be necessary a year in advance for the peak summer season. Facilities include croquet, horseshoes, tennis courts, rental boats, a swimming pool, and 410 feet of sandy beach.

A little further away is **Quaaout Lodge**, a small, secluded lodge on Little Shuswap Lake Road, 8 km (5 mi) east of Chase. It's close to the world-famous Adams River salmon run and features a restaurant with First Nations cuisine. Prices range $79–$150. Write Box 1215, Chase, V0E 1M0; or call (250) 679-3090 or (800) 663-4303.

CAMPING

Dry, sunny weather encourages camping in Okanagan Similkameen. **Okanagan Lake Provincial Park**, on Okanagan Lake 11 km (7 mi) north of Summerland on Highway 97, would have been a desert were it not for 10,000 trees planted on the dry hillside. It's open from March through November, with cash fees of $15.50 (four persons) charged between April and November. It has a good beach, a boat launch, and hot showers. Reservations are recommended at the Discover Camping phone number for B.C. Provincial Parks, (800) 689-9025; or write Box 399, Summerland, V0H 1Z0. Similar conditions prevail at **Bear Creek Provincial Park**, 9 km (6 mi) west of Kelowna on Westside Road off Highway 97, (250) 494-6500. If you want to watch wildlife, choose **Vaseux Lake Provincial Park** at the north end of Vaseux Lake, 4 km (2 mi) south of Okanagan Falls, (250) 494-6500. Cost is $9.50 for four people.

There are many private campgrounds in the Okanagan. Some of the best are: **Lakeshore Tent and RV Park**, 15419 North Lakeshore Drive, RR1, Summerland, (250) 494-8149; open May through September, this park has 120 meters (394 ft) of beach for swimming and boating, a playground, and game room. Four persons, $17.25. **Hiawatha RV Park**, 3787 Lakeshore Road, Kelowna, is quiet, family-oriented, and near a sandy beach open March 15 through October 15. Security is important, and the gate is closed at night. Rates are $27–$35 for two. Also recommended for family camping on a sandy beach with a free boat launch is **Shady Lagoon Campsite**, RR1, Osoyoos. In Lumby, in a lakeside, terraced mountain setting, is **Echo Lake Fishing Resort**, 2126 Creighton Valley Road, (250) 547-6434, open May through October.

NIGHTLIFE

I'd opt for a dinner-dance cruise on Lake Okanagan aboard the **MV *Fintry Queen***, but those who like to gamble can play blackjack, roulette, Sic Bo, Red Dog, and Caribbean stud poker at **Lake City Casinos** in Kelowna, (250) 860-9467; in Vernon, (250) 545-3505; and in Kamloops, (250) 372-3334. There are enough pubs, bistros, coffeehouses, and clubs in Okanagan Similkameen to satisfy summer and winter vacationers, but the region is known for its appreciation of the arts as well: sample Vernon's **Powerhouse Theatre**, (250) 542-6194; Newport Beach Resort's **Sen'Klip Native Theatre**, (250) 549-2921; and Armstrong's **Caravan Farm Theatre**, (s250) 546-8533.

APPENDIX

METRIC CONVERSION CHART

1 U.S. gallon = approximately 4 liters
1 liter = about 1 quart
1 Canadian gallon = approximately 4.5 liters

1 pound = approximately $\frac{1}{2}$ kilogram
1 kilogram = about 2 pounds

1 foot = approximately $\frac{1}{3}$ meter
1 meter = about 1 yard
1 yard = a little less than a meter
1 mile = approximately 1.6 kilometers
1 kilometer = about $\frac{2}{3}$ mile

90°F = about 30°C
20°C = approximately 70°F

Planning Map: Western Canada

Tatshenshini-Alsek
Wilderness Park

Yukon Territory

1

Atlin
Provincial
Park

97

Juneau

37

Muncho Lake
Provincial Park

Telegraph
Creek

8

Alaska

Mount Edziza
Provincial Park

Spatsizi Plateau
Wilderness Provincial
Park

37

Tatlatui
Provincial Park

Ketchikan

Stewart

Hazelton

Naikoon
Provincial
Park

Prince
Rupert

16

British
Columbia

Queen
Charlotte
Islands

7

Hecate Strait

Kitimat Ranges

16

Tweedsmui
Provincial
Park

South Moresby
National Park
Reserve

Pacific Ocean

Bella
Coola

6

2

Cape Scott
Provincial
Park

Ts'ylpos
Provincial
Park

Port Hardy

Campbell
River

Vancouver
Island

Strathcona
Provincial
Park

19

4

5

4

Pacific Rim National Park

Nanaimo

0 SCALE   250   250
         KILOMETERS MILES

—— ROAD   .... FERRY
═══ DIVIDED HIGHWAY   ---- AREA OR PARK BOUNDARY

You have permission to photocopy this map.

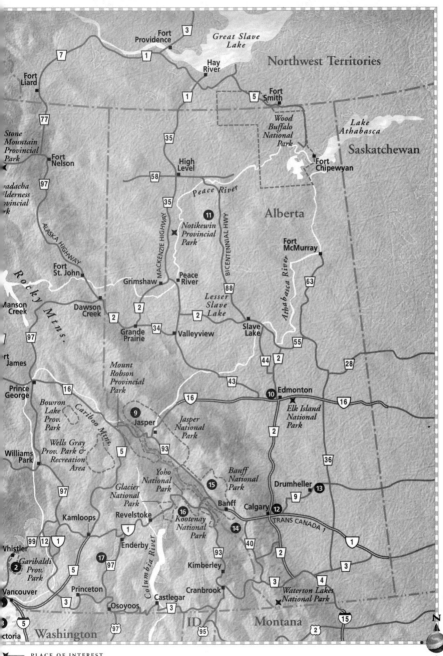

PLACE OF INTEREST

Planning Map: Western Canada

Yukon Territory

Tatshenshini-Alsek
Wilderness Park

1

Atlin
Provincial
Park

97

37

Muncho Lake
Provincial Par

Juneau

Telegraph
Creek

Ałaska

8

Mount Edziza
Provincial Park

Spatsizi Plateau
Wilderness Provincial
Park

37

Tatlatui
Provincial Park

Ketchikan

Stewart

Hazelton

British
Columbia

Naikoon
Provincial
Park

Prince
Rupert

16

Queen
Charlotte
Islands

7

Hecate Strait

Kitimat Ranges

16

Tweedsmu
Provincia
Park

South Moresby
National Park
Reserve

6

Bella
Coola

Pacific Ocean

Cape Scott
Provincial
Park

Port Hardy

Ts'ylpos
Provincia
Park

Campbell
River

Vancouver
Island

Strathcona
Provincial
Park

19

4

4

Pacific Rim National Park

5

Nanaimo

0 SCALE   250   250
      KILOMETERS   MILES

━━━ ROAD   ·········· FERRY
═══ DIVIDED HIGHWAY   ---- AREA OR PARK BOUNDARY

PLACE OF INTEREST

INDEX

Map Index

ABOUT THE AUTHOR

Born and raised in Australia, Lyn Hancock has been living in and writing about Western Canada for almost 30 years. She has traveled widely throughout the region and recorded her adventures in thousands of international newspaper and magazine articles. Her many book titles include *There's a Seal in My Sleeping Bag*, *Yukon*, *Nunavut*, *Northwest Territories*, and *Winging It in the North*. She has won numerous awards for writing and photography. In addition to traveling and writing, Hancock gives lectures throughout Canada, Australia, and the United States.